Touching Second

MCFARLAND HISTORICAL BASEBALL LIBRARY

Marty McGee *and* Gary Mitchem, *Editors*

1. Cobb, Ty. *Busting 'Em and Other Big League Stories* (1914). 2003
2. Axelson, G.W. *"Commy": The Life Story of Charles A. Comiskey* (1919). 2003

Gary Mitchem *and* Marty McGee, *Editors*

3. Ellard, Harry. *Base Ball in Cincinnati: A History* (1908). 2003
4. Richter, Francis C. *Richter's History and Records of Base Ball* (1914). 2003

Gary Mitchem *and* Mark Durr, *Editors*

5. Lanigan, Ernest J. *The Baseball Cyclopedia* (1922). 2005
6. Evers, John J., and Hugh S. Fullerton. *Touching Second* (1910). 2005
7. Rice, Grantland. *Base-Ball Ballads* (1910). 2005

John J. Stuart

Touching Second

by John J. Evers *and*
Hugh S. Fullerton

McFarland Historical Baseball Library, 6
Gary Mitchem *and* Mark Durr, *Editors*

McFarland & Company, Inc., Publishers
Jefferson, North Carolina, and London

Frontispiece: John J. Evers

Library of Congress Cataloguing-in-Publication Data

Evers, John J.
  Touching second / by John J. Evers and Hugh S. Fullerton
  [Gary Mitchem and Mark Durr, series editors]
      p. cm. — (McFarland historical baseball library ; 6)
  Originally published: Chicago : Reilly & Britton, 1910. With
  new editor's note.
  Includes index.

  ISBN 0-7864-1869-9 (softcover : 50# alkaline paper) ∞

  1. Baseball.   I. Fullerton, Hugh S. (Hugh Stuart), 1873–1945.
II. Title.   III. Series.
GV867.E8   2005
796.357—dc22   2004002929

British Library cataloguing data are available

Cover photograph: Johnny Evers in 1903 (National Baseball Hall of Fame
Library, Cooperstown, N.Y.)

Manufactured in the United States of America

McFarland & Company, Inc., Publishers
  Box 611, Jefferson, North Carolina 28640
    www.mcfarlandpub.com

Contents

Contents

Illustrations

Editors' Note

On September 23, 1908, as the Pittsburgh Pirates, the New York Giants and the Chicago Cubs were locked in a pennant race, the Cubs and the Giants faced off at the Polo Grounds in New York. With two outs in the bottom of the ninth, the game tied and Moose McCormick on third, Giants rookie Fred Merkle was on first. After Al Bridwell singled to center, Merkle watched as McCormick crossed the plate, and then seeing the crowd spill onto the field, peeled off toward the Giants clubhouse. Johnny Evers called for the ball and the attention of the umpires, then touched second. Merkle was called out on the force play. At first declared a tie, the game was replayed when at season's end the pennant race was still undecided. The Cubs won the second meeting, as Mordecai Brown outpitched Christy Mathewson, and the team would eventually defeat Detroit in the World Series. Evers' play had radically changed the outcome of the season. In the months that followed, according to Al Spink, the phrase "touch-second" fell into general use.

When a year and half later Reilly & Britton released a book written primarily by Chicago sportswriter Hugh S. Fullerton, but capitalizing on the name of Evers, the book's main title, *Touching Second,* would seem to have suggested itself.

A facsimile of the dust jacket of the 1910 Reilly & Britton edition of *Touching Second* **(facsimile Dust Jackets, L.L.C., San Francisco).**

The first edition was published in April 1910 and was so popular that it quickly went into a second printing—sometimes incorrectly described as a second edition—in May. The book was reissued as *Baseball in the Big Leagues* by the same company in 1913. It wouldn't be the only foray into publishing for Evers, whom many called the brainiest ballplayer of his day; he also contributed more than 30 articles to publications such as *Baseball Magazine* and in 1917 wrote a small instructional book entitled *How to Play Second Base,* released by American Sports Publishing.

John J. Evers joined the Cubs in September 1902, when the club purchased his contract from the minor league team in Troy, New York, Evers' hometown. By September 14 the famous Tinker-Evers-Chance double play combination was in place. The trio would remain together until 1910, when they were memorialized in Franklin P. Adams' poem "Baseball's Sad Lexicon."

Over the course of his career Evers would finish among the National League's top ten in on-base percentage five times, in runs scored four times, in stolen bases three times, and in batting average twice. He won the league's MVP (then called the Chalmers Award, after the automobile manufacturer) in 1914. Playing behind some of the deadball era's greatest pitching staffs—from 1903 to 1910 the Cubs pitchers allowed only 1.11 walks and hits per inning, compared with 1.24 for the league—it is perhaps no surprise that Evers, Tinker and Chance never led the league in double plays turned. But there are indications that the trio's reputation for skillful defense was based on more than Adams's verse: All three had career fielding percentages and range factors above the league average. And in the 11 seasons they were with the Cubs, Evers or Tinker would finish in the National League top 5 for Fielding Wins seven times, twice making the list together.

After three brief, undistinguished stints as a manager, Evers was elected to the Hall of Fame in 1946 by the Veterans Committee, along with both of his double-play partners.

For *Touching Second*, Evers paired with another Hall of Fame honoree, the 1964 J.G. Taylor Spink Award recipient Hugh S. Fullerton. Now remembered as the man who broke the 1919 Black Sox scandal, Fullerton was at the time a well-known baseball writer for the *Chicago Examiner*, with a reputation as a stylist. In *The National Game* (1911), Al Spink called him "perhaps the ablest baseball writer in America." He was active within his profession, having helped found the Baseball Writers Association of America (BBWA) in 1908, and staunchly supported young writers in whom he saw talent— among them Ring Lardner, and Charles E. Van Loan.

Increasingly hard to find since the early editions fell out of print, *Touching Second* nevertheless remains one of the handful of vintage baseball books familiar to present-day fans. With its balance of insightful anecdotes and rigorous logic, the book is prized as a primer on "inside baseball" by two of the men who knew the most about it.

The McFarland edition of John J. Evers and Hugh S. Fullerton's *Touching Second* exactly reproduces the text of the original, including any peculiarities of spelling and punctuation, and any historical inaccuracies. The pagination has been adjusted to fit series specifications, and some photos have been re-sized, their placement in most instances minimally affected. An index and this note have been added. Any additional modifications are enclosed in brackets.

The editors thank Mike Emeigh, SABR member and contributor for the weblog Baseball Primer, for sharing his knowledge of deadball era defense, and particularly his assessment of the Tinker, Evers, and Chance double-play combination; Trey Strecker, editor of *Dead Balls and Double Curves* and *The Collected Baseball Stories of Charles Van Loan,* for allowing us to check the player names of our index against one he created; and baseball booksellers Wayne Green and R. Plapinger, for information about the publication history of *Touching Second* and *Baseball in the Big Leagues.*

Gary Mitchem
Mark Durr

Introduction

A ball player who has served on a championship baseball club for seven seasons and a reporter who has followed the fortunes of winning and losing teams for twenty years decided to pool their knowledge of the game and its players and produce a book. They agreed that past generations of ball players and reporters have left only garbled traditions and scattered fragments of their knowledge of the game and that the science of baseball, as understood now, should be preserved in some way for future generations to use or to improve upon. They designed the book not only to be a history of the present day development of the American game, but also as a high text book for the lovers of baseball, for players in the amateur and school fields, and for the "fans" generally. That they do not know all about baseball, they freely concede, but present a general study of the inside science of the game based on long experience, dozens of the great players past and present being unconscious contributors.

The manuscript was originally written by the reporter and was rewritten, added to, corrected and revised, by the player. In it are included several articles originally printed in THE AMERICAN MAGAZINE under the reporter's name, with corrections and additions by the player. The whole was rewritten into its present form by the authors, working together, and is presented with the hope that it may assist "fans," younger ball players and all lovers of baseball to a better appreciation of the finer points of the national game, and enable them to see behind the moves of the men on the field, the generalship and brainwork of "inside play."

April, 1910.

CHAPTER I

The Game

Baseball is a game typically American, played by more than 60,000 clubs comprised of approximately 750,000 men and boys over 12 years of age, with practically the entire population of the United States as spectators.

The game is the most highly developed, scientific and logical form of athletic pastime evolved by man, and the ultimate evolution of the one universal game. For some form of pastime or contest involving the use of balls and sticks is indulged in by every tribe of the human race now found on the face of the earth, and historical research reveals both in writings and in pictures that ball games have been played from the earliest known times by every race of man. Egyptian drawings dug out of the Nile storehouses, show angular athletes tossing and catching balls. The Romans played ball with spheres of ivory, bone, wood and softer materials. We know that the Greek hosts before Troy amused themselves with contests at throwing balls. The chances are our earliest ball players learned the game hurling nuts at each other from tops of palm trees. It does not require much of a stretch of the imagination to believe that Abel probably gave a bad decision in favor of the Ham Giants, and that Cain slew him with a bat.

Touching Second

The tribes of the South Sea islands play ball. The Hottentots use the ball in their games and their dances. The Australian Bushmen, long before the British brought them cricket, played a game with a ball, a bat and a base. The tribes of India have their games with balls; the Patagonians use the ball in throwing and catching, and American soldiers found among the tribesmen of Mindanao, in the Philippines, natives whose ability to catch and throw balls would have done credit to a professional baseball player. Every civilized nation has its game, in which the ball, either sphere or spheroid, is the common object. It remained for the inventive American to develop and systematize the universal game, choose the best from scores of other games, and create the greatest of all pastimes: baseball.

The game is the only one played which is founded upon exact and scientific lines. The playing field is laid out with such geometrical exactness, and with such close study of the natural speed of foot and power of arm of the human animal as to give the defensive team an exactly equal chance with the attackers, and to compel both attacker and defender to approach the extreme limit of human speed and agility in every close play. If first base was ninety-two feet from the home plate, instead of ninety, baseball would be ruined because, in the present high development of the game, two feet additional distance would make it almost impossible for a team to score. If the distance between the bases was 88 feet the scores would run into double figures in almost every game. The distances have been so calculated and the players so distributed, that each of the nine men on defense has exactly the amount of ground to cover that the fastest runner possibly can cover with a flying start.

As a problem in geometry, baseball, in any of its departments, may be reduced to exact figures. In algebra the laws of choice and chance may be applied directly to the game. As a scientific pastime, involving the laws of physics and mathematics, the game appeals to the studious. As an exhibition of physical skill and endurance it attracts all lovers of athletics; involving quick thinking, a high degree of generalship and brainwork, it draws the attention of many who ordinarily care nothing for sports or games.

Baseball once was defined as "nine durn fools clubbing a ball around and nine other durn fools chasing it." The definition, while trite, is erroneous, for, in the present day, a fool would have as great a chance to succeed in any of the professions as he would in baseball.

Charlie Bennett, the once great catcher, who lost both legs in a railway accident at the height of his career, illustrated this fact in making a bull. He was watching a game at Detroit when a young base runner, trying to steal second, slid straight at the baseman, who was reaching to take a high throw. The baseman blocked him with one leg, caught the ball and touched the runner out.

"I could have beaten that myself," muttered Bennett in disgust.

"Without legs, Charlie?" inquired a friend.

"Yes—without legs," snorted Bennett angrily, "for I would have had brains enough not to slide where he could block my feet."

Besides interesting almost all classes of Americans, including every imported race after the first generation, baseball has an added interest which, to a great extent, explains its widespread vogue, and this is the element of local popularity. The game in America has reached an almost feudal stage. Each city possessing a ball team takes the same pride and interest in it and accords it the same loyal support that the cities of mediaeval Europe did to their chosen bands of warrior knights. To what extent this pride and loyalty exists is scarcely understood, a close race between teams representing rival towns sometimes creating a condition not far removed from civil warfare.

Touching Second

Probably there is not one person in one hundred over fourteen years of age in the United States who does not understand at least the basic principles of the game and scarcely one native born American in a thousand who has not at some time played the game. A canvass of the House of Representatives at Washington made by the late Joe Campbell during one session of Congress revealed the fact that every man in the House understood baseball and all except two had played the game. One of the two was crippled and the other was partially blind. Campbell obtained from each member a story of his baseball experiences. At that time there were seven members of Congress who had played professional baseball, one of them being Senator Arthur Pugh Gorman.

The extent to which the game has seized upon the people, regardless of class, may be judged by the fact that the number of persons who paid admission to see major league baseball games in one season exceeded the adult population of the United States. In one day (a week day) the total attendance upon baseball games at 107 parks under organized baseball was given at 543,200, and the largest crowd was given at 24,800. How half a million persons could leave business for half a day to attend games was not explained. These figures are from the records of games in leagues under the National agreement, operated as a business. How many were attending amateur, semi-professional and college games on that same day cannot be estimated. Nor can anyone tell accurately how many baseball teams there are in the United States. The city of Chicago alone, with two major league clubs, and twenty-six semi-professional teams, has registered over 550 baseball clubs with nearly 75,000 players. A close estimate of attendance upon baseball games in Chicago one Sunday with both the American and National League teams playing at home showed that about 400,000 persons spent part of Sunday afternoon watching ball games. The scores of 278 games played

I. The Game

on that Sunday in and around Chicago were received by one newspaper. This proportion of interest scarcely can be maintained throughout the country. Chicago is a Sunday ball town and the game on that day is the chief amusement of the people. And every town and hamlet, city, college, almost every church, young people's society and club, every farm hamlet and cross roads village has its baseball team.

The extent to which the people are familiar with the game and interested in it may be judged by a story. A few years ago the clubs representing Chicago in the American and National Leagues won the championships in their own leagues and met to play for the World's Championship. Chicago was in a turmoil for weeks, business was neglected, and work in many cases abandoned. The foreman of one of the great newspapers was compelled to send all the American League adherents in his office to one department and the National Leaguers to another, keeping them apart so the paper might be printed without delay. Police records showed hundreds of arrests of men who fought while disputing the merits of the two teams.

The Sunday editor of one paper sent three reporters out into the city to discover some adult male citizen who did not know that the White Sox and Cubs were to play. After five days of canvassing many sections of the city and all classes of its cosmopolitan population the man was found. He was a German butcher and he became famous in a day as the only man in Chicago who was ignorant of baseball and the approaching series. But even he became a convert, for Comiskey sent him a season ticket to the American League games and before the next June he was one of the regular White Sox rooters.

During the same series, when the West Side and the South Side were engaged almost in civil war, there was an Irishman named Faugh, a Ballagh Finnegan, better known as "Fog," who had made

♦ 11 ♦

a small fortune in trade on the West Side, and who, although he never had seen a game, was one of the most loyal supporters of the West Side team. On the day of the first game "Fog," gloriously arrayed, and with much money to wager, was the center of a group of ardent West Siders assembled in one section of the South Side stands. Standing on his seat he defied the White Sox supporters and flaunted his money in their faces.

"Wan hundred to sixty on the Wist Side," he shouted.

"Wan hundrid to fifty. Wan hundrid to forty."

The South Siders, who were not betting on their team, ignored him. He shouted, challenged, and yelled the praises of the West side. Presently the umpire brushed off the plate and announced:—

"Ladies and Gentlemen—The batteries for today's game will be Reulbach and Kling for the West Side. Walsh and Sullivan for the South Side."

For an instant "Fog" blinked hard, wavering between loyalty to the West Side and love of Ireland. Then, leaping up again, he shouted,

"Walsh and Sullivan—thim's they byes I meant. Wan hundrid to sixty on the South Side."

The interest in that struggle in Chicago was duplicated over the entire country the following year when Chicago and New York engaged in their bitter contest for the National League championship. The presidential campaign was at its height, but the interest in the baseball race overshadowed it. Norman Mack, chairman of the Democratic National Committee, met one of the club owners on the street.

"When is that baseball season going to end?" he inquired anxiously.

The club owner explained the situation.

"Well," remarked Mack, "Hurry up and get it over with. We want to stir up some interest in the campaign.

I. The Game

On the day when the teams played off their tie for the championship, the Democratic National headquarters was turned into a baseball meeting. A committeeman from Oregon, entering to report, complained to Mack that he could not get a hearing.

"They're in the sixth inning now," remarked Mack. "In about an hour we can start to do business." And he joined the crowd at the ticker.

Baseball, under that name, had its beginning at Cooperstown, N. Y., in 1839, although afterward the name was changed, the game being called the "New York game," with the "Massachusetts game" following later, the rules being somewhat different. Before the invention of baseball the English game of "rounders" and "town ball" and "three hole cat" had been played in America with balls, bats and bases. In 1839 a West Point cadet named Doubleday, appointed from Cooperstown and probably at home on furlough, invented the game. Doubleday afterwards was a brigadier general in the army and famous as a mathematician. He organized a team of seven boys to play the game, first against two batters, then against any number present and not engaged in fielding. Later he placed nine men on a side, assigned their positions and played games. As to whether Cadet Doubleday introduced the game into West Point upon his return to the academy there is much dispute. It is said by several army veterans that the class of 1841 played a game believed to be the Doubleday game against another class team, but this has been denied.

Alexander J. Cartwright, of New York, proposed a similar game in 1845, mathematically calculated the distance between bases, and singularly enough, adopted 90 feet as the correct distance, exactly as Doubleday had done. The wisdom of the mathematical calculations of these pioneers is vouched for by the experts of to-day. Cartwright wrote rules for his game and organized a club, first trying seven players, then nine.

Touching Second

Baseball, under the name of the "New York game," became popular at once and was played widely through the eastern states, the rules, however, varying in almost every district so that it was difficult to arrange matches. Each team was forced to concede some rules to the other, and lengthy conferences preceded inter-city matches before the rules could be agreed upon. In some towns 21 "aces" (or, as we call them, "runs") constituted a game. In others, especially where cricket had been played, 100 "rounds" or tallies constituted a game and frequently many days were required to complete a match.

The Knickerbocker club, of New York. Framed a complete code of rules in 1845, the basic principles laid down in the rules being the same as those now prevailing. The rules placed the bases 42 paces apart and 21 "aces" constituted a game. The new game had taken well in Brooklyn, which was the center of athletic activity, and the Knickerbocker rules prevailed among the Brooklyn clubs. The Hudson river towns and cities adopted the game, and adapted the rules to suit their own views. It was played entirely by amateurs, and while called "baseball" in some places it continued to be called the "New York game" or "New York" until it was introduced into Boston by the Tri-Mountain team in 1858.

Boston, having been a cricketing center, objected to the New York rules, changed them and played the "Massachusetts game," in which 100 runs constituted a game. The records of games played in Boston and Cambridge show that sometimes five days were required to complete a match. Harvard teams engaged in the "Massachusetts game" soon after its introduction in Boston and became leaders in the new pastime.

With the organization of the National Baseball Association in 1858, the game began to approach uniformity. The rules were amended and codified and baseball quickly succeeded cricket as the popular sport. From the first, local patriotism played an important part in the sport. Matches played for as high as $1,000 a side were frequent. Brawls, clashes between partisan crowds, and assaults upon umpires are recorded even in those days.

In 1860 baseball had become almost national in scope, and the rules were constantly modified as the play developed necessities for restricting certain practices. The game spread westward rapidly, and made much better progress in western cities than in the east. The civil war, however, arrested the development of the new game for a time. It was played during the war in camps all over the south, regiments and companies having their teams. Sergeant Dryden, of an Iowa regiment, relates that during the long waits in the trenches before Vicksburg, the Union and Confederate soldiers jokingly challenged each other to play baseball, and that during the brief truces the men of his company and the enemy played catch from line to line.

"We were throwing and catching the ball belonging to our company team one day" he relates, "when firing commenced afresh and the men dived into their holes. There was a big fellow named Holleran who, after we had got under cover, wanted to go over and whip the 'Johnny Reb' who had stolen our ball. The next morning during a lull in the firing, that 'Reb' yelled to us and in a minute the baseball came flying over the works, so we played a game on our next relief."

The returning soldiers gave the game new impetus in 1865 and within a few years the West became the important factor in the development of baseball. Chicago, Rockford and Freeport, Ill., Cincinnati, Youngstown, O., and many of the small cities produced famous clubs, while in the East, Providence, Troy, Lynn, Mass., Hornellsville, N. Y., and cities scarcely heard from since became prominent because of their teams.

The first move toward professionalizing the game was made in

1864 when Al. J. Reach, afterwards famous as a player and manufacturer of sporting goods, was paid a salary to play with the Philadelphia club. In the late sixties the Cincinnati Cricket Club, of which Harry Wright was the leading spirit, organized a professional baseball team called the Red Stockings which toured the country, advertising the Queen City and demonstrating the commercial possibilities of the game.

In 1871 a move was made which came near bringing baseball into disgrace and preventing its growth. This was the organization of the National Association of Professional Baseball Players. This body established itself in power, the players governing the game and themselves, and continued to rule until 1875. During that time gamblers, in collusion with certain players, gained control of baseball, and open gambling and the selling of pools was conducted in connection with many parks. The confidence of the public was destroyed, and except as a gambling institution baseball attracted little attention in the professional field. Grave charges of selling games, and in some cases proof of crooked playing, resulted from the reign of the gamblers and the dishonest among players and managers.

The game suffered in popularity, even in the amateur field, and the players who were in charge of the organization proved failures. When in 1876 the National League of Professional Baseball Clubs succeeded to the control of baseball and took the game out of the hands of the players, the promoters made a stern attempt to punish players guilty of selling games and to stamp out gambling as the only means of salvation of the pastime.

William H. Hulbert, president of the league, saved the game by a radical move. He summarily expelled and placed upon a blacklist every player accused of being connected with the gambling frauds, whether the charges were proved or not. Some innocents may have suffered, but Hulbert drove the gamblers from the parks.

Again baseball recovered and flourished, increasing steadily in popularity until 1890, when an insurrection of the players against the National League club owners checked its progress. The cause of the rebellion was the attempt of the club owners to limit all salaries. The players for a time seemed triumphant, but leaders among them treacherously sold them out to the club owners and the Player's League collapsed, leaving the owners heavily in debt and the game discredited in many places.

Slowly the era of prosperity returned. Interest increased rapidly. Baseball was flourishing more and more until 1900, when a war between the two great leagues of the country gave it another serious reverse. With the re-establishment of peace and uniform laws governing all clubs and players the game made wonderful strides forward year by year. The owners of the major league clubs themselves were surprised. The development of interest in the game during the last ten years has been so rapid that men financially interested found themselves unable to accommodate their patrons. From the field in the pasture lot at Cooperstown, where Doubleday stepped off 90 feet, an era of million dollar plants, each seating up to 40,000 spectators, shows the change in the game.

As an amusement enterprise baseball today is scarcely second to the theater. It caters to millions of spectators and represents an investment of perhaps $100,000,000 in property and players. The property holdings of the National and American Leagues alone represent an investment of about $15,000,000. The sixteen major league clubs pay over $1,000,000 a season in salaries to players and spend nearly as much in securing and trying out new players. Add to this the salary lists of thirty-eight minor leagues, and wages paid by thousands of semi-professional clubs, and the immensity of the baseball business as an amusement enterprise may be imagined.

♦ CHAPTER II ♦

The Players

There is scarcely a sport known to the world in which professionalism does not exert a lowering influence. Cricket, golf, even the turf, draw strict lines between the amateur and the professional. In most branches of athletics to become a professional means to take a step backward in the social scale and in the estimation of fellow men.

The great exception to this rule is baseball. The chief reason for this is that baseball in the United States and Canada no longer is upon a doubtful basis, but ranks as an established and honorable trade. In addition the game requires exceptional qualities of body and mind, and in consequence perfect physical condition, involving moral restrictions, not only is insisted upon, but brings exceptional rewards.

In the earlier days of the game professional players were looked upon, in many cases justly, as ruffians or at best itinerant ne'er-do-weels. In many towns and cities of that time the atrocious conduct of the hired athletes, their carousals and misbehavior on and off the field, gave the sport and its players a bad name. Players of that day were recruits who looked upon the game as a means of gratifying nomadic tastes. Few of them expected to continue in the sport, and regarded an engagement as a summer outing, to be devoted to having a good time.

The end of that era came when baseball became a paying commercial venture and was placed upon a business basis. During the early days of the National League, as well as the smaller leagues, club owners, managers and backers invested in the game for the love of the sport itself and without much thought of getting any monetary returns. They expected to lose money; or possibly to regain it through the advertising the team would give them or their cities, rather than in actual receipts at the gates. They organized and operated their teams from that standpoint. Some of the owners were wealthy men, backing teams as an amusement or from a personal pride. There was no recognized basis for salaries, but the average was low, and attracted only the adventurous or the tough, scrappy athletes from the back lots and bottoms of cities. While here and there were men of character and of education, decent clean young men who loved the game, the average of the players was low, morally and intellectually.

When the owners began to perceive that the sport was the latent rival of the theater in financial possibilities and possibly might become the greatest amusement enterprise in the world, the necessity of curbing rowdyism among the players and of obtaining men of higher moral and mental equipment impressed itself upon some of them. A few still held out for the old order of things. The majority, however, became wiser. They had seen crowds suddenly cease to attend games; whole cities turn in disgust against teams and their tactics; as happened in Cleveland, Baltimore, and once in New York. The owners then decided to cater to the patrons; to protect them from the insults and revilings and the coarse words and acts of some of the men.

Much as the "commercialization of baseball" is to be regretted from some standpoints, the fact that it has abolished rowdyism, brought a higher, cleaner and more sportsmanlike class of players into the game and put a premium on brains, commends the business administration. With the beginning of financial prosperity to owners, who had long struggled against loss and sometimes ruin, a higher class of men was attracted to the profession. The colleges sent some of their best men; young athletes who under ordinary conditions would have remained at home and entered business were lured to the game by the chances of big salaries and some honors.

This revolution of conditions began before the Brotherhood fight which culminated in the revolt of the players in 1890. The game was beginning to prosper after years of struggle, salaries were growing higher and higher, and club owners were bidding against each other for the services of the best players. In that respect, baseball is one of the oddest of all business ventures. Eight club owners in the league are partners in business, sharing receipts, sharing prosperity and adversity. Yet all the time these business partners must strive to beat each other on the field and to take each other's players away from them. The National League has almost from the start been mercenary, and this unavoidable condition, which reduced profits largely, the club owners sought to abolish by agreeing to enforce a salary limit, whereby the highest salary paid to any player was to be $2,000. The players revolted against this reduction of salaries, organized a rival league, and salaries leaped to five times that figure, bringing disaster upon everyone concerned.

The restoration of peace reduced salaries again, but they increased steadily during the next ten year period, as the game grew in popularity and returned large financial receipts. The National League had inaugurated another salary reducing campaign in 1899, which ended abruptly when the American League invaded the field and sent salaries to a war-time footing again by bidding for players. At the restoration of peace salaries had reached so high a figure that baseball offered a chance of quick riches to a high class of youths who speedily enlisted. Salaries fell after the peace pact, but have continued to increase steadily and healthily to the present time.

The reforms among the players which the National League had striven in vain to bring about were accomplished as a result of the war between the American and National Leagues. Up to that time the rowdy element in professional baseball had been rampant; and the players of greatest prominence considered themselves almost beyond control of their managers. The young players entering the profession in many instances fell under the influence of the disorderly element and became their allies. The American League, raiding the National, took away most of its star players, but also got most of the disorderly element. These men, scattered through new clubs and sharply curbed, lost much of their power and influence. The American League found itself compelled to adopt stern repressive measures while the National, with clubs of young and aspiring recruits, was relieved of the necessity of repressing them, and started right with the new men by placing a premium on decency and good behavior.

The owners and managers came at last to realize that players of the carousing type could not maintain themselves in good playing condition through an entire season, while the sober and hard working players, even when less brilliant, were found to bring better results.

The establishment of two major leagues of equal or nearly equal caliber immediately doubled the demand for first-class players, and developed the fact that, with perhaps 100,000 active players in the minor leagues, college, semi-professional and strong amateur teams, it was extremely difficult to find 325 men good enough, and with experience enough, to fill the sixteen clubs of the two major leagues. This famine in athletes not only acted to increase the demand for players, and to add to salaries, but it impressed upon both owners and managers the necessity of keeping good ball players in condition. The live stock, upon which the fortunes of the owners depended, had become so valuable that any depreciation found its way into profit and loss figures, and the watchful care of managers over the morals and physical grooming of players insured good behavior. As the game advanced and developed toward perfection, the demand for men above the average in mentality as well as in strength and speed became greater and greater, and the value of the players rose steadily.

The finding and developing of players is the greatest problem of the modern game. There is a dearth of really good players; men of brains, speed and strength, coolness and character. The major leagues alone demand nearly two hundred new players each year to fill gaps in the ranks, and of these not more than twenty, or one in ten, is good enough to remain with the major league teams as a substitute even, and perhaps not more than an average of eight for the sixteen clubs secure regular positions, replacing veterans.

It is almost impossible to purchase players of worth, but outside of all monetary considerations it is certain that the manager of a weak major league club cannot, even if given his choice of all the players in America outside the major leagues, get together a team good enough to raise his city into the first division unless phenomenal luck attends his efforts and a half a dozen players develop suddenly after being promoted.

There have been instances of teams being thrown together that fitted exactly, but they are baseball miracles. The modern manager has as much chance of putting together a winning team in one season as he would have of throwing a handful of mud into the air and having it come down as a Sevres vase. John Grim, who has managed baseball clubs in almost every league and state in the United

States, once put together a team of ten men to represent Portland, Ore., in the Northwest League. He had two weeks in which to create a team out of nothing and a few thousand dollars. In ten days he gathered from all over the United States ten players, most of whom he never had seen before and new little about. He moved on Portland with his squad. Every man in the squad developed into a good ball player. All ten remained with the team through the entire season, and with only one recruit they won the championship from three other teams of experienced players.

Sometimes players are found in coveys, like quail. Hornellsville, N. Y., once gave to the major leagues six players in one year. Lowe, Long, Ganzel and Bennett went from one team into fast company. There was a team which at one time represented Franklin, Pa., in the Iron and Oil League which, without making any spectacular showing in that humble organization, proved a gold mine. In one season that team developed and sent into the major league Jimmy Slagle, Claude Ritchey, Emmet Heidrick, Bill Taylor, "Sox" Seybold and Nichols, the Pittsburg left-handed pitcher, every one of whom at once sprang into prominence and most of whom afterwards came to be regarded as famous players.

In the fall of 1909, Connie Mack, finding his all star Philadelphia Athletics decaying rapidly and threatening to become a hopelessly slow club, discarded practically his entire team, and starting afresh to build a new club, retaining only a few of the veterans to balance the new men and teach them the tricks of the trade, had the phenomenal luck to develop a team which came near being of championship caliber. He discovered Collins, whose infield play was the sensation of the American League in 1909, and Krause, a left-hander, who stepped directly into the front rank of the pitchers of the country. Besides these he found several men better than those he had cast off. But such records are freaks. Usually when a team passes its prime and begins to retrograde, years are required—years and fortunes—before another winning team is produced.

In the earlier days of the game players usually came in pairs, a pitcher and a catcher together; and were mainly recruited from cities. The reason for this was that they started together, throwing and catching back of the shop during the noon-hour recess. Half the players entered the profession either as pitchers or catchers and found their other positions after joining the team and failing in battery positions. Such a thing is next to impossible under modern conditions, because baseball today is one of the most highly specialized of all trades. A second baseman is as distinct from a shortstop as the paying teller of a bank is from the individual ledger man. The right fielder may be able to play left field, but not nearly so well as he can his own position. Why a player is fitted for one position and useless in others is explained later in the individual study of the positions, the men and their duties.

The supply of players of major league caliber is so small that the owners of clubs in the American and National Leagues, and the higher minor leagues have resorted to dragnet methods to discover them and to pull them from the back lots, the college fields and the country playgrounds. Each club employs a scouting force, usually composed of veteran players or retired owners. The duty of these scouts is to scour the entire country, league after league, club after club, seeking men who by their playing show promise, or who by their actions or hitting ability give signs of future development.

Each club receives hundreds of letters every week proclaiming the skill of players in distant places, and immediately the name of the player is listed, his records examined, his past history looked into, the evidence of persons who have watched him play is sought, and finally, if he seems to give promise, a scout is dispatched to see him work, and to report every detail of his build, his speed, his personal character and his habits. Money is not considered if the player shows sufficient ability, in the opinion of the scout, to play in the major leagues, either that year or within the next year, and the man is purchased outright immediately, often at surprising figures.

The extent to which this scrutiny of players is indulged in by the owners and managers of major league clubs is almost unbelievable. Barney Dreyfuss, owner of the Pittsburg club, has books in his offices in which are recorded the names, addresses, descriptions, batting and fielding averages, character and general makeup of thousands of players of whom the baseball world never has heard and probably never will hear, except when they are produced in the form of a Wagner, a Leach or a Jay Miller. The country schoolmaster, playing ball at recess with the boys, may be watched by a major league scout who sits on the fence. The minor league player may lay off some day to rest a sore finger and discover afterwards that a scout, who had traveled thousands of miles to see him play, was in the stands, and that he lost his chance of promotion by remaining idle on that day.

It is related that Dreyfuss was sitting in a buggy on a dusty country turnpike near Goshen, O., watching the schoolmaster playing "Anthony-over" with the boys. The schoolmaster caught the ball, wound up, and instead of throwing it back over the roof of the school, curved it around the building and hit one of the boys in the back. Dreyfuss thereupon climbed out of his buggy, and signed the schoolmaster to pitch for Pittsburg, thereby discovering Sam Leever, one of the greatest of pitchers.

Dan O'Leary, when he was manager of the Indianapolis club, arranged an exhibition game with the team representing a small town near the Indiana capital. The small town team looked fairly strong, but complained that their best player had been forced to work that day, refusing to remain idle when he could make $2 at his trade.

O'Leary volunteered to persuade the player to get into the game. He hired a horse and buggy, drove three miles into the country and found the player busily engaged in shingling a barn. O'Leary agreed to pay him $3 if he would play against Indianapolis that afternoon. In the game the lanky Hoosier twice hit the ball out of the pasture in which they were playing. O'Leary offered him a position on the Indianapolis team and took him away with the club that night. The carpenter was Sam Thompson, who developed into the greatest batter of his day and one of the hardest hitters the game ever has known.

Hans Wagner became a ball player because George Moreland, who owned the Youngstown, O., club needed a pitcher and could pay only $35 a month. Wagner's brother, Al Wagner, suggested that he try Hans, who accepted the offer.

There was one discouraged scout about ten years ago who lost one of the greatest pitchers ever developed because the pitcher was under a heavy handicap. Frank Bancroft, still-hunter after baseball talent of all sorts, was informed that there was a pitcher named Charlie Pickerel at Lynchburg, O., who was as good as any man on the Cincinnati list. Bancroft hastened into the country and watched Pickerel pitch. He was amazed at the speed and curves of the amateur and was on the point of making him an offer when he discovered the one weakness of the man. He could not pitch with his shoes on. Every inning when he went to the slab Pickerel removed his shoes, took a toe hold on the rubber and was another Rusie, but Bancroft feared complications and allowed him to escape.

Tom Ramsey, who perhaps was the most remarkable left-handed pitcher in the history of baseball, was discovered scientifically. He was a brick-layer, and being accustomed to gripping brick with his left hand while breaking them with his trowel, he had cultivated a marvelous power in thumb and forefingers. The Louisville club secured him on the report of a player who had seen Ramsey

Tyrus Cobb, the great exponent of the modern "speed-game" and a heavy batter.

twist the cover of a baseball by pressure of his fingers. The player figured that a man with such power in his throwing hand ought to be a great pitcher, and Ramsey within a short time after joining the team, pitched curves of such wonderful speed and such quick breaks that he became the sensation of the game. James A. Hart, when he was managing Louisville, studied the secret of Ramsey's success and instead of looking for ball players in minor leagues, went scouting for left-handed brick-layers, trailing them to the tops of buildings, but he never discovered another Ramsey.

Nat Hudson, who won the World's Championship for St. Louis in the famous series between the St. Louis Browns under Comiskey and the Chicago White Stockings under Anson, was found in a peculiar manner. Comiskey was a Chicago man, and in the middle of a season he went to Chicago with his St. Louis club, being in desperate need of a pitcher. He was in a barber shop when the barber suggested that he try Hudson, of whom Comiskey never had heard. On hunting for the pitcher Comiskey found that he lived directly across the street from his own home, so after searching the entire country for a pitcher, he got his star at his own doorstep.

But there are few such discoveries made under modern conditions. The men are watched by scores of clubs; and records of their habits, dispositions, speed, hitting ability and intelligence are kept almost from the day they start to play. At one time in the early part of 1907 four scouts representing four major league clubs were in the stands at Springfield, Ill., at one game, watching Doyle, for whom eight clubs had already made bids. The New York club, fearing some other club would get the player, paid $4,500 for him by telegraph without seeing him play, thus securing a great second baseman. In 1909 eleven clubs were bidding at one time for Blackburn, of Providence, who went to Comiskey's Chicago team. "Tad" Jones, the Yale catcher and football player, received offers from every major league club in the country during his senior year, but he refused to become a professional.

Competition for the services of players became so great that club owners of the major leagues threw out dragnets and bought or drafted every player in the minor leagues who had shown signs of promise, frequently recruiting as many as fifty players for one club. The practice, of course, strengthened the strong and wealthy clubs and weakened the poorer ones, until in 1909 an agreement was reached by the club owners limiting the number of players each club could recruit. This step was taken to protect the financially weaker clubs of the major leagues, as well as to prevent the major leagues from disrupting all the smaller organizations by wholesale raids upon the players.

Of the 325 (approximately) players carried on the pay-rolls of the major leagues during a season, not more than one hundred are really finished and competent players. It is extraordinary if ten out of the army of recruits tried out each spring develop even enough strength to hold a substitute position with the major league clubs, and the discovery of a really great player is as unusual as the finding of a Koh-i-noor. There is a moderate supply of "good" players, men of the ordinary ability, but extremely few of the Cobb, Wagner, Speaker, Mathewson, Brown, Kling, and Leach class.

This scarcity of "great" players as distinguished from "good" players has been one of the sources of trouble to organized baseball, because it has served to make both classes dissatisfied. The "great" players think they should be paid proportionately great salaries, and the "good" players, even when admitting the superiority of the others, cannot be persuaded to figure the difference of ability in dollars and cents. Beyond doubt, also, there has come with the securing of absolute power over the game and its players, a desire of the club owners to hold down salaries, especially of young and ambitious players. Frequently the aspiring player is offered far less by the major league club than he received in the smaller leagues. He sometimes accepts in order to win promotion, but the policy has served to reduce further the supply of really good players.

The close specialization in the modern game would amaze persons who rate all players merely as "ball players," forgetting that the president of a railroad is a "railroad man" just as the brakeman is. Players now come as specialists in certain positions and insist upon signing to play that position alone. There are rare men, such as Leach of Pittsburg, Parent of the Chicago White Sox, Hofman of the Cubs, and Wagner, who can play in almost any position. In a way this specialization has assisted the makers of teams greatly. Each team-builder knows exactly in what position his club is weak, and under the close classification in the modern game he is not compelled to look over the entire field for his man. If he needs a second baseman he seeks through that class instead of among "infielders."

Yet some of the biggest baseball "finds" of years have resulted from the fact that managers knew better than men themselves where their proper positions were. In many instances men taken from one position and placed in another immediately showed remarkable improvement. Frank Chance, the "Peerless Leader" of the Chicago Cubs, was a catcher. He declared he could not play first base and refused to play there, threatening to retire from baseball when Manager Selee ordered him to that position. Even then he balked until Selee offered him an increased salary, when he reluctantly consented to make the attempt. Roger Bresnahan imagined he was a pitcher, tried the infield, failed at both places, but then developed into one of the greatest of catchers. Fred Parent, after a brilliant career as a short stop and a fair showing as a second baseman, late in his career discovered that he was a better player in the outfield than in the infield. Joe Tinker refused to play short stop, insisting that he was a third baseman, and was persuaded with difficulty to try the position at which he became famous.

Sometimes this specialization by players is imagination on the part of players who fail to study their own physical shortcomings and advantages in order to fit themselves into the proper place. A third baseman, for instance, does not need the speed required to play short stop, but he must have weight, be able to start forward quickly, and have the strength and the courage to block hard line drives. Besides these things he must be able to throw either underhand or overhand ball, and a hard, fast thrower.

A short stop must be able to move toward his right rapidly, start forward quickly, and at the same time must be able to move to his left, toward or back of second base, and recover quickly after making stops in a necessarily awkward position. Above all things, he must be able to throw either underhead or overhead from any position. An example of the possibilities in short stop acrobatics was a play made by Doolan of Philadelphia, who while in the act of throwing to first base spiked in the neck a base runner en route from second to third. He must have thrown with both feet off the ground.

The second baseman must have a fast snap throw from any position, especially an underhand snap throw while scooping slow balls at top speed, and he must be able to move faster toward his left than to the right. The outfielders specialize in regard to their ability to come in or go out, and whether they run faster to the right or to the left, the center fielder always being the best of the three in going outward and catching balls over his head.

The needs of each position are treated later in detail, in studying the peculiarities of the duties of each part of the machine.

Baseball players of the major leagues now are an intelligent, clean, set of men; this of necessity, regardless of their moral scruples. They are being recruited from higher levels of social and educational development and they occupy a position unique in sports. They are professionals, yet are received and regarded as higher amateurs. The player who reaches the major leagues has reached the post-graduate course of a moral and physical training school and proved his worth. He is the surviving fittest of the game. A few unfit survive, but not for long. Ball playing, as a profession, is now regarded as an honorable means of livelihood and a field for profitable use of talents.

◆ CHAPTER III ◆

Baseball Law

Understand in the first place that baseball "law" is illegal, contrary to civil law, in direct violation of the Federal laws regulating combines and the blacklist, and in principle, directly in defiance of the Constitution and of the Rights of Man. Yet, because of the nature of the peculiar business, the greater part of baseball law is necessary.

Having accumulated at great expense and enormous labor a baseball team capable of winning, and upon which depends the value of large investments in land and structures, the owner of a club is entitled to some protection. And from the first it has been the principle of all baseball organizations that there shall never be an appeal to civil law. No contract, drawn in the form adopted in organized baseball, will hold in civil law. The owners of clubs playing under the National Agreement openly bind themselves to the policy of blacklisting offending players and depriving them by written conspiracy from their means of making a livelihood. They enforce their claims of absolute ownership of the services of players by an iron-clad agreement never to employ any player who in any way offends against the other parties to the agreement and compel the players to sign contracts which, in theory and effect, are life contracts and are unconstitutional.

These facts are indisputable and admitted. Baseball club owners and officials have placed themselves beyond civil law by agreement; have pledged themselves not to appeal to the courts, and to punish anyone who makes such appeal. They justify this action on the grounds of the peculiar nature of the business.

The professional baseball player, having once signed his name to the contract offered by any club, becomes the perpetual property and asset of that club until sold, released on ten days notice, traded into the bondage of another club, or drafted by a club of higher class. He may be sent to any club, regardless of his own wishes and welfare, may be fined, suspended or blacklisted for a term of years or for life. He has no voice in his own career beyond ineffectual protest, and should he attempt to appeal to civil law it is hardly possibly any club owner would dare employ him, as by so doing the club owner would forfeit his rights to protection and to territory.

Whether or not baseball law is a necessity to the welfare and safe conduct of the game is scarcely a question for argument here. The greater part of the baseball code was adopted because of necessities arising from situations involving property rights. Baseball is a peculiar business, and because of its peculiarities the club owners and the officers of leagues claim their laws are necessary.

If the owners of newspapers throughout the United States were to adopt a separate code of laws and attempt to enforce a "reserve" contract, which compelled writers to sign another contract at the expiration of the existing one, the agreement would be smashed in a day. If the theatrical trust should attempt to reserve all actors, the contracts would be worthless. The necessity for the reserve clause among baseball players is great; the combination between owners is much closer than in any other business in America and perfectly effective. In baseball a reserve clause enables club owners to hold together a team, prevents competitive bidding for the services of extraordinary players, enables owners to enforce, in many leagues, a strict salary limit. Without the reserve clause it is doubtful if any twenty players could be held together long enough to create a strong, coherent team, with perfect team work. Without the reserve, and the illegal agreements between owners, some players would receive high salaries for a few years, possibly bankrupt some clubs without much improving their playing strength, destroy the power of owners and managers to discipline players, and, for a times at least, weak clubs would be weakened and strong ones strengthened.

The question is whether contracts for a term of years would not accomplish the same ends. Undoubtedly a sudden change of the system of government would be followed by a period of destructive bidding, but many think that within a short time the salary and contract questions would adjust themselves, the scale of wages being what the business would justify, and the players be certain of greater justice.

The theory upon which baseball's legal code was framed was the protection of the weak leagues, the restriction of salaries within the means of each league, the prevention of contract jumping and violation of agreements by players. Many of the most iniquitous laws in force resulted from defensive action by the owners to prevent the repetition of disgraceful acts by players.

Legally, the baseball player is a slave held in bondage, but he is the best treated, most pampered slave of history, and while there are many cases of oppression, the majority of the players received just and equitable treatment.

As far as baseball law has been honestly and fairly administered it has aided greatly in the improvement of conditions in the sport, increased its stability as an investment, and, in spite of its illegal phases considered from a common law standpoint, it has had a beneficent effect upon everyone concerned, even upon the average player.

But, as usual in all combines, the rulers of the game soon saw that laws framed to protect all could be used by some to oppress others; as an instrument of the rich to benefit at the expense of the poor and the weak, against players by employers, against small leagues by large ones. The only protection existing for players is the fear by club owners, with huge sums invested in the amusement enterprise, that players, if not treated well, or if oppressed, will not give their best efforts on the playing field.

Close examination of the records of the supreme court of baseball since its establishment in 1903 (no reference to the justice of any case being made), reveals the fact that about 82 per cent of cases between major and minor leagues have been decided in favor of the major leagues, and almost ninety per cent of cases involving cases between players and club owners have been decided against the players. The ratio of decisions favoring the strong against the weak appears disproportionate.

An expert in civil law, taking fifty decisions of the National Commission as recorded in their own reports and examining them, reported that, in his judgment, the National Commission had no jurisdiction in twenty-eight, exceeded its powers in nine, made the law fit the case in six, while in three the commission decided against its own laws, as set forth in the agreement. The man who studied the cases knew nothing of baseball except what appeared in the commission's reports, and considered the cases from a legal standpoint.

The vast majority of decisions, however, were accepted without question and recorded as final in baseball. Players either submitted to the rulings or found other employment.

Few persons outside those engaged in the game understand what baseball law is, or how it is administered, or how it affects teams and players. Before 1903, when the National Agreement was written and ratified by most of the organized clubs in America, baseball had been chaotic because of the war between the National and the American Leagues, which after one year of desperate conflict settled down into steady guerilla warfare. The financial standing of almost every club was shaken, and with salaries and expenses at the highest mark in history, receipts were heavily cut. The owners, weary of the ruinous strife and compelled to cease their efforts to ruin each other for safety's sake, met at Cincinnati in September, 1903, and reached the "National Agreement" which is the basis of all baseball law. The National and American Leagues and the National Association of Minor Leagues ratified the agreement as the supreme law of the game, arranged for the establishment of a supreme court of baseball to sit en banc (or en bunc) on disputes of all kinds, agreeing to accept decisions as final.

This court was called the National Commission, and it constitutes perhaps the most extraordinary judicial and legislative body in the history of America. It was provided that the commission should be composed of the presidents of the National and American Leagues, and a third man, who was to be chairman and chosen by the two presidents. August Herrmann, owner of the Cincinnati club and a ring politician of prominence, was chosen as chairman.

Students of political economy possibly would imagine that the court was a farce, the principle behind its formation being laughably in defiance of the accepted theories of government. Instead of choosing judges because of their impartiality, they were chosen because of their interest in, and knowledge of cases to be decided. The consent of the governed was not asked at first, though later the minor leagues were asked to enter into the agreement; but the consent of the players, over whom the commission was given full and extraordinary powers, never was requested. The interests of forty leagues, perhaps 350 clubs and 8,000 players, were thrust into the hands of three men, one an owner, the others representing owners.

Further, this court was empowered not only to hear cases and pass judgment, but to enforce punishments, collect fines and execute their own decrees. Going further, the commission, a judicial body, was made executive and legislative, empowered to pass laws governing themselves, the club owners (their employers), and players, even to pass laws to decide cases already in hand, to pass laws to correct abuses, and to make these laws retroactive and punish for offenses committed prior to their enactment. In the first year of the existence of the court, it went back and punished for offenses which were committed, or were alleged to have been committed, before the National Agreement was signed and the court created.

This procedure was explained, or excused, as such proceedings now are excused, on the plea that the action was necessary for "the good of the game."

The National Commission, while laughable from a standpoint of civil law, has proved effective, has safeguarded the game in many ways, and has corrected many evils.

The National Agreement, which is the constitution of base-ball, is one of the most remarkable of existing legal codes. The first remarkable phase of the constitution is found in Rule 23, which provides: "These rules may be changed at any time by a majority vote of the commission."

That one rule gave the National Commission the most absolute power in all cases, without referendum even to the club owners, made two men supreme to enact laws to punish all offenses, and to create offenses for which punishment might be inflicted. The chief objection of players to the high court of the game is that they believe too much power has been given to two men, both naturally influenced in favor of the employers.

The reservation clause is the vital principle of organized base-ball. The owners claim baseball could not exist without it, while the thinking players insist that long term contracts, safeguarding the interests of both parties, would accomplish as much.

The general public does not understand the system on which the baseball business is built. The agreement between the club owners of all leagues provided for classification of the leagues, each of which was to remain separate and independent, making its own rules except in cases where power was claimed for the central government. The National and American Leagues were rated as the major leagues, the Eastern and American Association as secondary major leagues, and the others were divided into classes A, B, C, and D, with provisions for even lower ratings if necessary.

Each league is allotted a fixed value per head on its players, and an annual period is fixed during which any league of an higher class is privileged to draft players, to a certain number, from clubs of a lower class league by paying the fixed sum.

The National and American Leagues may draw upon any league for any player, and take him upon payment of the sum fixed as the per capita value of players of that class. If the clubs fail to draft the player during the stated drafting period, he must be acquired by purchase. In theory, this classification was made to protect the smaller leagues from being disrupted by drafts upon them by the major leagues. During its workings it has done much injustice to some clubs of the lower class, but on the whole, the smaller leagues have profited greatly at the expense of the richer clubs because of the over-eagerness of the large club owners to obtain players. The vast majority of players drafted or purchased from the smaller clubs are sent back after brief trials in the major leagues, usually for smaller sums than those paid, so the minor leagues have little cause for complaint against the direct workings of the drafting laws. The evils are found, not in the rules, but in the evasion and the abuse of them generally indulged in.

Both the larger and smaller leagues have taken advantage of flaws in the arrangement. The principal abuses of the system have been by major leagues taking players from lower class leagues, not for themselves but for other clubs of lower rank with which secret agreements have been made. The injustice to the players is apparent in all such arrangements. The drafting laws give the player no voice in his own career. Not only must he go where he is ordered, but must accept whatever salary is offered him by the club which drafts him. The growing practice of the larger leagues in offering recruits smaller salaries than they were paid in the minor leagues is another fertile cause for complaint.

Each league is empowered to regulate its own affairs—and further, to fix salary limits. Nearly all the low class leagues have written agreements limiting the amount that may be paid in salaries per month to players. On their face, agreements such as these would seem an intolerable injustice to players, but as a matter of fact, little cause of complaint is given the players, as usually eight clubs in each league violate the agreement almost as soon as signing it.

The strength of the organization that rules the players and clubs was tested within a short time after the adoption of the National Agreement when players, rebellious at heart, commenced to demand non-reserve contracts as the price of signing any contract. Many players proposed to sign the regulation contract for a term of years provided they were not reserved and were made free agents at the end of the contractual period. The commission ordered all clubs to sign players under nothing but the approved form of contract, containing the reserve clause. Players who were in demand still insisted upon non-reserve contracts and many received contracts with the reserve clause stricken out. The result in many cases was peculiar, for at the end of the contract term the player discovered that instead of being free, he still was under reserve. The commission had made a law which said:

"Where the contract contains a reservation clause, the player shall in no instance be held to be free from reservation unless the clause is stricken from the contract."

The players then discovered that, instead of striking out the clause, the club owners had presented them with contracts in which there was no printed reserve clause and that the law of baseball says:

"Where the contract does not contain a reservation clause, every club, nevertheless, has a right to reserve a player unless the contract itself contains a written stipulation that the player is not to be reserved."

Some players discovered they had been reserved by a trick which in any other business would be held as fraudulent, and that he still was a chattel of the club which, he thought, had agreed to set him free. And there were no Ohio River cakes of ice over which he could escape.

The administration of baseball law is peculiar. There are several cases recorded in which players, who accept terms, report, and play even one game with clubs, then refuse to sign the contracts offered, become the property of that club, subject to perpetual reservation.

Nor in baseball law is it necessary even for a player to sign a contract, or enter into any agreement to become as asset of a club. In the case of A. A. O'Brien, of the Ilion, N. Y., club, the supreme court of baseball ruled on the subject. O'Brien played with Ilion, but refused to accept any contract and, after playing for a time, left the club to attend to more profitable business. In spite of that fact, Ilion placed him under reservation, and accepted the draft price from the Philadelphia Athletics in payment for the player. The National Commission decided O'Brien belonged to Ilion, that Philadelphia had the right to draft him, and barred O'Brien from any voice in the matter.

In no case, as far as the records show, has the question of the justice or injustice of the salary offered been taken into consideration by the court in deciding cases. The club itself is made sole judge of salaries, and that has opened the way to injustice. In several recorded cases players have been offered less than half the salaries paid them the previous year. There was one major league pitcher who received $3,500 a season. In a game he hit the manager of another club three times with pitched balls, finally injuring him severely. The manager accused him of hitting him purposely. Two years later the manager traded for the pitcher, offered him a salary of $1,500, explaining that he was getting revenge, and drove the man out of baseball.

Only the bitter rivalry between club owners, and the desire to satisfy players and keep them satisfied in order that they will do their best work, prevents wholesale horizontal decreases of salaries in the major leagues, where the combination is most powerful.

The players do not oppose baseball law, regarding some final court as necessary to the welfare of the game. It is the frequent abuse of the power and its use to oppress that foments the rebellious spirit among the players. One constant source of friction is the rule governing reporting for spring training. Many players have other business interests and object to spending six weeks training, without pay, when the time might be profitably occupied. Their contracts require them to report at a stipulated time before their salaries begin, and special laws provide heavy fines for failure to do so. Recently laws have been enacted by the commission to prevent players from engaging in games out of season, the club owners desiring to retain absolute control over players for the twelve months of the year.

The complaint of the players is not so much against baseball law itself as against the manner in which it is administered, and against the custom of not allowing the defendant player an opportunity to present his side of the case either to the president of his own league or to the National Commission. The player who has failed to report to his club in the spring or violated (perhaps technically) some fractional part of his contract, finds himself in trouble. His case is taken up behind closed doors by the National Commission and he is fined without a chance being given him to present a defense, or to offer an explanation. A club owner, who is called before the court, is told to prepare a defense against the charge which has been made against him. Frequently the Commission, or one member of it, states weeks in advance of a hearing what the decision will be, and that before consulting other members of the commission.

The demand of the players is for an impartial court of three or five men not vitally interested in baseball, men who have no baseball connections, especially no financial ones. The players desire that this court shall codify and print all existing laws, and submit them to all members of the agreement for ratification. Finally, they demand that the court shall sit openly at stated intervals to hear causes, and take the evidence on both sides.

◆ CHAPTER IV ◆

Creating a
Winning Team

Creating a championship baseball team is a question of luck, patience, brains and money, with patience and luck the principal elements making toward success. Critics of weak teams complain always, "Why don't they buy some ball players?" Nothing more suggestive of ignorance of the game and conditions prevailing was ever voiced than that wail. The scarcity of players was explained in a preceding chapter, yet that is only a portion of the difficulty of the man upon whom it devolves to make a team.

Baseball players are not for sale. No really good player ever is sold unless behind the sale are reasons well known to the seller. If a good man is placed in the market something is wrong. Either the player is dissatisfied, has had troubles with other players, has taken to drink or has developed some ailment or weakness. Investigation of every case of sales by major league clubs will reveal some such cause.

Often clubs will trade one good player for another because they are over-supplied in one department and weak in another, or because they believe another man will fit into the team better; but money will not, alone, make a team. Experience seems to show that a manager may best strengthen his team when by knowledge of the inside conditions existing on the other clubs—learning which men are dissatisfied, or have quarreled with their managers or team mates, have a grievance or a "grouch"—he may make advantageous purchases or trades. Players worthless to one club often prove valuable to another. Practically every winning major league club of recent history has been made in that way from the discards of weaker clubs.

In spite of the optimistic announcements early each season few managers believe their teams will win pennants. Most of them are content to improve a few positions, and continue to improve each year up to a stage of development which justifies straining every nerve to win highest honors. The team that finishes sixth one year, fifth the next and third the next may be expected to make a strong fight for the championship, but it is seldom that more than three clubs have any real hope of winning.

Usually ten years, frequently more, are required to create a pennant-winning team and it is of pennant-winning caliber not more than three years before it begins to retrograde. Occasionally after reaching its highest form a team collapses entirely in one season and the work must be begun all over again. The New York Highlanders, after coming within a game of the championship, collapsed the following season to nothingness. The St. Louis Browns, with strong pennant possibilities, fell two games short of the 1908 American League championship and the following year was the most wretched team in either major league.

No team of young players ever has won a major league pennant, although Boston and Philadelphia in 1909 came near upsetting baseball tradition in that respect.

Teams are built on various theories. Comiskey, who has led more pennant-winning teams than any other man, works on the theory that pitchers and condition will win. His teams always are kept in top condition throughout the season and he will go to any lengths to get "air tight" pitchers. Detroit and Pittsburg both are teams built with the idea of hitting power first. The Chicago Cubs are built on the theory of team work, inside play and base running. The Boston American team is an aggregation accumulated with the idea that speed of foot will capture pennants. The solid foundation of a good and lasting team is rather along the average in hitting, base running, fielding and pitching and the highest possible development of team work. Harmony, united effort, brains and condition will win over speed, individual brilliancy and heavy hitting.

The first problem of the owner of a franchise is to get a leader, for without leaders who can get the best work out of every man, teams cannot win. The next is to get the team, then team work, and having all these there remains nothing to do but to pray for luck and good umpiring.

Teams have been thrown together that fitted perfectly. Pittsburg closed the season of 1908 needing a second baseman, a first baseman, either a third baseman or a center fielder, and pitchers. Jay Miller developed into a sensational second baseman and two minor leaguers, Abstein and Barbeau, played like stars for more than half the year. Barbeau was first to explode, but his place immediately was filled by Byrne, and Pittsburg won a lucky pennant. It was the first team in baseball history to win after starting to "go back." The three veterans of the team, Clarke, Leach, and Wagner, each played the greatest game of their careers. Philadelphia, in the National League, has not won the pennant since 1871. Cincinnati never has won the championship. Chicago, which monopolized baseball in the early eighties, was twenty years getting together another pennant-winning team. Perhaps the best way to show how hard it is to get together a championship team is to take some one club and relate its struggles before final triumph.

IV. Creating a Winning Team

The sale of Clarkson and Kelley to Boston destroyed Anson's championship club. The cause of that sale never was made public, but the real reason was a woman, and the club was compelled to sell the men, although the act brought down the wrath of the city upon them. The remnant of the team fell into a rut. When James A. Hart became president he saw that the first step necessary was to get rid of all the old stars—even Anson—and begin making a new team. He could not get rid of Anson until 1898, when he brought back Tom Burns, who proved a failure in two years. Tom Loftus was tried for two years—and failed. Frank Selee, adopting Hart's ideas, began at the bottom to create an entirely new club. It is extremely doubtful whether Selee ever would have made the team a pennant-winner, on account of prejudices against certain players. Selee's health failed and Charles W. Murphy, who had just purchased the club, discovered a leader.

The real beginning of the Chicago Cubs was in March, 1898, when a big, bow-legged, rather awkward young player come from the Pacific coast to be tried as a catcher. Quiet, good-natured, rather retiring off the field, serious, and in deadly earnest while playing, honest and sincere in everything, Frank Leroy Chance reported at training quarters at West Baden, Ind., carrying a bunch of gnarled and wrecked fingers at the end of each hand. Anyone who at that time had predicted that Chance was to become the leader of the greatest club ever organized would have earned a laugh. He had no experience except the little gained in amateur games in California. He played with the Fresno High School team in 1893, for two years with Washington University at Irvington, Cal., and he participated in the great amateur tournament played between all the school teams of California, catching for Fresno, which team finished close to Oakland and Stockton. Bill Lange, then with the Chicago club, saw Chance and recommended him for trial.

While awkward and unfinished, pitchers who worked with him declare that Chance from the first showed his genius for leadership and great skill in handling pitchers and watching batters. His fearless recklessness brought him many injuries as a catcher and twice he was nearly killed.

There was not much sign of promise of a championship team in Chicago then, for Hart, in spite of his theories, still had his old stars; and it was not until 1900 that the club, with all its scouts, its purchases and trades, made another rich strike. This lucky find was John Kling, who was born knowing baseball in Kansas City. He was manager, pitcher and first batter of the Schmeltzers from 1893 to 1895, when he went to Rockford, Ill., as a catcher and lasted one pay day, being released as a failure. Returning to Kansas City, he led the Schmeltzers three more years. In 1898 he joined Houston, Tex., under the name of Klein, and quit because the team would not pay him his salary. He again caught for the Schmeltzers until 1900, when he went to St. Joseph, Mo.

Ted Sullivan, the veteran scout, went on a secret visit to St. Joseph to buy Sam Strang, later of Chicago and New York, and was so impressed with Kling that he also was purchased, Chicago securing the greatest catcher the game ever has known.

The season of 1901 passed without permanent improvement of the club, which was disrupted by the war between the American and National Leagues. A host of players were purchased, but not one was of championship caliber; and it was not until the coming of Selee that the prospects of a winning team brightened. Selee and Hart reached an agreement as to the management in the fall of 1901, and Selee immediately laid plans to strengthen Chicago. His first step was a bit of strategy to secure Slagle, who was wanted to lead the batting list.

Slagle was a quiet, cool, left-handed batter with much patience and judgment. His career in baseball had been full of vicissitudes. He started playing with Clarion, Pa., in 1889, and afterward went to Ohio Wesleyan University at Delaware, where he played the outfield two seasons. In 1894 he signed with Franklin, in the Iron and Oil League, then played with Omaha for one season; next went to Houston, Tex., where a scout discovered him and took him to Boston in the fall of 1896. Boston banished him to Grand Rapids, from which place he went to Kansas City. Pittsburg bought him, but before he played there he was traded to Washington, and when the National League was reduced to eight clubs in 1898 Slagle was sent to Philadelphia, where, in the greatest aggregation of batters ever organized, the little fellow led the list. He was sold to Boston in 1901 and near the end of the season broke a finger. Selee, having a scheme, sold him to Baltimore. The release to Baltimore was part of the plot to get him to Chicago, for as soon as Selee became manager of Chicago he brought Slagle back.

That same spring Selee found the man to stop the gap at short stop which had existed for years. The man was Joe Tinker, who began playing ball with the John Taylors in Kansas City in 1896. He was so good even then that the next year Hagen's Tailors paid $2 for him, and he helped that team win the city championship in 1898. Then he went to the Bruce Lumbers, with which team he met and conquered Kling's Schmeltzers. The next season Kling traded two uniforms and a bat for Tinker and brought him to the Schmeltzers, but in June he went to Parsons, Kans., and later in the summer to Coffeyville. Denver purchased him and tried him at second base, but he was so bad that he was sold quickly to John McCloskey, who was managing the Great Falls team. It happened that Great Falls was in financial straits, and needing money, McCloskey sold Tinker to Helena for $200 and Joe Marshall, saving the team and the league from bankruptcy. He was taken to Portland, Ore., in 1901, by Jack Grim. Playing third base, he helped win the pennant of the Northwest League. He played so well that scouts for both Cincinnati and Chicago bid for him. Jack McCarthy, who had been ill-treated by Cincinnati, advised Tinker to try Chicago and he joined the team as a third baseman. Selee insisted upon making a short stop of him, and after a long dispute Tinker agreed to try—and became one of the greatest in the league.

Perhaps the greatest luck the Chicago club ever had was in forming an alliance with George Huff, athletic director of the University of Illinois, for the association of Huff with the club as scout marked an era in the making of the championship team. Huff's first contribution to the team was Carl Lundgren, the University of Illinois pitcher who had twice won the Intercollegiate championship for the school. Lundgren was quiet, studious and the "Human Icicle," one of the most careful observers of batters ever found. He was of the type that studies three aces and a pair of tens for two minutes before calling—and studies a pair of deuces just as hard. When he calls, he wins, and he pitched wonderful ball for Chicago.

(The following is by Fullerton.)

Late that same season Lowe, the famous second baseman, injured his leg and the team was left without any man for the place. A scout was in Troy, N. Y., to get Hardy, a pitcher, and in despair Selee wired him to get a second baseman, and forward him C. O. D. When the scout returned bringing John J. Evers almost everyone laughed. Evers was then not nineteen years of age. No one suspected that he was destined to become the greatest second baseman that ever lived and the foremost exponent and developer of the "inside game," for neither his appearance nor his experience indicated any great promise. He began playing ball when eight years of age, with the Cheer Ups at Troy. After playing on school and amateur teams, he was signed, in 1902, to play short stop for Troy, the opportunity with Chicago coming before he had played a season in the minor league.

All there is to Evers is a bundle of nerves, a lot of woven wire muscles, and the quickest brain in baseball. He has invented and thought out more plays than any man of recent years. He went to second base to fill Lowe's place the first day he reached Chicago, played twenty-two games to the end of the season without an error, and became the baseball idol of Chicago.

(Evers wanted that left out.)

Prospects for getting a winning team improved, but luck deserted Selee's banner in 1903. However, a change was made which was of as much importance, possibly more, than anything before or since. Selee persuaded Chance after long resistance to play first base and transformed him into a great first baseman.

With Chance, Evers and Tinker in position, the team began to be formidable, but Selee was sick, and really unable to perform the duties of manager. His sickness forced him to rely more and more upon the judgment of Chance, who suddenly developed a genius for handling men. Lowe was out of the game and a captain was needed. Selee decided to try something unheard of; to submit the election of a captain to the vote of the players themselves. There were three candidates, none especially active. Selee's choice was Casey; Kling and Chance both had admirers among the men. The election was held in the club house, Selee actively exerting his influence for Casey, while some of the players were urging Chance as the veteran of the squad. The result of the vote was Chance, 11; Casey, 4; Kling, 2. Selee was dumbfounded and for a time annoyed, but events proved the players had made the wisest selection and the vote was the turning point in the career of Chance and in the development of the club.

Chance, although only advisor to Selee, at once assumed the

task of building up the team. He seemed to know just what men he wanted, and how to get them, as well as the weaknesses of his own team. His first move was to get Mordecai Brown. The Omaha management, desiring to keep Brown, told Selee his arm was bad, but Chance declined to believe it. Chance had been watching Brown and wanted him, but was overruled and St. Louis filed prior claim and secured him—but only temporarily. Chance was persistent, and when Jack Taylor fell into disgrace after the loss of the city championship, a deal was arranged whereby Taylor and McLean were given to St. Louis for Brown, who had not pitched well there.

Late that same season Scout Huff discovered three more men of championship caliber. The story of Huff's work that season reads like a Sherlock Holmes adventure, especially the tale of his pursuit of three ghostly pitchers. The story properly begins three years earlier, when Ed Reulbach, a giant youngster, was pitching for Notre Dame, Indiana, University. Reulbach is as near a physically perfect man as possible. Huff had seen his terrific speed and wonderful curves in college games and set watch on him. The next year, while beating the underbrush for young players, Huff began to receive reports from Sedalia, Mo., of a pitcher named Lawson and finally went there to see him pitch. The day before he reached Sedalia, Lawson disappeared, leaving no trace or clue. Huff wanted a pitcher, needed him, and hurried to find Reulbach, but imagine his surprise when, immediately after the close of school, Reulbach disappeared as utterly as Lawson had done, leaving no trace.

The Huff began to receive reports from Montpelier, Vermont, of a young pitcher who was winning everything in the Green Mountain League and whose name was Sheldon. Huff disguised himself as an alderman and went to Montpelier to see the new prodigy perform. The mystery was solved—Sheldon, Lawson and Reulbach all were pitching and they were one man; all Reulbach under assorted names. Huff straightened out the tangle and returned to Chicago with one of the greatest modern pitchers.

Hart had heard that McChesney of Des Moines was worth having and sent Huff to observe. Huff reported McChesney only a fair ball player, but that Hofman, short stop, was one of the greatest players in the country. Both were purchased and Chicago thus accidentally secured the best utility man of modern times. Hofman played every infield and outfield position for Chicago during three pennant-winning seasons, being so good a substitute that Chance could not afford to use him as a regular until 1909 when he went to center field. Two seasons he saved the pennant for Chicago by understudying every man on the team who was injured, playing almost to the standard of every man he replaced. In one week he played six positions on the infield and outfield.

Hofman came into baseball from the amateurs of St. Louis. He played with Smith Academy team for a time, then with semi-professional teams in St. Louis and finally got into the Trolley League, where he became a contract jumper. His contract with East St. Louis guaranteed him $8 a game when weather conditions permitted play. One day the sun was shining, the weather warm, and everything favorable, but the Mississippi River had risen and flooded the grounds. Hofman contended that weather did not prevent the game and claimed his money. The management refused to pay and Hofman jumped to Belleville, where Barney Dreyfuss found him in 1903, and took him to Pittsburg, but immediately released him to Des Moines where Huff discovered him.

Huff made one more important discovery that season. McCarthy's legs were giving way, and an outfielder was needed. Huff went to Syracuse to see Magee. He telegraphed Selee to get Schulte, a quiet, droll York state boy, and Mike Mitchell. Both were secured, but Chicago offered Mitchell less money than he was getting at Syracuse.

He was forced to accept the offer, but openly stated he would not give his best efforts to the club, and so was lost to Chicago, Cincinnati securing a great player. Schulte quickly developed into one of the best players in the National League.

If anyone could have found Schulte up to 1898 a more detailed map would be needed. He was born in Cochocton, New York, and started playing ball with Glen Aubrey. From there he went to Poseyville, from Poseyville to Poseytuck, to Hickory Grove, to Blossburg, and finally in 1897 got upon the edge of the map at Waverly, playing there two years. Then he went to Lestershire, and reached Syracuse in 1902.

Schulte proved to be the man needed. In him Chance had found one of the rarest baseball treasures, a "third batter." The third batter in any team is the most important. He must hit long flies, hit hard, bunt and run, because ahead of him in a well constructed team are two batters who are on the team for their ability to "get on," and the third man must be able either to move them up or hit them home.

The team, after eighteen years of effort, was growing strong, but not steady. It fought hard for the pennant in 1905, but was beaten. Chicago at last had a contender in the pennant race. Selee was sick, and he did things he would not have done had he been well. Having a team almost complete, he was kept from wrecking it only by Chance. Selee wanted to release Slagle; he wanted to let Evers go; he was so anxious to get rid of Hofman that he refused to permit him to practice on the diamond with the other players. In the middle of the season Selee's illness forced him to surrender and Chance was chosen as manager. The big, awkward youngster who had joined the team at West Baden seven years earlier, suddenly showed himself a great baseball leader. The day he took charge of the team he said: "We need pitchers, we must have a new third baseman, and a hitting outfielder before we can win the pennant."

Casey was playing a fair third base and Maloney was a sensational, if erratic, outfielder, and was the idol of the crowd. That winter the team was sold by Hart, who had spent so many years trying to create a winner, to C. Webb Murphy, who gave Chance absolute power as far as playing and getting players was concerned.

Chance knew the men he wanted. He wanted four; and three of them he got. To get the first one he made one of the most spectacular deals ever recorded in baseball history. This man was James Sheckard, a brilliant, clever and much wanted outfielder who had disturbed the Brooklyn club by playing hop scotch with the American League during the war. Here the gossip of the club proved valuable. Sheckard was dissatisfied with Brooklyn, and Chance knew it. The Brooklyn management did not think Sheckard was giving his best services, but feared to trade a man who was popular with the spectators. The trade Chance made to get Sheckard stunned Chicago followers of the game. He gave Outfielders McCarthy and Maloney, Third Baseman Casey and Pitcher Briggs, with $2,000 added. Chance was satisfied. His outfield was complete at last. He swung Schulte to right field, his natural position, put Sheckard in left, and with Slagle in center regarded the work as finished.

Chance realized third base must be filled or his pennant hopes would filter away at that corner. He knew the man he wanted, Harry Steinfeldt, who was playing indifferent ball with Cincinnati. He was slow, a heavy hitter, a good fielder and a wonderful thrower. Again inside gossip directed Chance to a man while older managers, not closely in touch with players, listened to other stories. Chance knew Steinfeldt, had played with him two winters, in California, and knew also that internal dissentions were causing the trouble in the Cincinnati ranks. The Cincinnati club was anxious to trade Steinfeldt, but gossip among his enemies in Cincinnati had kept other clubs from bidding for the player. Chance asked Murphy to make a trade.

Murphy went to Cincinnati, but the stories whispered to him sent him flying back to Chicago without the player. A few days later Murphy asked Chance: "What third baseman can we get?"

"Steinfeldt," said Chance.

Murphy argued, but went to Cincinnati and again returned without the player, but with even more startling stories to tell Chance. "Who shall we get?" he asked.

"Steinfeldt," replied Chance, unmoved.

So Murphy, still unconvinced, went to Cincinnati and traded Weimer, a left-handed pitcher for Steinfeldt.

The team was complete at last. The day Steinfeldt signed Chance remarked that if he could add a little pitching strength the team would win the pennant.

Huff was sent in frantic search of the additional pitching strength and recommended Jack Pfiester, a big left-hander who, after a career extending all over America, was pitching well for Omaha; well and often. Pfiester had a non-reserve contract with Omaha, so he owned himself, and when Huff and Chance tried to get him they dealt with him direct and purchased him for $2,500. Still Chance was not content. He wanted another strong catcher to assist Kling and he traded for Pat Moran, who had for five years hit well and caught steady ball for Boston. They he profited again by his knowledge of players and the inside gossip of teams. He knew Overall was a fine pitcher, and he knew that the reason Overall was not pitching well for Cincinnati was that he was being overworked and was weak. Chance had played with Overall in California, had attempted to buy him from Tacoma, when Cincinnati secured him, and had kept constant watch on the giant young pitcher. He knew better than Manager Hanlon of Cincinnati how to handle the man—and believed he could win. A deal was made—Chance giving Wicker for Overall and $2,000, a deal which proved the joke of the season.

IV. Creating a Winning Team

The team was complete; finished in every detail and with the pitching staff working like machinery, it swept through the season of 1906 breaking all records, winning 116 games and losing only 36. Two more years it won the National League championship and twice the World's Championship, before it was beaten out by Pittsburg in 1909.

The experience of Chicago in making a club is the experience of all winning teams; the details of the finding, developing, buying and trading show those who complain because their home team fails to win, why the management cannot follow their advice and "buy some good players."

♦ CHAPTER V ♦

Managers and Their Duties

The laws of baseball, calculated to create dissatisfaction and ill-feeling among players, require that a buffer be erected between the player and the owner which shall lessen the friction and entirely separate the ball field and the business office of the club. Upon the manager devolves the duty of persuading players that salaries and fines are part of business and not associated with playing baseball.

Managers of baseball teams that win are born to command men, and they are the rarest products of the game. To make a team win a manager must rule with a firm hand, lead with a spirit and dash that keeps the other members of the club spurred to highest speed, deal fairly, win without gloating, die fighting and be ready to congratulate his conqueror. He must have tact, patience, gameness. The good manager is a general, gifted with the power to rule men as well as to lead them in battle, and his duties upon the field are the lightest part of his work—the part that has least effect upon the result of the pennant race.

Managers are divided into two distinct classes; bench managers who, if wise, direct and counsel rather than order their men; and playing managers who demonstrate the plays and lead their men in person. The former is a general directing the battle from headquarters in the rear; the latter a Navarre with white-plumed helmet always in the thickest of the fray. The playing manager is the more brilliant. When he falls he falls harder, although with spectacular effect, while the bench manager lasts longer and his successes and failures are more likely to be attributed to others.

As to the respective value of the two classes this much can be said: more pennants have been won by playing managers in modern baseball than by bench managers and, within the last decade, the wisest club owners have turned to their playing ranks to find managers rather than to employ bench managers of known ability and reputation. The bench managers who have succeeded, in every instance, have possessed a great field general to carry out the orders; so that really the man on the field deserved a share at least of the honors of victory.

Almost every successful field captain who acted under bench managers later became a successful manager on his own account. Ned Hanlon, after a victorious career, during which men like Kelley, Jennings, McGraw and Wilbur Robinson executed his orders and led his men, failed when he had no capable leader of the field forces. McAleer, his peer in knowledge of the game, Frank Selee, and John McCloskey, for whom Long, Lowe, and other great players executed orders, failed when their field generals fell. They could direct, but needed field generals to lead. Jennings, a great leader when a player, succeeded in Detroit because, while in fact a bench manager, he was on the field and almost in as close touch with his men as a player could be, besides having men of brains and ability as his aides.

The playing manager is far more effective on the field, all other things being equal, but as a permanent investment he is more likely to prove a sudden and spectacular failure. The moment he reaches the stage where he cannot execute and demonstrate the plays he commands his men to make, they will turn upon him. He may retire to the bench then, but it is a question whether a field manager will become a bench manager, for the old desire to be in the game and do things himself will handicap him in his work on the bench. Fred Clarke, of Pittsburg, and Frank Chance, of Chicago, owe their great success to the fact that they can, and will, do anything they order their men to do, and have the nerve and the courage to go even further than they would order another to go.

Comiskey, perhaps the greatest field general the game ever has known, as well as the most successful silent manager, is proof in himself that the playing manager is the one that wins. Comiskey always is the guiding spirit of his teams, no matter who the manager may be. After retiring from active play, he had the good fortune to discover able lieutenants to lead his teams and execute his orders, besides thinking for themselves. Each time he has chosen the wrong aide, his team has lost; each time he has found an able man, the team has been victorious. After the overwhelming defeat of his team for the Championship of Chicago in 1909 Comiskey remarked quietly:

"This hurts. They had the better team. What we needed was a leader, then we could have beaten them even with a poorer team. I have made money in baseball, but I would give everything I have to be able to go out there before my people, who are pleading with me to win, and lead that team."

The position of manager of a team in a major league is one of the most nerve racking, exhausting and desperate in the calendar of work. Primarily, the manager is responsible for the creating and assembling of the team, in which duty there are hundreds of opportunities to make mistakes. He is responsible for the condition of the

men, both in preparation for the season and during the entire playing season. He is responsible for the selection of the pitchers every
day; in this alone a bad manager could cause a team to drop from
first to last place in a month. Upon him rests the burden of deciding what style of attack and defense shall be used in any game or in
the crises of the game. More than that, he is held responsible by the
spectators and by the press, which is severe, and by the "fans," who
add cruelty to criticism, for every defeat.

Ishmael would have felt as if he was the guest of honor compared to the manager who with a strong "paper" team finishes far
down in the race, and Lazarus and Job could not have felt as sore
and boiling as he. In addition, the manager frequently must either
endure or suppress criticism and open opposition in his own ranks.
The day Job's biggest boil broke he must have felt exactly as did Tom
Burns one afternoon when he was managing the Chicago club.

"Push it off to right field," he ordered the batter who was starting to the plate.

"Why, you old gray-headed stiff, you hit 212 the last season you
played," responded the player.

The crowd which cheers the players has little conception of the
trials and tribulations of the manager who, perhaps, crouches unseen
and forgotten (by the crowd) in the corner of the bench. The public does not realize that he is dealing with twenty-two ultra-inde-
pendent athletes, vulgarly healthy, frankly outspoken and unawed
by any authority or pomp. Only persons who have one child, which
possess four grandparents, and twenty or thirty aunts all trying to
spoil it, can understand in full the difficulties of the manager's job.

Ball players are about as spoiled, unreasonable and pampered
as a matinee idol, and are worse because they are usually young and
have not even the saving grace of experience to guide them. The
average major league player is a youth who has jumped from small

Roger Bresnahan, a great catcher and a successful manager.

wages to a comfortable income in a few weeks, from the criticism of the home crowd of a few dozen persons to the applause and cheers of perhaps twenty thousand persons. He is sought after, flattered and pampered. He meets men and women of high standing who thoughtlessly praise him. The surprising thing is that ball players who succeed are not worse spoiled.

The young ball player has a brilliant day; he is exalted. He has a bad day, and the excited abuse heaped upon him by the crowd burns his sensitive soul. He becomes cynical and bitter. In a short time he either is a "bug" or a "grouch." He has all the day, except a short time in the afternoon and perhaps an hour in the morning, to exult over his triumphs or mourn over his errors and in his bitterness he loses faith both in friends and enemies.

That stage requires several years to wear away. In about five seasons the player realizes that the public is fickle, that it does not mean its applause any more than it means its abuse. He begins to understand that in its excitement the crowd is "cussing the cards, not the players." Then he generally grows more philosophical. This does not always happen, however. There was one player who, after years of playing, was going to desert the Chicago team because one night he was assigned to lower berth number five instead of to number seven.

It is small wonder that the major league players become spoiled. The hotel arrangements all are made for them; their baggage is checked, the train connections, berths, and carriages are all arranged for by the manager or secretary. The player is told when to go, where to go, and how to go and some players after years of traveling are almost as helpless as if they never had been on a train. On many occasions when a player wants to make a journey by himself the manager is compelled to purchase his tickets, find his train, and send him to it in a carriage. There was a player with the St. Louis club a few years ago who asked permission of the manager to lay over on Sunday at Cincinnati en route from Boston to Philadelphia.

The trials of a manager with twenty men, the majority of them grown children, under his charge, who is forced to soothe their injured feelings, condole with them in their troubles, cheer them in their blues and check them in their exuberance, may better be imagined than told.

One evening after Frank Chance had won two World's Championships, he sat gloomily silent for a long time. The big, hearty, joyous boy who had come from California a dozen years before was battered, grizzled, careworn and weary. Still young, his fine face showed lines of care and worry and a few gray hairs streaked his head. He was thirty-two and looked old. For a long time he sat musing. Then he looked up and smiled grimly.

"This business is making a crab out of me," he remarked.

Two years of managing a team of recalcitrants proved enough to turn Clarke Griffith's hair from black to white. Fred Lake said he aged five years in leading the Boston American team through five weeks of a spring training trip.

If one could know all the pranks, all the outbreaks and troubles of one ball club in one season he would wonder that any man responsible for the conduct of the team could keep his reason.

James A. Hart, when managing the old Louisville team, had perhaps the worst team from the standpoint of behavior and disregard of discipline ever gotten together. Almost every man on the team either was a drunkard or a "bad actor." It was almost laughable to hear Hart issuing orders.

"Ramsey," he would say in the clubhouse, "You pitch on Thursday and if you win you can get drunk until Sunday, when I'll expect you to be in uniform again."

That was the only way in which he could handle the team—

and his method worked. Ramsey would take his two days off, but he considered it a point of honor to report Sunday and he would come to the grounds ready for duty.

What Anson endured from skylarkers such as Tom Daly, Elmer Foster, Hernan, Ryan, Mike Kelly, Lange and the now sedate Dahlen, only he knows, and he mercifully has forgotten much of what they did to him. Every new man or reporter, who sojourned with the team risked not only limb but life.

One spring the Chicago team had been disrupting Texas and the southwest on the pretense of training and reached Kansas City to finish the work of preparation for the season. On April 1, the day on which pay commenced, Anson announced his intention of fining any man he caught taking a drink or keeping late hours. The players did not fear Anson but they knew him well enough to realize that the first one caught, at least, would suffer heavy punishment and no one desired to be the first. That evening after the game not one player dared order even a bottle of beer sent to his room, and there was gloom all over the training camp.

After supper an innocent reporter was busy in his room when Foster, Ryan and several others of the choice spirits of the team began to drop in, as if casually. When the meek scribe inquired what mischief was afoot, they told him to go on writing and not to get inquisitive. A short time later a porter wheeled an eight gallon keg of beer into the room, the reporter's papers were brushed off the table, he was informed he had written enough for that evening, the keg was tapped, and cards produced. The poker game lasted until long past midnight and the beer was consumed. Anson meantime was camping in a chair at the entrance of the hotel, keeping grim watch. Occasionally he would stalk back to the bar room to make certain none of his players dared take a drink.

The party in the reporter's room was continued every night,

while Anson congratulated himself that at last he had effectually curbed the rowdies on the team. One evening when the keg was partly empty and the poker game full, Foster wandered to the open window and looked down four stories.

"Well, I declare," he said in surprise, "If there isn't Captain Anson seated by the doorway." Picking up the keg he dropped it out the window.

The keg struck the sidewalk twenty feet from where Anson was seated, with a report like the discharge of a fourteen-inch gun. It bounded twenty feet and crashed down again upon the sidewalk, but by the time it struck again Anson had dived to safety. Anson never really obtained evidence enough to convict anyone, but he had an idea.

"I know it was Ryan, Daly or Foster," he said, "but which one I'm not certain."

On that same trip the team was departing from a hotel when Foster, polite, apologetic and courteously embarrassed, drew Anson aside.

"Captain," he whispered, "I regret exceedingly an unfortunate predicament into which I have been forced, as it compels me to ask a great favor."

"What is it, Foster?" inquired Captain Anson.

"To tell the truth, Captain," (Foster actually hesitated and blushed), "I am a bit short, and—and—I wanted to ask you, as a great favor, if you will settle my laundry bill."

"Certainly, Foster, certainly," replied Anson heartily as he strode toward the desk. Foster hastily grabbed his hand baggage and disappeared as rapidly as possible from the hotel. When Anson received the bill he staggered. It read: "To laundry, $42.55." Foster had charged up extra meals, drinks and every other item as laundry.

Tom Daly, another irrepressible who never became entirely

subdued during all his long career, added gray hairs to the heads of many managers. Nothing stopped Daly and few things ever caused him to hesitate. Mischief bubbled out of him. One hot summer day he was riding westward with the team when the train stopped at a small station. Standing on the platform was a farmer with a benign, fatherly expression and enough whiskers to stuff a chest protector. Daly, leaning from the car window, accosted the farmer most politely, engaged him in conversation regarding crops, the effect of the drought upon the corn, prices and the weather outlook. Just as the train started Daly stretched out his hand. "Well, good-bye," he remarked and, grasping the astonished farmer by the whiskers he dragged him half the length of the platform.

The game has improved wonderfully in respect to the behavior and manners of players since the commercialization era. Condition has become such a vital element in the success of clubs that drinking and carousing cannot be tolerated. Besides that, the players have come to realize that they must care for their bodies if they are to continue in the profession.

An incident that happened in Philadelphia near the close of the season of 1908 shows the control of modern managers over their men and the discipline existing. The race was close, and to Chicago even one defeat seemed to mean the loss of the pennant. The Chicago club had just finished a double header and had lost one of the games in heart-breaking manner when it seemed won. New York had beaten Pittsburg twice, and it appeared as if the results that day had decided the championship. The Cubs, returning to the hotel in carriages, were silent and downhearted. Not a word was spoken for a long time. Suddenly Tinker remarked to Chance: "Well, Cap, I guess it's all off. Let's break training and make a good night of it."

For an instant Chance was silent. Then he said:

"No. We were good winners last year. Let's show them we are good losers and play the string out. We may win yet."

The following day Chicago won two games and New York lost two, and the Cubs were back in the race. When Tinker made the remark the team had twelve games to play and, by winning eleven of them, it tied New York for the championship and then won the deciding game. Chance's insistence upon continuing in training and delaying celebration brought the victory.

Managers finally realized that to win they did not need the brilliant but erratic stars, and chose players of decent character and enough intelligence to keep themselves in condition without being watched. The great success of Chance and Clarke and Comiskey have resulted from the selection of men who will keep in condition.

The increasing prosperity of baseball has served to relieve the manager from much labor, as business managers and secretaries have taken many of their duties away. They are still left in charge of the physical, moral and often financial welfare of their men, besides directing their playing on the field. Discipline the manager must have. Five major league managers failed in 1909 because they were unable to enforce discipline among their players. Sometimes stringent measures are necessary to hold players in check, especially after a team has gained the upper hand and discovered the weaknesses of the man in charge. If they think a manager is unfair, or has favorites, he is lost. He must hold their confidence, as well as respect.

Chance, for instance, permits poker playing with a twenty-five cent limit, but all games must stop by eleven o'clock. He stepped into a hotel room at midnight once and discovered five of his players and a newspaper man playing dollar limit.

"That will cost you each $25," he said quietly, "not so much for playing as for deliberately disobeying the limit rule."

Every man in the game was a veteran.

"I wouldn't mind you older players doing it," Chance continued, "but you're setting the worst kind of an example to the young ones. As for you," he added, turning to the reporter, "I'll not give you a piece of news for a month."

"Can't I pay the fine and get the news?" inquired the reporter.

"Sure, that will punish you and not the paper," replied Chance.

A few weeks later Chance was playing poker. Everyone had forgotten the time limit, and it was nearly midnight before it was noticed.

"I'll have to fine myself this time," remarked Chance, and he reported himself fined $25 for violating his own rules.

Fining, however, has not been found the most effective way of curbing disobedience. Suspending players, putting them on the bench for an indefinite period, or in extreme cases, trading them, or sending them to some minor league, has proved more salutary. Chance's players once began to feel too prosperous and independent. A pitcher, who had been a famous figure, was sent home to prepare to pitch an important Sunday game. The team arrived home on Sunday morning and Chance discovered the pitcher had not been at the grounds at all. He immediately wrote the unconditional release of the pitcher. He never had an uprising afterwards.

Possibly the most effective disciplinary system is the one by which Bill Rourke controls the Omaha club. He never fines a player. If the man will not listen to moral suasion, Rourke invites him back of the clubhouse and enforces discipline with his fists. Once Rourke was compelled to invite out a big player who proved a Tartar. He gave Rourke a bad whipping, then while Rourke was patching up his damaged features, the player hastened away. As soon as Rourke removed traces of the conflict he sought the man and found him at his hotel packing his trunk.

"What are you doing?" he demanded.

Touching Second

"Why—well," stammered the player, "I didn't see how I could stay with the team after what happened."

"Stay?" ejaculated Rourke, "I should say you will stay. I need you to manage this club."

Rourke's theory was correct. The manager who cannot rule his men might as well retire in favor of the man who can.

♦ CHAPTER VI ♦

Catching

Catching is the pivotal position and the most important in base-ball. The catcher is the director or transmitter of all messages, the key-board used by manager or pitcher to flash orders to all others, and the chief wigwag station on the battlefield in the defensive game.

Oddly enough, this important position is the only one in which the players have failed to improve mechanically, and keep pace with the physical development of the national sport. The statement in no way is meant to reflect upon the catchers themselves. The game has changed so much in the last decade that the heavy increase in the duties thrust upon the catchers has not only diminished the supply but overtaxed the physical capacity of all except the extraordinary men. The position has become so vital to the game, and its duties so numerous and trying, that it is difficult for one man to carry them all with any degree of success.

There are not ten really first-class catchers in America and the team which lacks one of these ten, no matter how great its strength may be in other departments, is doomed to failure before it starts. A weak, uncertain, erratic or brainless catcher can ruin the best pitching corps in the land in a few weeks, and break up a perfectly organized team in even less time. The number of passed balls, muffed flies, failures to touch base runners at the plate and other mechanical mistakes form no criterion by which to judge a catcher. His greatest errors are those of judgment, his worst blunders are the ones the spectators never see. For not only must he direct the pitching and signal for each ball, signal for each play made with runners on the bases, watch runners and signal the pitcher to make throws, but also he has innumerable opportunities to throw or not to throw when the slightest hesitancy or uncertainty will mean defeat. He can make a pitcher "wild," force the best pitcher to give bases on balls, break up all the teamwork and infield play, by a moment of excitement or panic. A cool, brainy pitcher sometimes can steady a catcher, or take the control of the game out of his hands and, changing signals, hold the team steady and save the catcher, but the majority of pitchers prefer to pitch to orders, rather than assume responsibility of changing them.

To understand the manifold duties of the catcher requires not only brains, coolness, generalship and good memory, but also the mechanical ability to catch balls of any speed, to judge distances accurately, throw from any position on the line and with a short, snap motion of the arm, to throw off the shoulder towards first base with scarcely a glance in that direction, to direct team work, observe the positions of every player before every ball pitched, signal fielders before making a throw, watch runners closely and signal the pitcher when they venture too far off the bases, to know which men will steal, and on what ball, to win the friendship of umpires, and above all to know the tricks and habits of batters.

Because of the intimate knowledge of batters and baserunners required in successful catching, experience is the greatest factor in the position, and it is impossible for young catchers to meet with great success. Usually three years of experience with a major league team is needed to make a catcher competent. As the catcher's throwing must be done with a jerky motion of the arm and from unnatural positions, as the position is the most wearing one in the game, and the most dangerous, only a minority who begin as catchers continue long enough to gain the experience. The catcher who can go through two seasons without crippling injuries from spikes of base runners, foul tips or wild pitches is lucky.

The number of times a catcher is injured in a season is surprising. At one time in 1909, George Gibson, in spite of chest protectors, shin guards, and heavy pads, had black and blue spots imprinted by nineteen foul tips upon his body, a damaged hand, a bruise on his hip six inches square where a thrown bat had struck, and three spike cuts. Yet he had not missed a game and was congratulating himself on his "luck." Pat Moran, of Chicago, in four games was hit seven times on or near the knees by fouls, struck once on the throwing arm, and once on the shoulder; yet he stuck to it until a foul broke through his mask and tore his face. Under such conditions of wear and tear the wonder is that the supply of catchers even approximates the demand and it is small wonder that the men who might make really great catchers prefer some other position where the risk is not so large.

Chance, while a catcher, had the record for getting hurt. He was injured five times in one game at New York and that night, lying in his berth lamenting his ill luck, with a torn ear, a bruised arm, and with a finger stuck into a lemon, he was struck by a disc of tin sailed up the aisle by a roisterer and suffered a severe cut on his upper lip.

The first and most important duty of the catcher is to know batters, and the power of observation and quick judgment necessarily involved is enormous. Veteran batters, of course, are known by all, as their weaknesses and strength are matters of common gossip. The catchers must remember what kind of balls they hit, and in what direction they are likely to hit any special kind of ball. Also they know that batters change gradually and must be on the look-out for signs of such changes. Occasionally batters who always have hit to left field and are "easy" on slow balls, suddenly begin to hit slow and low balls hard and to right field.

Besides first hand knowledge of a batter's possibilities, the catcher must look closely each time he comes to bat, first to see what kind of a bat he carries; second, to observe the position of his feet and body, upon which positions the direction of his hit depend, and third to see how he is gripping his bat, in order to guess his designs. Frequently the catcher, after observing the position of the batter, must order the pitcher to pitch straight and fast toward the batter's head, the object being to force the batter to shift position quickly and destroy his plan of attack. Batters never before seen are judged by the position of their feet and their grip upon the bats and then the catcher must experiment to discover the weakness of the batter. Frequently players watching during batting practice find the weaknesses of new men before the game starts. Boston brought a young outfielder to Chicago who had a reputation for being able to hit. Kling and Brown watched him closely during batting practice.

"He'll fish," remarked Brown.

"Anything low—in or outside," whispered Kling.

Brown pitched low curves outside the plate and low fast straight balls inside during the game and the new man "fished," i.e., swung at balls he could not reach. Brown, when asked to explain how he knew this said:

"He showed nervousness and pulled his left foot. I knew he would swing at anything that broke quickly."

"He held his hands with the wrists turned too high," added Kling, "and fully an inch too far apart to get a good swing at a low ball inside."

VI. Catching

The slightest shift of position of hands, feet or body of a batter must be noted by the catcher, and interpreted. The first nervous motion to bunt, the first impulsive step forward, reveal the intention of the batters and the catcher can order the ball pitched exactly where the batter is not expecting it.

Spectators are not aware that one of the greatest and most effective balls pitched is the "bean ball." "Bean" is baseball for "head" and pitching at the batter's head, not to hit it, but to drive him out of position and perhaps cause him to get panic stricken and swing at the ball in self-defense is an art. Even hitting batters is advocated by many pitchers. Tony Mullane, in his day one of the greatest pitchers, owed much of his success to the fact that he hit batters who tried to crowd the plate. One of the Chicago pitchers, at the start of his career, was timid, and the batters kept encroaching upon the plate and hitting his curve ball. Chance instructed the pitcher to hit one batter in the first inning of every game he pitched until the batters were driven back. The pitcher followed orders and after he had pitched once against each opposing team the batters were driven back until he became a success.

After experience has brought to the catcher a knowledge of batters and an intimate familiarity with his own men, their capabilities and their mode of play, the catcher begins to be valuable. Being the only player facing all the others he must either originate or transmit all orders. He must know every signal used, either by manager or men, and have courage enough to assume responsibility for issuing orders when in positions where it is impossible to get them from the manager. In this respect the playing manager has the advantage of the bench manager again, as he is in position to signal the catcher constantly, and afford much assistance, especially to a weak man.

The catcher must conceal carefully every signal given, not only hiding his signals, and "covering up" to prevent coaches, batters or base runners from seeing them, but frequently when he observes he is being watched, he must give false signals to mislead the opposition. In the scheme of attack of all teams is the great strategical principle, and the alert eyes of the attackers often detect signals and compel quick changes, so that the catcher constantly is on the alert to outgeneral the men who are watching him.

Possibly the most intricate part of the catcher's work, as well as the most important, is throwing to catch runners, not when they are stealing, but while they are leading off the bases. The number of runners actually caught matters little, but the throwing has for its principal object the prevention of stealing, and holding the runners close to their bases. The catcher watches the runner edging away from first base. He knows to an inch how far the runner can go and return in safety. The catcher signals, by turning his mitt over and back rapidly, that on the next pitched ball he will throw to first. As the ball is pitched the first baseman dashes behind the runner to the base, the pitcher throws shoulder high and outside the plate, and the catcher, without looking, grabs the sphere and hurls it at first base, where the baseman meets it on the run. If the runner has hesitated an eighth of a second in diving back, he is blocked off the base and put out.

Catchers like Archer, who throw with a snap of the arm while standing flat footed, catch scores of runners each season, and practically stop the stealing of second base by preventing the runners from getting a flying start. After a catcher once establishes a reputation for throwing, he has few throws to make.

A throw of that kind made by Kling that caught Herzog off first base in the famous game between New York and Chicago when

Opposite: "Red" Dooin, one of the greatest of catchers, taking a wild pitch "raw."

they played off their tie for the championship gave Chicago the pennant in 1908. Two men were on bases, Bresnahan was striving to bunt. Kling caught the bunt signal, the ball was pitched out and like a flash Kling hurled the ball to Chance. Herzog was caught, hesitating eight feet from the bag and New York was stopped in the midst of a rally that ought to have netted half a dozen runs.

The Cubs worked a variation of the same play with great success one season until Evers was sent to hospital by it. The play was planned to kill the sacrifice bunt. With a runner on first base, and the intent of the batter to sacrifice self-evident, the pitcher curved the ball far outside the plate. Chance would desert his position and dash forward as if to field the bunt, giving the base runner freedom to move away from the base. Evers then came at top speed behind the unsuspecting runner and Kling threw to first base, Evers taking the ball and catching the runner. The play proved effective until one of Kling's throws went wild. Evers attempted to block the ball, and Blankenship, of Cincinnati, who was the runner, collided with Evers and sent him to hospital for six weeks.

The play when made to catch a runner off second base, requires the unerring cooperation of the short stop and second baseman who, jockeying around the base appear to be striving to hold him close. The object of this is to spur the runner to an added effort to take a few feet of ground. The short stop tries to get behind the runner again and again, apparently without success. The instant the catcher signals his intention of throwing, the short stop apparently ceases his efforts to hold up the runners, and, retiring to his natural position, speaks to the runner in an effort to divert his attention. When the catcher throws, the second baseman takes the ball on the run and crosses the bag to block the runner. Frequently the catcher will change the plan quickly during the jockeying and signal the pitcher to whirl and throw to the base.

VI. Catching

In the attempted double steal, which is used by all teams almost without fail when runners are on first and third and two out, the decision of the catcher as to where to throw is vital. He must decide whether to throw to second base, to third base, or to the pitcher, whether to throw clear to third base, or throw short, in order that one of the fielders may come forward, meet the throw and return the ball to him. His decision must be made after the runners start, and it is dependent upon the way in which they act, or upon their speed or peculiarities.

In this the veteran catcher has much advantage, as he knows from experience just how certain runners make the play. With Leach on third base, for instance, every catcher throws fast to third base, because it is well known Leach has a habit of making a false start for the plate. If Wagner is the runner at third the catcher will throw short, and the short stop or second baseman will dash forward, meet the ball and throw back to the plate. They know Wagner will start at the right instant, and that he will come home fast and slide to the finish. With a bad baserunner on third, the catcher will make the long throw to second base, and head off the runner going from first. Every variation of the play depends for its success upon the quick thinking of the catcher, and the least delay means a run scored.

There always has been much argument and contention regarding the relative abilities of the great catchers. The best authorities agree that Mike Kelly, Buck Ewing and John Kling were the best of their respective eras, but conditions have changed so much comparisons between them are impossible. Ewing and Kling were men of much the same type—quiet, cool and calculating; Kelly was different, being a volatile, brainy, inventive Irishman. Kelly, who played back and took the ball on the first bound most of the time, had twice as many passed balls in a month as Kling would have in a season, but his armor was lighter, and he faced different styles of pitching. He caught in the days when great powerful, often wild, pitchers, took a five foot run through the box and hurled the ball fifty feet. Ewing who really came between Kelly and Kling, was cool, studious, steady, helpful to pitchers, and threw with rare judgment and ability. Kling is a brilliant general who worked perfectly with pitchers and the infield, and his throwing was as near perfect as could be. How much Chicago's wonderful infield helped in making Kling a great catcher is hard to calculate. One eastern catcher remarked:—

"I would catch for half the salary I am getting if I had that infield to throw to and work with."

Kling is a past master of the art of working umpires on balls and strikes, which is one of the duties of a catcher that is not suspected by the spectators. The importance of "getting the corners" is realized by all players, and the catcher who gets this advantage is invaluable to his club. Some umpires call strikes on both corners, some the outside, some the inside, and some force the pitcher to put the ball squarely over the plate. Many and varied are the schemes worked by catchers to "get the corners." The best tactics however, are those employed by the catchers who seldom kick, and who win the friendship and confidence of the officials. The other players may kick, or rage and shoot shafts of sarcasm at the umpire, but the catcher knows he must be diplomatic. Sympathizing with the umpire, or openly rebuking his own team mates for kicking, assuring the umpire he was right, or speaking his objections in a low tone, serve many catchers in their effort to get a "shade the better of it" on ball and strike decisions. The umpire does not care much what the players say to him, or how much they kick, if they do not arouse the crowd to anger. Kling's method was to be friendly with all umpires, siding with them, telling them they were right, and frequently whispering to them to be on the guard for a certain curve that was coming. He urged them not to pay attention to other players, and while never openly criticizing umpires, he occasionally whispered that he thought the ball might have been over the corner.

Roger Bresnahan, one of the greatest of catchers, works on exactly opposite lines. He seldom says much to an umpire (that anyone save the umpire can hear) but he invites the crowd to sympathize with him against the official by looking pained and grieved. When an umpire calls a ball which Bresnahan thinks was a strike, spectators have the impression that Bresnahan has just lost his dearest friend. He can assume a look of outraged, grieved and hurt surprise that would win a fortune for him on the stage. Even the batter who knows that the ball was a foot outside the plate, feels sorrowful when he sees Bresnahan's look of woe. Louis Criger, another marvelous catcher, adopts another method. He talks all the time he is catching, forcibly expressing his opinion of the umpire on every ball and strike, and he keeps up a running fire of argument and criticism. The long suffering umpires have grown so accustomed to him that they merely allow him to rave. "Red" Dooin, the hardest working and one of the best catchers in either league, always talks, smiles, and fights at the same time. He is in deadly earnest and when he does quarrel with an umpire it is not for effect. One day in 1909 an umpire threatened to put him off the field.

"Put me off. Put me off," he screamed, "put me off, then I won't have to associate with a fellow like you."

Of all methods, Kling's is the most effective, for after all, umpires are human and one kind word helps.

◆ CHAPTER VII ◆

Pitching

Pitching is the most highly developed, most skillful and most important part of baseball, requiring more thought, more strength and more brains than any other position demands. Good pitching is the absolute essential to victory, and considered in relation to the "inside game," is vital, for unless the pitcher understands every move of his fellow players, and adjusts his pitching to the plan, the "inside game" becomes worse than useless.

The development of the science of pitching has, from the inception of the game, been in advance of the development of the other departments of play and to such an extent that the rule makers from the first have found it necessary to legislate to handicap the pitcher to prevent him from becoming absolute master of the game. In spite of the rules the pitchers have by persistent work and thought kept in advance of the progress of the national sport.

Involving the study of wind pressures, dynamics, physics, and mathematics, in addition to the principles of the game itself, pitching is an art demanding closest attention at every instant, the concentration of every energy upon the game, so much so that in almost every game the pitchers lose all track of the number of innings played, of the score itself, forget the crowd, and neither hear the cheers nor hisses, because their minds are so focused on the batters.

The story of the development of the art of pitching from the days of the straight arm, underhand pitch to the present is one of constant discoveries and triumphs, until, in the educated fingers of the great masters of the art, the ball seems endowed with life.

The days of the underhand pitch were the kindergarten days of the game, and with the coming of overhand pitching the science began to develop. The discovery of the curve ball marked another era, and gave the foundation for modern pitching. Pitchers use, primarily, two kinds of pitches, the "straight one," and the curve. They are the basis of all pitching, but there are all kinds of "straight" balls and as many varieties of curve as there are pitchers. The majority of pitchers begin their careers with no other varieties than speed and a curve, and the strength of youthful arms to win success. The "straight" ball is a misnomer, for there is only one kind of ball a pitcher cannot throw and that is a "straight" one, as every ball curves, regardless of the will of the pitcher. It is the study and development of these curves that makes great pitchers.

The fast ball is sheer speed, its success depending entirely upon its velocity and the control the pitcher has of it. It is pitched with the sphere gripped with the thumb underneath and the first two fingers on top, and is thrown either underhand or overhand with full force. Pitched directly overhand, with the fingers held directly on top, the ball goes as straight to the plate as it is possible to make it go, the speed and the downward angle make it difficult for the batter to hit, unless it comes in "the groove," which is the natural angle. Pitched with the hand held sideways, the ball, taking friction from the finger tips, swerves slightly from its course and breaks in towards a right handed batter. If the ball is gripped tightly with the finger tips at the moment it is released from the hand its speed piles up a billow of air in front of it, and at some point before crossing the plate, the air resistance becomes so great that the ball "jumps" an inch or more upward or in the direction the greatest amount of pressure of the fingers was applied.

Every man who pitches fast balls successfully has a powerful grip and a strong arm, the stronger the greater the jump to the fast ball. President Cleveland once received a crowd of baseball players in the White House and shook hands with all. When the ceremony was over he laughingly picked out the three pitchers, and explained that he knew by the grips of their hands that they were pitchers.

The curve is a ball held exactly in the same way in which the fast one is gripped, but the ball is released over the side and end of the first finger. The amount of curve or shoot depends upon the manner and strength of the grip of the hand and the way in which the wrist is turned at the moment of release, as well as upon the amount of power applied by the pitcher.

These are the elementary principles of pitching, so well understood that every school boy knows them. They are the beginning of the wonders of baseball pitching. After them come the change of pace, the slow ball, the "spit ball," the "knuckle ball," the "fade-away," a score of curves and varieties of curves, and to tell how these things are done it is necessary to tell who does them, and how.

Cy Young and "Kid" Nichols were the leading pitchers of fast balls, although both used curves while depending upon the "straight" one for their greatest success. They pitched the ball alike, throwing directly overhand, with the hand held as straight as possible and, at the instant of releasing the ball each gripped it tightly with the finger tips and loosely with the thumb. The finger pressure increased the speed of the natural revolution of the ball and caused it to jump more. It is odd that Young and Nichols who probably came nearer pitching "straight" balls than any other pitchers ever did, were so

Willis, just after releasing a slow curve intended to turn in toward the batter.

successful and it proves that the batter does not hit at the ball at all, but swings his bat at a spot where he expects the ball to cross the plate. The success of the fast ball lies in this, and in the fact that it is coming so rapidly the batter has no opportunity to change the direction of his swing before the ball passes.

The curve pitchers are a host. Every one has a different curve, faster, sharper, slower, with heavier twist, or some individual peculiarity to distinguish it. The first curves pitched were of the variety now known as the "barrel hoop." It was a slow curve, pitched underhand, with the hand swung nearly to the level of the knee, fingers downward and hand held almost at right angles with the wrist. As the hand was swung the wrist was jerked sharply and the ball, sliding off the first finger, revolved rapidly and the air pressure on one side of the sphere and the partial vacuum on the other caused by the rotation, forced the ball to move in a slow wide arc. All curves are developments of the "barrel hoop," the same principle entering into each, whether it is Mordecai Brown's marvelous "hook" curve, George Mullin's meteoric shoot, or the wonderful curves of Camnitz, Overall, Wiltse, Krause, Adams, Ferguson and others.

Brown's "hook" curve is the highest present development of the fast overhand curve pitch which breaks sharply down and outward. Brown probably owes much of his success to a feed chopper which cut off part of his right hand, leaving him without an index finger and with the middle finger bent at right angles at the first joint. Brown pitches the "hook" overhand, releasing the ball at various points after his hand swings past his body. By the point at which he releases the ball he regulates the point at which it breaks in the air. He can make the ball either describe a wide fast arc, or by jerking his hand at the proper instant, make the ball go in almost a straight line, perhaps fifty feet, and then dart suddenly down and outward.

There are many players, however, among them members of the

Detroit team who faced him in the final game for the World's Championship in 1908, who believe Overall's curve a more marvelous one. In that game the Chicago giant had one of the most remarkable curves ever pitched. At times the ball darted down two feet and struck the ground while the batters struck more than a foot over it.

Overall pitches his curve with a wide, sweeping overhand swing, releasing the ball over the side of the index finger as his hand turns downward. His swing and curve are duplicates of those used by Terry, McCormick and some of the great pitchers of the past, and when his jerk motion at the finish of the wide swing is sharp, the curve actually darts downward.

But speed and curves alone will not win and pitchers, baseball generations ago, discovered that there was not enough of an assortment to long puzzle batters. The batters guessed correctly too many times whether the ball would be curved or fast, and often detected by the position of the hand that a curve was coming even before it was pitched. With the necessity of a greater assortment came the "slow ball," one of the paradoxes of the game. Slow balls are of three different kinds, with a huge number of varieties of each kind. The original slow ball was merely a ball thrown slowly, the pitcher depending entirely upon a false motion to deceive the batter into believing he was pitching a fast ball. The pitcher would swing his arm, check it suddenly and "lob" the ball to the plate. The ball did not deceive the batter in the slightest after it left the pitcher's hand, but before that he was thrown off his balance, deceived by the arm motion, and was out of position to lunge forward and hit the ball.

Keefe, O'Day and most of the old time pitchers used that kind of a slow ball, but after batters began to watch the motion and shift their feet so as to run forward and meet the slow pitch, they were compelled to find something new and the development of the slow ball followed. The difficulty was to pitch a ball with full force and with the exact motion used in pitching a fast ball, and yet make the ball travel slowly. It was discovered that if the ball be held far back in the palm of the hand, with the little finger and the thumb clinched on opposite sides of it, or the little finger and the third finger on one side and the thumb on the other, with the other fingers held so as not to touch the ball at all, the result could be attained. Held that way, and with the arm swung at full speed and force, the finger and thumb gripping the ball tightly at the moment of release, the result is peculiar. Instead of revolving and going rapidly the ball wabbles from side to side, scarcely turning over, and allowing the full atmospheric pressure to strike the forward side with no revolution to lessen the friction. The result is the air pressure stops the ball and it loses speed rapidly, obeys the call of gravity and drops quickly toward the earth after expending its force. The harder the ball is thrown and the tighter the finger pressure at the instant of release, the more sharply the ball drops. Expert after expert developed the slow ball, until its perfection was reached in the hands of Brown, Frank Sparks, of Philadelphia, and "Doc" White of the Chicago Americans.

The odd thing about pitching is this:—a ball which revolves in the air appears much smaller to the eye than one that fails to revolve and the more rapid the revolution of the sphere the smaller it appears. The slow ball, floating in the air and "dead," looks as "big as a balloon," as everyone in the bleachers remarks, and it does not deceive the eye. In fact if slow balls of that variety are pitched three or four times in succession they look so large that an amateur can hit them out of the lot. Successful use of that kind of a pitched ball consists entirely in surprising the batter, fooling him when he expects something else. The batter may miss the ball a foot, yet his eye is not deceived. He saw the ball perfectly but was off balance, just as he was for the slow pitch.

The discovery of another kind of slow ball, and the most

successful pitched ball ever used, arose from the fact that to deceive the eye the ball must be made to appear small, and that revolution, and rapid revolution at that, is necessary to deceive the eye into the idea of smallness and speed when it is slow. "Hoss" Radbourne working on that theory, began to develop a slow ball that revolved rapidly. It seemed impossible, because a ball that revolves rapidly usually has great speed, the greater the speed, the greater the revolution. But Radbourne, pitching for Providence, kept practicing until he found his slow ball. He had been a good pitcher before that, and after his discovery he became one of the greatest the game has ever known.

No one could understand his success, yet his discovery was simple. He found that if he held the ball exactly as if pitching a fast ball, with the thumb on one side and the two first fingers on the other, and at the moment of releasing it from his hand clinched the fingers tips tightly into the seams of the ball and jerked backwards with the hand, the ball not only would revolve rapidly but would travel almost on a straight line—yet slowly. The revolution, which was the reverse of the natural twist, helped the ball to hold its straight course, and it lost speed quickly after exhausting the reverse revolution and fell rapidly towards the ground at a point in front of the batter. The secret of his discovery, Radbourne imparted to Clark Griffith, now manager of the Cincinnati club, and for years after the passing of Radbourne, Griffith was one of the premier pitchers of the country, holding practically a monopoly on his slow ball and using it with wonderful effect.

But the ultimate and greatest development of that slow ball was left for Mathewson of New York, in whose hands it became the most effective ball ever used; the "fadeaway," which is only a development of the idea and the style used by Radbourne and Griffith, is a ball which almost all the pitchers in the country are trying with more or less success to imitate. Yet before Mathewson learned the trick of pitching his "fader," there was one who pitched the same ball in even more wonderful style. Virgil Garvin, a tall, slender young Texan, with extraordinarily long fingers, pitched the ball before Mathewson, but he did not understand its use or worth. He pitched it with his middle finger lapped over the index finger and when he released the ball his hand was turned almost upside down. He jerked the hand downward and backward, the ball going over the sides of the lapped fingers, giving it a rapid revolution that resulted in the impression of great speed.

Mathewson achieved his "fadeaway" by holding the ball exactly as Griffith did his slow ball and releasing it over the side of the middle finger. By the sharp holding pressure and "draw" of his fingers he put the "reverse English" on the ball, causing it to revolve rapidly for a distance, then lose speed and "fade" towards the ground and inward like a left handed pitcher's slow curve. The action of the ball is exactly that of a massed billiard ball, and when the ball "fades" it really is striving to get grip enough on the air to return toward the pitcher.

Scores of pitchers have imitated Mathewson's "fadeaway," some with success. Flakenberg, of Cleveland, Willis of Pittsburg, and Reulbach of Chicago can pitch it well. "Vic" Willis, a veteran, ranks as one of the cleverest of pitchers, and his use of slow curves is a revelation to young players. Chicago signed a youngster once who thought he could hit. Willis, who never had seen him before, teased him with slow curves and drooping slow pitches, and the youngster struck out three times.

"Are there more like him?" he inquired anxiously.

"He's only a second rater," complained an angry player.

"Then," said the youngster with immense cheerfulness, "I won't be here long."

Opposite: Ed Walsh, just after a side-arm pitch.

With all these varieties of speed and curves, pitchers were not satisfied and each kept seeking more varieties of slants warranted to prevent hitting. There came into baseball in 1903 a ball that came near revolutionizing the game. The Chicago White Sox had signed Elmer Stricklett. While the team was training at New Orleans, Stricklett was pitching to batters in practice when he pitched a ball which, whirling rapidly for a short distance, suddenly ceased revolving, commenced to float and wabble like a slow ball and then darted down and out like a fast curve, leaving the batter staring in astonishment. Stricklett repeated the pitch and immediately every man on the field was clamoring to see the ball and bat at it, suspecting some trick. That night correspondents sent messages filled with wild theories regarding the "spit ball." It is odd to recall the "call down" one of the correspondents received from the managing editor who telegraphed:

"Please confine yourself to facts. No such thing as a spit ball is possible and the expression is vulgar."

The managing editor was partly right; the ball is not a spit ball but a thumb ball. It is pitched with two (sometimes with three) fingers held on one side and the thumb on the other. The ball is made slippery at the point touched by the fingers, so that it slides off the fingers with the minimum of friction. The thumb, gripped tightly against the seam on the opposite side, gives the maximum of friction at that point, the result being that the ball, leaving the thumb, takes "reverse English." It whirls rapidly for a short distance, until the heavy friction begins to overcome the natural rotary motion of the ball, when it stops rotating, as if a struggle between the two forces was going on, then the thumb "English" gains control and the ball darts just as it would have done if curved naturally, shooting in the direction the heaviest friction was applied. A "spit ball," when pitched directly overhand, darts almost straight downward, and when pitched sidearm, with the thumb toward the body, it darts as a fast curve does, down and outward. Immense power and speed are required to pitch the ball successfully as the faster it is pitched the faster and sharper the curve will be.

The "thumb ball," pitched without moisture, was used before Stricklett found saliva would negative the friction of the fingers, but the object was to get heavy friction on the thumb, rather than to decrease friction on the other side. The principle of the "spit ball" was used in Griffith's and Radbourne's slow balls. Those who saw Griffith pitch will remember how he always tapped the ball upon his heel spikes, and tried to persuade umpires he was knocking dirt out of the spikes. His object was to make small cuts or abrasions on the surface of the ball, against which to press his thumb and get more friction at the desired point. He never thought of greasing or wetting the ball to lessen friction on the opposite side.

Obtaining more friction at one point was the object of many pitchers. Some rubbed the ball on gritty dirt, others carried small files to use surreptitiously. One sharp rasp of the file and the ball was "winged," at a certain point. The pitcher gripped his fingers against the "winged" spot and not only was the sharpness of the curve accentuated, but the "wings" by offering more resistance to the air, caused the ball to make eccentric shoots in the air.

Al Orth used a "thumb ball" and saliva with astonishing success, but oddly enough never hit upon the most successful manner of using it. Orth came nearer pitching an upcurve than any pitcher ever did, and many think his underhand ball really curved upward. He at least made the unnatural rotation of the ball overcome gravity to such an extent that the ball did not drop, whether it rose or not. In pitching he held his thumb on top of the ball, pressed tightly against a seam, and two fingers under it, not touching the seam, and he spat upon the place where the fingers came in contact with the leather. Then he pitched underhand with great force, his hand swinging almost straight downward at the level of is knee. His object was to make the ball angle from his knee to the batter's shoulder and the false revolution imparted by his thumb was to make the ball "ride" the air and help maintain the angle. In seven years the number of "popups" hit off Orth's pitching was one of the wonders of the game, being almost twice the normal, batters continually hitting under his "thumb ball," which in reality was a "spit ball" pitched upside down.

The overhand "spit ball," with its marvelous shoot, brought an army of strong armed pitchers into the game, revived veterans whose careers seemed over, and ruined many great hitters. Almost every pitcher learned to use it—and in the hands of Ed Walsh, the giant of the Chicago White Stockings, it reached its highest stage of development and made him the pitching marvel of the decade.

Immediately variations of the ball were developed. Slippery elm, talcum powder, crude oil, Vaseline were used to lessen the friction of the fingers while other pitchers, to get more friction on the thumb, used gum, pumice stone, resin or adhesive tape.

Stricklett had founded a new school of pitching. "Spit ball" pitchers who can control the ball need few other curves, and the ball, when it breaks at the right stop, practically is impossible to hit. But it was soon found to have drawbacks. Some pitchers abandoned it because it injured their arms. The catchers dreaded it because it was hard to handle, and harder to throw. The fielders opposed it because the slippery ball was hard to throw, and because, when hit, the ball takes doubly unnatural English, both from the bat and when it strikes the ground, and darts in weird manner. The batters objected, naturally, as it stopped their slugging.

Frank Chance disliked the ball and during one spring training trip every team the Cubs played presented a "spit ball" pitcher. Chance wanted batting practice and was aggravated. One day at

Memphis a giant "spit ball" pitcher made his debut. Early in the game he pitched a "spitter" to Chance. The ball failed to break and Chance drove it back with terrific force. The pitcher threw up his hands. They were driven against his head, the ball caromed on to center field and Chance, spluttering with rage, remarked:—

"There's one blanked 'spit ball' pitcher I put out of business."

Walsh, master artist of the "spit ball," pitches it in the most common way. He uses a trifle of slippery elm bark in his mouth and moistens a spot an inch square between the seams of the ball. His thumb he clinches tightly lengthwise on the opposite seam and, swinging his arm straight overhand with terrific force, he drives the ball straight at the plate. At times it will dart two feet down or out, depending upon the way his arm is swung.

The American League, during the early days of the "spit ball," used it so much that Charlie Dryden, angler and scribe, remarked that: "The American League consists of Ban Johnson, the 'spit ball' and the Wabash Railroad."

The "knuckle ball," a freak, promised much, and is successfully used by some long fingered pitchers, but it cannot be a general success because it is impossible for the fingers to grip the ball firmly enough to control its direction. The ball is pitched with the three middle fingers bent under, the ball resting against the first joints, and held by the thumb and little finger on opposite sides. Somers, of Detroit, pitches the ball with great effect at times, but it is uncertain, being nothing more or less than a "spit ball" pitched in freakish manner.

The "wrist ball" is only a contortion of the wrist and hands, resulting in a slow curve, and the "finger nail ball" is another freak effort at a slow ball.

There is more to pitching, however, than curving or inventing curves, and some of the most effective pitching is by angles rather than by curves. For some reason, unexplained, the deadly "cross fire" used with wonderful effect fifteen years ago, almost has been abandoned. The left-handers of former generations "cross fired" almost as often as they curved the ball and many right-handers used it. The ball was pitched sidearm, the hand being extended as far as possible, and while the pitcher's hand was swinging he stepped to right or left in the direction of his pitching arm and hurled the ball back across the inside corner of the plate, at an angle. The balk rules caused the left-handers to abandon the pitch partially, and the passing of the side arm right-handers, probably explains its abandonment. Pfiester, Leifield, "Doc" White and Krause use the ball effectively but not frequently.

Pitching from angles consists in angling the ball from high overhand to the batter's knee, from the pitcher's knee to the batter's shoulder and from the limit of the outstretched arm to the outside corner of the plate. One of the best exhibitions of pitching by angles ever given was in the now famous game between Chicago and New York in September, 1908, in which Merkle forgot to touch second base. Pfiester had strained a ligament in his pitching arm, and a lump had formed on his forearm two inches high, the muscle bunching. He could pitch straight balls and he asked Chance to let him try, as he always had been successful against the Giants. During the game he pitched three curved balls, all to Donlin, and all when he had to retire Donlin on strikes to save the game. After each time he curved the ball he had to be helped to the bench, as he was nearly fainting. By changing the angles he kept New York from winning until the famous mixup in which Merkle figured.

Shadowing the ball, which was an art in former days, is almost lost. A few pitchers try it, but without the skill of Bert Cunningham, Mattie Kilroy, Willie McGilland many of the old school. Griffith was the last pitcher to use it steadily. Shadowing consists of the pitcher sidestepping and placing his body on the line of the batter's vision, so that the ball has no background except the pitcher's body and the batter cannot see it plainly until the ball almost is upon him.

There was an odd instance of shadowing early in 1909 at Cincinnati. Reulbach was pitching for Chicago and a green umpire was officiating on the bases, with whom Reulbach became friendly. When no one was on bases Reulbach invited the new umpire to watch how his fast curve was breaking. That brought the umpire behind the pitcher, and Reulbach maneuvered him around until he was on the line of vision. For five innings the umpire helped beat Cincinnati nor did he discover why Reulbach was so friendly until the veteran umpire behind the bat ordered him to quit shadowing the ball and Reulbach laughed.

The study of backgrounds, air currents, and atmospheric conditions by pitchers is part of their business. They take advantage of every bad background, which may hamper the batters, and shift from side to side on the slab to make the ball come to the batter on a line with some blinding sign. The batters, being in the majority on each team, however, insist upon good solid green backgrounds to increase hitting, and overrule the pitchers who prefer glaring yellow, or white, or a motley of colors.

The direction and force of the wind affect pitching greatly. A cross wind from either direction may decide whether a left-hander or a right-hander will pitch. The weight of the atmosphere affects the curves and scouts looking for pitchers at Denver or Colorado Springs know that the curve balls in that altitude will curve hardly half as far as at sea level.

Al Orth was a student of such conditions. He was pitching for Philadelphia one hot day and was winning easily up to the seventh inning. The Philadelphia National grounds are surrounded by high

walls and stands and scarcely a breath of wind enters them. In the seventh inning Orth suddenly lost control. His "thumb ball" kept breaking away from the plate, he gave several bases on balls, and before New York was retired, the Giants were within one run of a tie. Orth was puzzled. As he started for the bench, where the manager was ordering another pitcher to warm up, he stopped, looked around, wetted a finger, held it in the air and grinned.

"Have those doors under the stand closed and I'll win this game," remarked Orth to the manager.

The doors were closed, Orth regained control and won without trouble.

The great exit doors under the stand had been opened, preparatory to letting the crowd disperse, and a half gale of wind, blowing around the stands, was driving Orth's underhand ball off its course.

In 1909 Mordecai Brown thought he had discovered a new curve, which he executed by releasing the ball with a sharp jerk of the wrist, while his hand was near his hip. He used it repeatedly in one game, the ball breaking down and in sharply and faster than his "fadeaway" would do. He started to practice it the next day and it would not work. He persisted for days, then he discovered that, when the wind was blowing from the southeast, moderately hard, he could pitch the ball. The curve was the result of the angle at which the wind was striking the circular stands.

The science of baseball pitching cannot all be known by one man, or by one team, as every pitcher has his own theories, and tricks, but this will show there is more to it than throwing a ball sixty feet.

Opposite: **Krause, after losing a slow floater.**

CHAPTER VIII

The "Inside Game"*

Once the City Editor sent me (Fullerton) to a meeting of an engineering society to report a lecture. In the course of his remarks the lecturer said: "At a distance of 185 miles this force, roughly speaking, is one two hundred and forty millionth part of a watt." Fearing he might begin to speak gently I decamped, but ever since then I have regretted that I did not stay and sign that rough-spoken gentleman to work out the mathematics of baseball.

I know that it is ninety feet from first base to second base, ninety feet from second base to third base, and that a baseball batted between those points is fair. I know that approximately 20 out of every 100 balls batted fair during the season are "safe hits." I know that of 1,284 ground balls batted during the season of 1909 in the American and National Leagues (1,284 chosen at random) 138 got past the infielders. I know that infielders of the National League (pitchers not included) fielded 9,382 ground balls errorlessly during the season of 1909. But how many millionths of a watt constitutes the chances of a hit being safe I cannot figure out. The average speed

*Reprinted from *The American Magazine* and copyrighted by it. Additions and corrections by Evers.

of fifty ground balls hit in three games during which three of us held twentieth-of-a-second watches we calculated to be 100 feet in one and three twentieth seconds. We know that the third baseman plays ordinarily 88 to 96 feet from the home plate, that the short stop playing "middling deep" is about 130 feet from the batter, that the second baseman is about two feet closer, and the first baseman 90 feet from the batter when a runner is on first base and 102 when no one is on bases. Given the speed and direction of the ball and the speed of the player, it is possible to figure to a millionth of a watt where his hands will meet the ball, but just as you start to write Q. E. D. the ball will take a bad bound. Given the average speed of the infielders, it would be possible to calculate beforehand approximately the number of base hits each team will make in a season—if the players were automatons.

The study of geometrical baseball is interesting in itself. Every ball player knows there are five "infield grooves" and four "outfield grooves," spaces between fielders where any ball hit with moderate force will be "safe" unless a marvelous stop intervenes. It is certain that the first base groove is a foot and a half wide at first base, and widens gradually through the outfield. There is a space 7½ feet wide between the territories covered by the first and second basemen through which the ball ought to be able to escape, as neither man can move fast enough to reach it. There is a gap in the defense directly over second base 7½ feet wide which is safe territory unless the pitcher, at the risk of his life, blocks the ball as it tries to pass him. The gap between the short stop and third baseman is 8½ feet wide, a foot wider than between the first and second baseman, because the ball goes faster in that direction, and the space between the third baseman's extreme limit of finger reach and the foul line is a foot and a half. Therefore, to get back to millionths of watts, as there is 26½ feet of ground unguarded out of 180 feet of defensible territory, Mr. Watt would argue that one ball in every $6^4/_{25}$ hit on the ground at an average speed of $1^3/_{20}$ seconds for 100 feet will be safe. The fact is that, in the major leagues, only about one in 16 gets past. Why?

In the season of 1909 I arranged with scorers to record hits of various kinds and secured the scores thus kept on 40 Central League games, 26 American Association games, and fourteen college games, to compare with major league scores kept in the same manner. In the college games one grounder in every $8^1/_3$ passed the infielders. In the Central League one in $10^7/_{12}$, in the American Association one in $12^2/_{43}$, and in the American and National Leagues (45 games of my own scoring) one in every $15^3/_{10}$. The figures were amazing, as they followed so closely the classification of the leagues. They proved that there is a reason for the "class," but the proof is not found in mathematics, but in two words (unless you hyphenate them), "*team work.*"

The truth is that the figures were truthful when baseball was in its swaddling clothes, but they lie egregiously now. The falsity of baseball mathematics is that the gaps in the infield exist just as wide as ever, but are closed by team work. The college player who reaches 8 in 9 grounders, may be faster than the major league player who gets his hands on 16 out of 17, but he does not understand the science of filling the grooves.

The best testimonial to the ability of Johnny Evers, of the Chicago club, to fill these grooves was given on the bench of an opposing team last summer.

"Hit 'em where they ain't," growled one player to another who had just been thrown out by Evers.

"I do; but he's always there," retorted the other.

This science of defensive work which enables four men to cover 180 feet of ground is the most fascinating part of modern baseball.

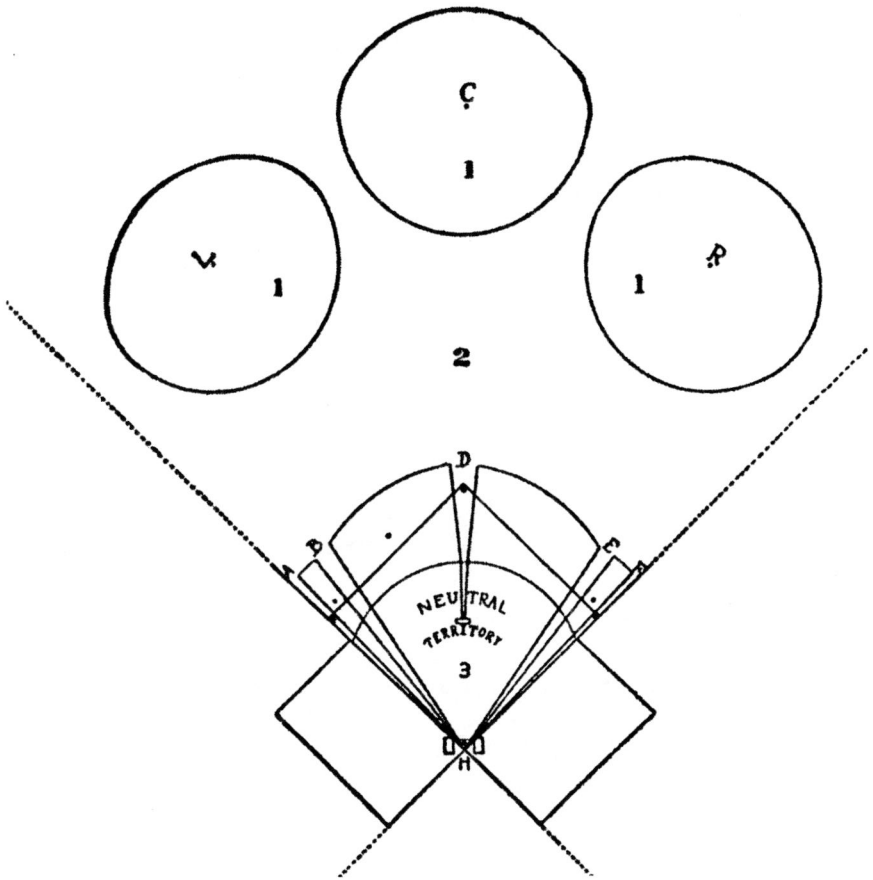

Diagram indicating territory where line hits ought to go safe. Calculations are made on the basis of the velocity of the ball being one and a half seconds per 100 feet and the speed of the players as six seconds for every 50 yards. A, B, D, E, F—Mark line drive grooves through the infield. L, C, R (1)—Ground covered by outfielders. In the territory marked 2, line hits will normally be safe.

It has become so intricate and involved that the spectator at a game of baseball between two highly developed teams really does not see the game at all. He sees the plays, the stops, the throws, the catches. He sees men shift and swing, change position, move forward, move back, move to the right or left, and then move back again, but all the beauty of the inside game is lost to him, nor does he imagine that behind each move is the master mind of a field general. The spectator yells himself purple in the face because Johnson fumbles a grounder and wonders why the manager don't "release that big stiff" for fumbling. Then he sits indignantly striving to imagine why the manager is plastering language upon Smith for failing to stop a ball he "couldn't have got anyhow."

"Inside baseball" is merely the art of getting the hits that "he couldn't have got anyhow."

Now watch this play closely. See whether or not you can discover what is going on. Pat Moran stoops behind the batter and hides his right hand back of his mitt. Ed Reulbach, pitcher, shakes his head affirmatively. Johnny Evers stoops, pats his hand in the dust, touches it to his knee and rests it upon his hip. Jimmy Sheckard trots twenty feet across left field angling in toward the diamond. Steinfeldt creeps slowly to his left; Tinker moves toward second base and Evers takes four or five steps back and edges toward Chance, who has backed up five feet. Reulbach pitches a fast ball high and on the out corner of the plate. Mike Mitchell hits it. The crowd yells in sudden apprehension. The ball seems a sure hit—going fast toward right field. Evers runs easily over, stops the ball, tosses it to Chance and Mitchell is out.

You saw all that. The ball was hit in "the groove" directly at the 7½ foot gap the geometrician will say is vacant, yet Evers fielded it. Now this is what happened; when Moran knelt down he put the index finger of his right hand straight down, then held it horizontally on the top of his mitt. Evers saw that Moran had signaled Reulbach to pitch a fast ball high and outside the plate. He rubbed his hand in the dirt, signaling Tinker, who patted his right hand upon his glove, replying he understood. Then Evers rested his hand upon his hip, signaling Sheckard, the outfield captain, what ball was to be pitched. Sheckard crept toward the spot where Mitchell would hit that kind of a ball 95 out of 100 times. While Reulbach was "winding up," swinging his arm to throw the ball, Evers called sharply to Chance (whose good ear is toward him), and Tinker called to Steinfeldt. While Reulbach's arm was swinging every man in the team was moving automatically toward right field, in full motion before Mitchell hit the ball. The gaps at first base, between first base and second, over second base and between third and short, were closed hermetically, while the gap between Steinfeldt and the third base line was opened up 22 feet. The ball, if hit on the ground, had no place to go except into some infielder's hands, unless Reulbach blundered and Mitchell "pulled" the ball down the third base gap. Every man on the team knew if Reulbach pitched high, fast and outside, Mitchell would hit toward right field. The only chance Mitchell had to hit safe was to drive the ball over the head of the outfielders, or hit it on a line over 7 feet and less than 15 feet above the ground. If Reulbach had been ordered to pitch low and over the plate, or low and inside, or a slow ball, the team would have shifted exactly in the opposite way.

Every club worthy the name uses the same system, but it is in the major leagues that it reaches its highest perfection. That is the explanation of the fact that college players stop *eight* out of *nine* grounders and big leaguers stop 15 out of 16 or thereabout. There is not much difference in the mechanical ability of players in the minor and major leagues, and the managers are men of almost equal experience, but the major league teams remain together year after year, while the minor league managers are forced to make an almost new team each season and teach the system to many recruits. The Milwaukee American Association team probably played as intricate and involved inside baseball in 1909 as any team ever did and it came near winning the pennant. "Stoney" McGlynn, the veteran pitcher, was chiefly responsible. McGlynn "hasn't much" (which means he does not pitch great curves and possesses little speed), but he can "put 'em where he wants to," and with a team behind him trained well enough to know every ball he pitches and to move in the direction the ball will be hit he is a great pitcher. With a broken up infield he is bad.

The system of signaling used by major league teams is so involved that it requires constant thought and a good memory to follow the signals, even after knowing them. No team dares use the same signals for any length of time. Some players become so skillful in detecting the signals of opponents that they sometimes compel the other club to change them two or three times during a game.

To show how complicated the system is, the Chicago Cubs catchers each have five signals which are plainly visible to the second baseman and short stop. If the pitcher gives the signal, the catcher repeats it by a different code. The catcher uses his hands, feet, knees or eyes in signaling. The commonest code is one finger in various positions for a straight ball, two fingers for a curve, a snapping of the thumb for a spit ball, a closed fist for a slow ball and the palm out if he wants a "pitch out," the ball being thrown wide to prevent the batter from hitting it when the defensive side suspects or knows a hit and run play is to be attempted. Sometimes the signal is given by the position of the feet. Schmidt of Detroit, using hands to signal when the bases are clear, signals with his eyes when runners are on bases, also using his hands to deceive them. In the World's Series between Detroit and Pittsburg last year Tommy Leach of Pittsburg tipped off Schmidt's signals repeatedly by guessing that

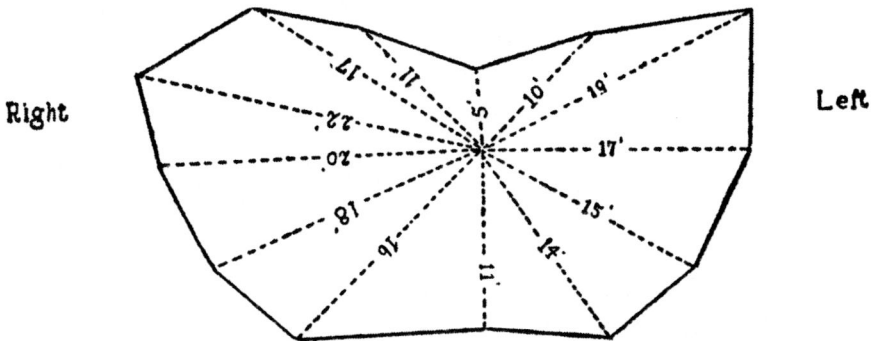

Diagram showing the relative distances an infielder covers in fielding balls of equal speed—calculated on the basis of the fielder's ability to move twenty feet to his right.

when Smith signaled one thing with his hands he was flashing the opposite signal with his eyes.

The second baseman and short stop see the catcher's signal and verify it by signaling to each other, deciding which is to cover second base. Also the intention of the pitcher is signaled to every member of the team.

One would think that the batter would notice the shifting of position and know what was to be pitched. He is, however, too intent on watching the pitcher to see anything else and, besides, the full motion of the defensive team is not noticeable until the pitcher starts to pitch, and then it is too late for the batter to realize anything except that the ball is coming. The coachers see the movement and half the time call out to the batter "Fast" or "Curve," but he does not hear until the ball is past him.

If you doubt this, try some day to see what becomes of the bat when a batter hits the ball and you will realize how had it is to watch anything except the ball.

In addition the second baseman and short stop have a code of their own, consisting of two signals, given with the hands, feet, arms or eyes,—sometimes by spoken words that are meaningless to any one else,—by which they understand which one is to take throws at second base. The manager also has his private set of signals by which he directs the movements of the team. Each man on the defensive infield has at least nine signals he must remember, most of which are changed, in meaning at least, every day. Each batter has six, three with the three preceding batters and three with the three men following him, making fourteen signals a day, besides the ones used by the manager. The second baseman and short stop have from 20 to 24 signals to keep in mind, most of which are changed every day and sometimes three times during a game. In 1909, when the hint had gone through the American League that the New York team was stealing signals, the Chicago White Sox changed signals nine times in one game, no signal meaning the same thing in any two innings.

There is no betrayal of secrets to explain how these signals are used or what they are, since they are changed so often that they may mean anything. Chance usually signals for a runner to try to steal by changing places with some one on the bench. He orders hit and run plays by looking over the bats. He orders double steals by lifting his cap and sometimes varies this by using the names of players. If he calls "Sheckard" he means steal, if "Schulte," hit and run, if "Hofman," go on the first ball.

Trained watchers at baseball games, men who have scored and reported hundreds of games, seldom observe the signals or understand what is happening. In one game a Chicago player, in defiance of Chance's orders, insisted upon remaining at first base after receiving an order to steal. Possibly the runner thought the opposing pitcher had caught the signal and was watching him too closely. Whatever the reason he did not run. The batter allowed two strikes

Napoleon Lajoie passing a signal to a batter. What does the position of his left hand mean?

to go over without moving to hit the ball. The crowd was howling at the batter, who was obeying orders, and the batter happened to be Steinfeldt, whose name that day was being used as the signal to steal. Chance was yelling: "Steinfeldt," "Steiny," "Steinfeldt," at the top of his voice and a veteran baseball man remarked:

"What is Chance yelling at Steiny for? He's playing the game. He ought to yell at that lobster on first."

But the signals used in attack have nothing to do with infield defensive work beyond showing how complicated the system is and how much the players must remember.

This infield defense involves much beyond knowing the signals. Its primary object is to enable the players to start before the ball is hit, as half the time required to reach a ball fifteen feet to one side is occupied in starting. The faster the second baseman can go to the left, and the short stop to the right, the closer they can play to second base, reducing the gap there without widening the others. The strength of arm of the short stop is another important factor in closing the gaps, for the deeper he can play the narrower the gap. With every foot he moves backward he gains a foot of territory. Also it must be remembered that every runner who reaches a base "ties up" one of the defense's players. On reaching first base, he forces the baseman to remain on the bag, and widens the right field gap by six feet at least. Runners on first and second tie up two men, and when this is the case and there is but one out, and a bunt expected or feared, the entire infield is "tied up" and the chances of the ball being batted safe are more than doubled.

The primary object in signaling is to enable the defensive players to start in the direction the ball is expected to be hit, and this is more important when runners are on bases than at other times. A player in motion can travel twelve feet while one who is "flat-footed" when the ball is hit is getting under way. If the pitcher blunders,

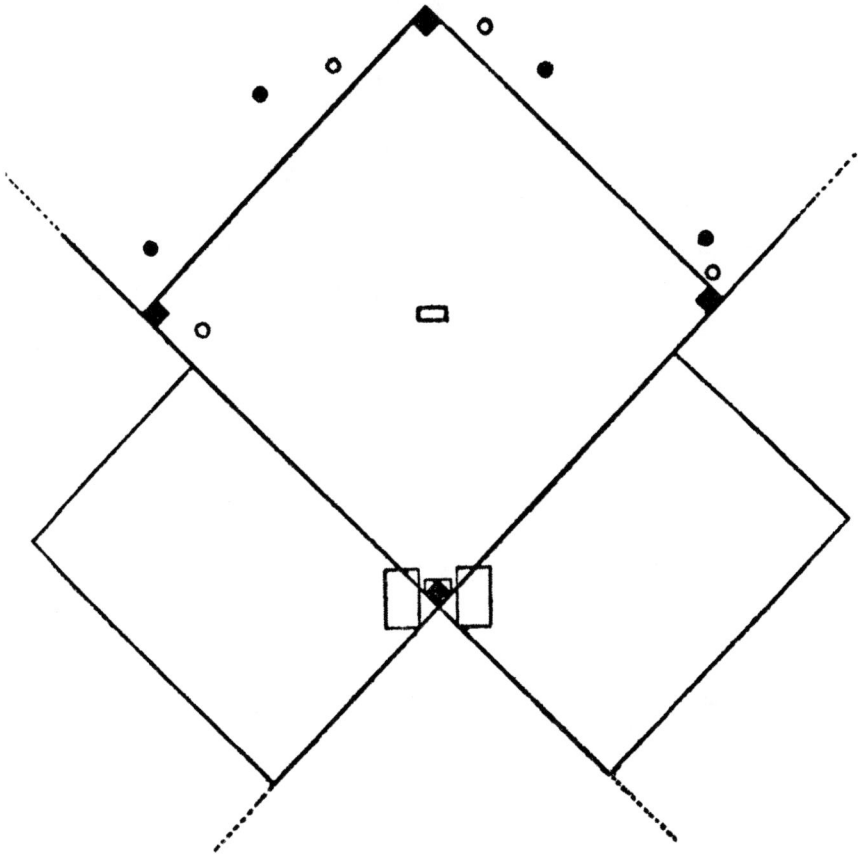

How runners on the bases "tie up" the fielders and make base hits more likely. Solid black dots indicate positions of players when bases are unoccupied. Circles show positions of infielders when runners are on first and second bases and the second baseman and short stop are "holding" the runner close to second.

disaster results, as the players in motion seldom can recover and field the ball if it is hit in the opposite direction. It is in that respect that "control" is the greatest element in a pitcher's success. But it is ability to hit all around the field that makes great batters. Men like JaJoie, Wagner, Leach, Evers and the late "Cozy" Dolan, who can "pull, push, and poke"—that is, twist their bats and hit in unexpected directions—break up the inside game and win many contests.

I always shall believe that Detroit lost the World's Championship of 1909 either through bad infield signaling or through too much signaling from the bench. Detroit's system is rather intricate and confusing because Jennings continually signals from the bench and the coaching lines. His signals to batters are given with hands during his famous grass-pulling, and with his legs while doing his famous "E-yah" act. From the bench, however, he uses sometimes spoken words, sometimes signals with his hands. I may be mistaken and some of his men wrong in charging the Tiger leader with the fatal blunders of the series. He may have given orders and the pitchers may have failed to get the ball where he wanted it to go, or the Pittsburg players may have performed the seemingly impossible and hit balls in the wrong direction. However that may be, Leach upset the entire defensive infield work of the Tigers. On three occasions, Moriority was running in fast when Leach, who was at bat, drove the ball past him, and once Bush was moving to cover second when the ball went down "the groove." Four of Wagner's long hits in the series were to left field and two of them at least were made off balls that were ordered to be pitched outside whether they were or not.

It is rather unfair to criticize infield work by exhibitions given in a series in which every man is strained to the limit and with immense crowds cheering and restricting the playing space, but the inside work of both Pittsburg and Detroit in the series was ragged and seemed to be wrong on many occasions. On two occasions, Bush and Delehanty were going in opposite directions when the ball was hit.

There is no play on the diamond in which the importance of infield signaling is so openly demonstrated to spectators as when a runner on first and another on third base are planning to attempt a double steal, either straight or delayed. When that situation arises short stop and second basemen exchange signals deciding which shall cover the base and which shall "cut in," which means, meet the throw before it gets to the base in order to return it to the catcher immediately should the runner at third start for home. Almost every team makes the play solely with regard to the strength of arm of the short stop or second baseman and the throwing force of the catcher. If the short stop has a "whip" strong enough to throw back the full distance, he covers second and the second baseman guards his territory. If either has a weak arm, the other runs in to meet the throw. Every player watches sharply for the exchange of signals from bench, from the coachers, batter and the basemen themselves and, if the signal is caught, the catcher instantly orders the ball "pitched out" high and fast in the best position for making a fast hard throw.

To show how closely the two teams watch each other in that situation: Cincinnati was playing Chicago with Frank Roth catching for the former team. Runners were on first and third. Roth signaled to the pitcher for a curve; Chance saw the signal and flashed a delayed double steal order. Huggins caught that signal, the Reds switched positions rapidly, and Roth signed for a pitch-out. The pitch-out signal was detected by Kane, who was coaching, and Chance signaled for a change. The result was the runners held their bases, and the pitcher wasted a ball. Roth signaled again, the infield changed, and Chance ordered the delayed steal. Roth was warned and ordered another pitchout, but no sooner had he flashed that signal and Chance had ordered another wait, than Roth ordered a fast

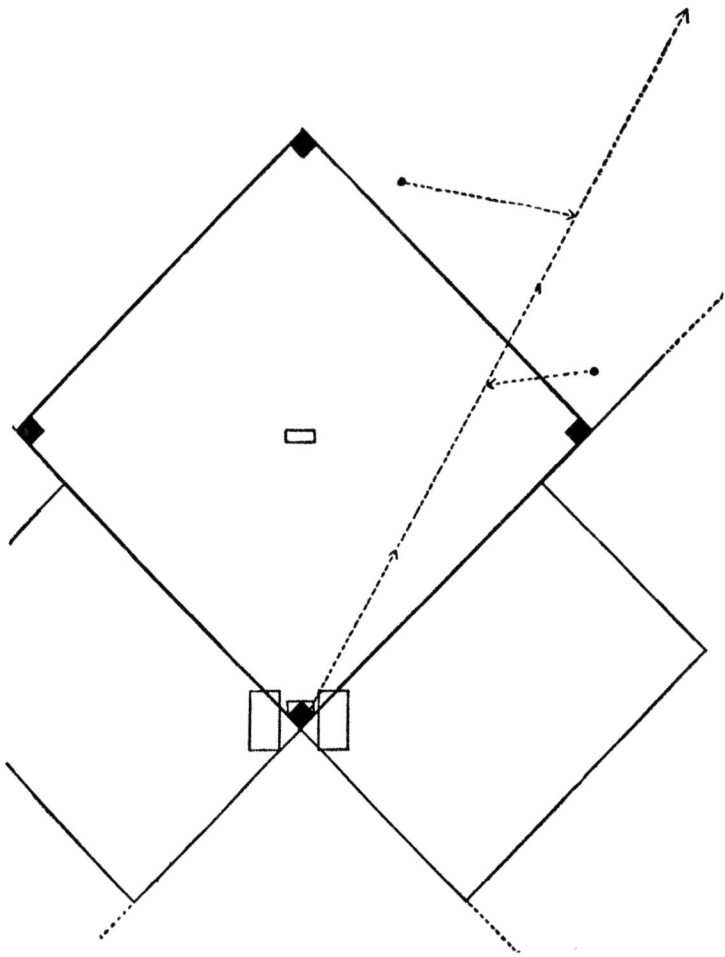

Diagram showing the angles at which the first baseman and second baseman naturally move in trying to intercept a hard bit ground ball passing between them.

straight ball pitched, thinking to out-guess Chance. But as Roth changed his signal Chance, guessing he would do exactly that thing, signaled a hit and run, with the result that a base hit tore through the infield and broke up the game.

The great danger to the defense on the double steal is that unless a pitch-out is certain both the short stop and second baseman are running to a line between home and second base and gaps 35 feet wide are left on both sides of the pitcher if the batter elects to hit. Consequently, if the attacking team decides to play hit and run instead of the double steal, and the defenders have been led to expect an attempt at the latter play, the chances of the batter hitting safe are tripled.

Late in the season, after the men know each other and the opponents perfectly, the infielders frequently discard the signals, having become so familiar with the plays and the style of making them that they know exactly what to do without signaling. Evers and Tinker of Chicago play entire games without looking at each other except when an unknown batter comes up to hit.

But to get back to that millionth of a watt and the geometry of the game. The average "fan" thinks that about four out of every batter hit fly balls. Managers growl all the time for the batters to "hit 'em on the ground," the theory being that more hits go safe on the ground than in the air. It is true more runners reach first base on ground hits than on fly balls, but the percentage of safe hits largely favors aerial batting. This is because so many grounders are fumbled and so few flies muffed.

This involves another study of angles, and an entirely new departure in infield defensive work. To discover what proportion of balls are hit on the ground, I took a mass of score books and classified 10,000 batted balls, every team in the National and American Leagues being represented in the figures. Really I scored 10,074

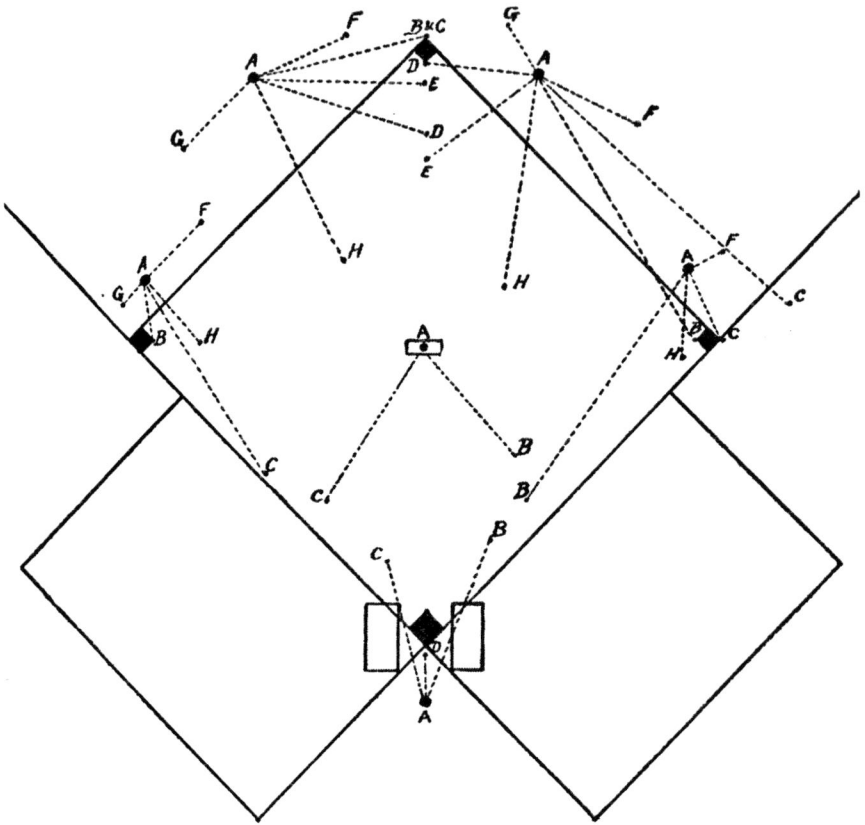

Diagram showing positions taken by infielders for different plays: A—
Normal position. B—Positions on bunt towards first base. C—Positions
on but towards third base. D—Positions on attempted double steal from
first to second and third to home with short stop taking the throw. E—
Same with second baseman taking the ball. F—Positions when right field
hitter is at bat. G—Positions when left field hitter is at bat. H—Infield
pulled in to catch runner at plate.

plays, because the number ran over unexpectedly and I did not know which 74 to deduct. Of them, 3,602 were fly balls, 5,171 were grounders, 344 were bunts, and 957 line drives, as distinguished from flies. Of the 10,074 balls batted, 2,067 were scored as base hits. Of the 3,602 fly balls, 747 fell safe and only 18 were muffed, which shows that the fielders catch almost everything they get their hands upon. Of the 5,171 ground balls, 424 were scored hits. Of the 344 bunts, 155 went safe, and of those 155 the fielders got their hands on 114. Of the 957 line drives, 741 resulted in safe hits.

But to show the ground-covering ability of the infielders further calculation is necessary. In scoring, I place a small "T" above hits I believe too hard to handle, and a small "D" over hits which are doubtful either through bad bounding of the ball or other cause. Of the 424 hits through the infield, 162 were marked "T" and 49 were marked "D." So the players reached the ball 211 times and failed to field it; and of the 213 times the ball went through untouched 46 were plain hit and run plays in which fielders were going the wrong way, in other words, blundering or being out-generaled by the batsman.

Out of the 5,171 grounders the players actually reached all except 213, or about .041 per cent., whereas on the natural chances of covering the ground they should have reached only about 800 per cent. instead of 959 per cent. of batted balls. The figures seem to show that by team work they were enabled to get in touch with 159 per cent. more batted balls than the geometry of the diamond would indicate.

The geometry of the game becomes more complex the deeper it is studied. Not only must the players on the infield know when to start in a given direction, but they must know exactly what angle to take to meet each ball. Further, they must change the angle to meet the running speed of each batter. If, for instance, "Larry" McLean, of Cincinnati, hits the ball, a second baseman will run backward, his path and the path of the ball meeting in an acute angle. If Miller Huggins is the batter he will run forward, making the lines meet in an obtuse angle. Moreover, they know to a nicety just where they must meet a ball of any given speed, and they start there almost instinctively. Oddly enough, the men can go much faster toward certain points than toward others, even when they are of equal speed, and they can, if they judge the speed of the ball and the runner, close up the gaps still further by reaching the spot in the ball's path toward which they can travel fastest. But all that is mechanical and habitual. It is the inside game which calls the brain into play to extend the reach of the arms.

Therefore, as Mr. Euclid, who invented diamonds, would say: If X covers 24 feet with his arms and legs and 18 with his brain, Y, the base-runner, is out, provided Z, the umpire, does not call him safe. Q. E. D.

CHAPTER IX

Outfielding

An English cricketer, a man renowned in his own country who had played for his county many years and was considered one of the best bats in all England, was sitting in the stands at the Polo Grounds, New York, watching his first baseball game. A batter hit a long, high fly to center field and Seymour jogging over unconcernedly, caught the ball and tossed it back to the infield

"Bravo! Bravo! Well caught! Well caught!" shouted the Englishman, clapping his hands.

His companion, an American, flushed with embarrassment while all the spectators in that part of the stand roared with laughter. The Englishman could not understand why the spectators regarded him as they would have a man who applauded during the death scene in a play.

From an American standpoint, the Englishman's outburst showed merely ignorance of the game, while as a matter of fact it proved that American crowds have become blasé. The spectators take for granted really wonderful catches and unless the outfielder is compelled to climb a tree, turn a double somersault, leap over a ten foot bleacher fence, or do something equally sensational, he scarcely attracts attention. The viewpoint of the Englishman really was the proper one. He realized that Seymour had performed a difficult feat and was applauding the skill of the American player in catching fly balls. He had watched cricketers ludicrously pursuing easy pop ups and floundering all over themselves in the effort to catch them, while the Americans, accustomed to seeing nearly every fly caught, regarded the feat as commonplace.

The marvelous work of the outfielders is perhaps the least appreciated part of the National game. Figures will prove how wonderful the fielding is. The fact is that any batted ball which remains in the air three and a quarter seconds will be caught unless it is hit over some fence, crowd, or stand. Ninety-nine out of 100 fly balls that stay in the air three seconds will be caught. In fact any fly ball, unless a sharp line fly hit in an unexpected direction, or one hit far over the head of a player, will be caught in nine cases out of ten. So accustomed have the scorers become to seeing fly balls caught that whenever the ball is hit into the air, the men who record the plays score the put out to the fielder before the ball strikes his hands, and when a fly is muffed, they are the last to see what has happened. Further, while often lenient with the infielders on fumbles, they charge the outfielder with errors no matter how far he may run, or what position he may be in, if the ball strikes his hands. They expect him to catch every ball he can get his hands upon.

Out of one thousand fly balls batted in games in the American and National Leagues during the season of 1909 (games chosen at random from score books) all except 27 were caught and nine of these were misjudged either because of the glare of the sun, the bad background or heavy shadows under the stands caused the outfielders to start in the wrong direction so they were unable to recover in time to catch the ball. Only five were plain muffs. Dozens of outfielders go through entire seasons without missing any ball upon which they can lay their hands.

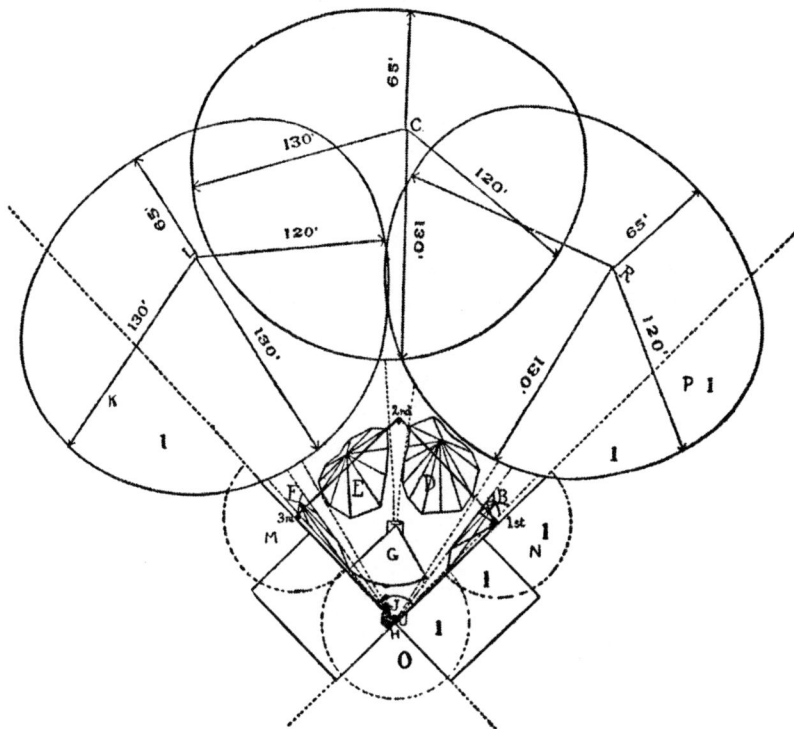

Diagram showing territory covered by fielders. The object of this diagram is to show the relative speed of players in various directions. The outfielders' ground covered is calculated on the speed of the men being 50 yards in six seconds and the ball being in the air three seconds. The infielder's ground is calculated on the same speed per man, fielding balls hit at a velocity of 100 feet in one and a half seconds. Note that an outfielder can run 130 feet to his right but only 120 feet to his left in the same time, as he starts quicker to the right. B—First baseman's territory. D—Second baseman's territory. E—Short stop's range. F—Third baseman's territory. J—Catcher's ground on bunts. G—Pitcher's territory on bunts and sharp grounders. K, M, N, O, P—Foul territory covered on three-second fouls. L, C, R—Outfielders' territory.

Catching flies is the least part of the work of outfielders. They must not only be able to catch fly balls, but catch them in position to make a throw the instant the ball touches the hands. They must have strength of arm, accuracy and absolute knowledge of the angles of the field and they must throw on the line and make the ball bound accurately into the hands of the catcher or baseman.

Primarily the outfielder must know the "inside game" as well as does the infielder, although not called upon to get into the play as often. He can make more mistakes and be more careless, but he should make as close a study of batters and base runners and watch the signals. If he is to succeed he must have an intuitive sense of direction, keen hearing, a quick eye; must make a study of backgrounds and take advantage of every light and shadow.

The "grooves" in the outfield are two in number, their width depending upon the positions and speeds of the outfielders. They run from a point directly behind the positions of the short stop and second basemen between the outfielders, widening rapidly after passing the line between the fielders. Down these "grooves" any hard hit ball is certain to go safe unless the fielder has anticipated the direction of the hit. He must do this either through knowledge of where the batter usually hits or through signals informing him what kind of ball the pitcher is going to pitch, from which he can judge the general direction in which the batter is likely to hit.

Intimate knowledge of batters, where they hit and how, is the primer of the outfielder. Each man must know how hard Fred Clarke, a left handed batter, is likely to hit a left handed pitcher's fast curve towards left field, and how hard he will pull the ball to right if it is pitched inside the plate. The left fielder must know that he must play fifty feet nearer the diamond when Keeler is batting than when Cobb faces the pitcher. Every batter in the entire league must be played in the same manner and the range of an outfielder in one game frequently is one hundred feet between his inside and his outside distances. Frequently, of course, a batter will hit where he is not expected to hit, but if the fielder is playing correctly no criticism is offered. It is regarded as one of the inevitable happenings.

Jimmy Slagle, for years regarded as one of the greatest judges of batters and the direction of their hits, went wrong one season. It was not because his judgment was at fault but because, for weeks and weeks, batters hit exactly where they seemed least likely to hit. The same thing happened to Sheckard of Chicago in 1909, and Mike Mitchell, of Cincinnati, in 1908. Sheckard, after a phenomenal run of these accidents, at the close of an inning one day took off his glove, closed his eyes and whirling around and around, let the glove fly.

"What's that for, Sheck?" called one of his teammates.

"I'm getting so I'm always wrong calling the turn on where batters will hit," he replied, "So I'm going to play wherever the glove lights."

The following inning he played on the spot where he picked up the glove. He was fifty feet out of proper position for the batter, but that unlucky man drove a hard line fly straight into Sheckard's hands, and from that to the end of the season Sheckard guessed right. He claimed the scheme changed his luck.

Different teams have widely varying systems of outfield play. Some play the "outside distance" on the theory that the fielders can come forward faster than they can go out after balls over their heads. Others play the "inside distance," on the theory that their throws will be more accurate and faster and that the number of short flies they will reach will more than offset the few long ones that will pass over their heads. Others play the middle distance and take chances both ways. The inside limit distance is more and more in favor among the thinking managers.

Harry Lumley, one of the brainiest of outfielders, after a throw to the plate.

IX. Outfielding

The Boston American team of 1909 played the outside limit all the time, but the speed of the outfielders saved the team. Pittsburg, playing the greatest shifting game of the year, used all the limits, changing their outfield distances with regard to the pitcher who was working for them. The Chicago National team played the "middle distance" and Detroit played the inside limit most of the time, although shifting frequently.

Of course outfielders adapt their distances to their own weaknesses or strength. Some men can move forward with great speed and are uncertain either as to direction or distance on balls hit over them. With Cobb, Clarke, Shulte, Leach, Davy Jones and Speaker, the distance chosen amounts to little, as they can retrieve mistakes in judgment by speed of foot. With men like Lumley, Sheckard, and Crawford, who lack speed, the study of direction is much more necessary. They are compelled to make up by brainwork what they lack in fleetness to equal the work of their faster competitors.

Willie Keeler, in his best days, was perhaps the greatest judge of where batters would hit that ever played, and in addition his quickness of perception gave him a running start after every fly ball. Walter Brodie, a great judge of fly balls, perhaps the greatest except O'Neill, could run with the ball, without looking, and catch it over his head, and he seemed to know from the crack of the bat exactly where the ball would land. "Big Bill" Lange had the same faculty of following balls hit over his head. "Kip" Selbach, in many respects nearly their equal, hardly could catch a ball that once went over him, and to defend himself he played the outside distance and came forward with wonderful speed. Clarke, leader of the Pittsburg World's Champions in 1909, is the rare combination who can go in any direction, especially toward the foul line for curving line drives. Cobb, although forced as a right fielder to follow curves in the false direction, almost is his equal in catching low line drives while going at top speed.

Touching Second

How deeply outfielders make a study of backgrounds and other conditions affecting their fielding is little understood outside the profession. Nearly all grounds are laid out so that the batter hits from south-west to north-east, in order that the lowering sun in midsummer may interfere as little as possible with the outfielders. But in games during late July, August and early September, the players work under a heavy handicap. After the middle of the game the sun, slanting over the top or through the stands and reflecting off them, glares into the faces of the fielders and gives the men in the outer line of defense much trouble. But the glare of the brassy sky, and the sun is not so much of a handicap as the heavy shadow that falls in front of the stands and stretches to the pitcher's box. The ball must rise out of this shadow before the fielder can gauge its flight accurately. In the construction of the modern skyscraper stands, the shadows have been deepened and greatly hamper the work of outfielders.

The devices and ingenuity of players in striving to overcome this handicap are revelations as to their powers of observation and the fertility and quickness of their brains. One game between Pittsburg and New York in 1909 illustrates the point. McGraw had a mediocre outfield and knew it. He was unable to strengthen the outfield so he devised a plan which made his outfield at least as good as that of the opponents in the games played on the Polo Grounds. New stands had been erected, and McGraw ordered them painted a washed yellow, a bilious-hued, glaring, eye-racking yellow. The background offered by the stand was a desperate one against which to field, but McGraw had the satisfaction of knowing that the other fellows, no matter how much superior mechanically, could not derive much satisfaction from their superiority on that field.

In the game with Pittsburg "Bull" McCormick was at bat and Clarke, in left field, seemed to be playing strangely out of position.

He knew the direction of McCormick's hits off left-handed pitchers, yet he was playing nearly fifty feet from where he should have been. McCormick hit down the left line and Clarke was compelled to make a spectacular running catch to get the ball at all, although it would have been easy had he been in place. When criticized for misplaying the batter he grinned and explained.

"Did you ever notice," he said, still grinning, "that over by the New York bench, back of first base, there is a little gate?"

"No, what has that to do with it?"

"Well, that gate is green. By moving around toward center field I could keep my eyes on that green gate. It rested the eyes and relieved them from the glare of the yellow, so I could see the ball the moment it was hit."

Players ordinarily dislike to play when the crowd, moving and turning, makes a dark shifting background. They welcome hot days when the majority of the spectators remove their coats and the women wear light colors, affording a better background. There was a young woman in Chicago who became unpleasantly conspicuous because Schulte used her as a background for fly balls, and when she moved from the box which she always occupied Schulte mentioned the fact that her green gown had helped him play. She was a loyal rooter, and in spite of the publicity, returned to her post to help the team, but sad to relate, she missed the point and wore a new brown broadcloth.

Green is the most restful color and many experiments have proved that it really aids both batting and fielding. There is one scientific player in the major leagues who has such faith in green that he carries a square of green cardboard in his uniform and gazes at it occasionally in order to rest his eyes.

Outfield throwing is one of the features of the modern game in which it is inferior to the game as played fifteen to twenty-five years ago. The reason is that outfielders of today do not practice distance throwing, preferring to save their arms. There are some fine and accurate throwers today, but probably not one who possesses the speed and accuracy of Jimmy Ryan, formerly one of Anson's champions. Ryan was left handed, and had the faculty of catching every ball in position and throwing with remarkable quickness, speed and accuracy. He threw to the plate from right field on the first bound, and twenty feet from first base, inside the diamond, he kept a little patch of the turf rolled smooth, watered and hardened. His throws were aimed at that prepared patch and off it the ball caromed like a shot into the hands of the catcher. Tommy McCarthy, in left field, threw to the plate, to first base, to second, and threw at every opportunity. Ryan and McCarthy after thirty years in baseball, still have good arms. Fifteen or twenty years ago outfielders gave exhibitions of throwing to the plate before games, throwing from long distances. The Chicago White Stockings had a target at the plate at which they would throw in practice. This practice made outfield throwing much more brilliant and effective than it is today.

The mechanical requirements for successful outfielding are numerous enough, but the difference between a good outfielder seldom lies in the mechanical abilities of the men. The chief difference is in the way in which they get into the team work, and close the gaps between the fields. Place the outfielders in their natural positions, that is, the center fielder directly on the line with the plate and second base, with the right and left fielders half way between him and the foul lines, and nearly every batter in the major leagues would be a 300 hitter. That shows the necessity of knowing all batters and shifting position with each pitched ball. The three fastest runners in the world cannot cover the ground between fielders on hits traveling 250 feet in two seconds, unless they have anticipated the direction of the hit, shifted position with the pitch, and made the start before the ball was hit.

IX. Outfielding

If the outfielders know where a batter hits, what ball is being pitched, and make one step before the ball is hit, so as to be in motion, the gaps are closed. Against some rank right field hitters the fielders can shift until all three are playing within reach of almost any ball hit to right, while the only gap existing is perhaps 100 feet down the left field line, in which direction the batter cannot hit the ball which is being pitched. With the man who hits all around the field the outfielder's only chance is to know just what the pitcher is doing, for there are certain kinds of balls that are batted in certain directions and hardly can be hit any other where.

Each outfield, therefore, has its captain, who takes the signal and transmits it to the other two, who shift positions according to his orders. Some outfield captains rely upon the keenness of their eyes to get the signal from the catchers, but when the opposing team is watching closely for signals this is impossible. The New York pitchers, for many seasons, reversed the process, and the pitchers pitched according to the positions taken by the outfielders. Other teams have done the same on occasion, but the practice of centralizing the signaling so that every member of the team knows what is being done is regarded as better.

The Pittsburg pitchers, because Manager Clarke is an outfielder, frequently take their cues from the position he assumes, and not infrequently during 1909, he signaled from the outfield to Gibson what ball to order pitched. Most outfielders, when they cannot get the signal for pitched balls, play entirely on their knowledge of the batsman. The Chicago Cubs originated the best system of any yet used. Sheckard, the outfield captain, received every ball and strike signal given, via Evers, who passed the signal of the catcher to Sheckard by varying positions of his hand upon his hip. Sheckard declares the signals contributed greatly to the work of the outfield.

When, in spite of all these precautions, the ball breaks through the outfield and goes "down the groove," perfect understanding as to which fielder shall "chase," and which shall relay the ball back to the infield is necessary, as a mistake or a second's delay will transform a three base hit into a home run; a double into a three bagger. The signal is passed in one word, and the one elected to chase, pursues the ball without question, although he may return swearing.

Each outfielder has special difficulties with which to contend, and of the three, the work of the right fielder is, perhaps, the most difficult. The reason for that is that balls hit towards right field curve sharply in the air and compel the fielder to extend his territory far over the foul line. The curve of the balls hit by right handers toward right field is especially troublesome. The left fielder has the difficulty in lesser degree. In the modern development of the game the left fielder has come in for some added troubles, especially as the result of the increasing skill of the left-handed batters in poking and shoving short flies over the infield into his territory. The center fielder has easier work as regards the curving of batted balls in the air, but he is required to cover more territory and to go in both directions. He has more chance to reach the home run drives "down the grooves." His chief trouble, however, is with line flies so hard that the wind pressure is likely either to make them dart downward suddenly, or shoot upward on some heavier current of air, giving him more opportunities for misjudging hard hit balls.

The study of air currents and wind directions is necessary for successful outfielding. The condition of the sky, the direction and force of the wind, whether it is steady or gusty, all are to be taken into consideration by the player before the game, and he must change positions with the force of the wind during the game. In one game in St. Louis in 1909, the wind blowing across the field crowded the fielders further and further over until all three were on the right side of the direct line through center field. There is a saying in baseball that "A high sky, a head wind and a home umpire will beat any team," and the outfielders vouch for the truth of the adage.

CHAPTER X

Batting

Batting is the aggressive part of the game; the true test of the nerve, courage and eye-speed of players, and the chief center of interest in every contest.

The importance of batting has, it is true, been largely overestimated, and few even of the managers and owners who have sought in every part of the country for that rarest of players the "Three Hundred hitter," realize the change that has come over batting in the last decade. The veterans who lament the passing of the sluggers of the "good old days," the old timer who recalls times when six .300 batters played on one team, and the student who looks back over the records of the mighty men of the ash, all have the idea that present day batters are inferior to the old time sluggers.

They are misled by figures. The batters of the modern game are better hitters, more scientific, and more effective than those of twenty or ten years ago. A close analysis of batsmen, their hits, and the results of their hits, will prove the point. If further proof is needed it is to be found in the strange acts of managers who, after scouring the country to find a .300 hitter, handicap him, restrain his batting, make a .250 hitter of him, and then consider him a better batter than when, perhaps, he batted .325.

X. Batting

The fact is, the batters of to-day are more scientific and resourceful, know more about handling bats, and better how to attack the weak points, than their predecessors did. The difference is the same as that between the slugging fighter, who rushed and pounded down his man by sheer strength, and the skilful boxer who, with one well directed blow, ends the battle.

The reasons for the decline of the averages of safe hits, and the number of long hits, are varied. The pitching, it is known, has improved steadily and rapidly, the defensive work of teams has been perfected until only a combination of terrific hitting power, skill, and luck will make any batter a .300 hitter. There were great pitchers in the old days; Clarkson, Keefe, Nat Hudson, Rusie, Ramsey; a host of them, but the general average of pitching was lower. Every team now has six or seven high class pitchers, where the old clubs had one good, perhaps, and three weak twirlers. But the pitching itself is not the chief cause of the general decrease of batting, as will be shown.

Frequently batters who slaughter the ball in the minor leagues, and hit any kind of pitching, fail utterly when drafted into the major leagues. Many followers of the sport imagine that the reason for this failure is to be found in the superiority of the major league pitchers, which is wrong. These men would hit in the major leagues, and hit hard, perhaps as hard as in the minors, if allowed to hit with the same freedom. There are, in the major leagues, many batters who could not hit in the minor leagues at all. The reason for both is found in team work, which is the chief cause of the decline in batting. Some batters are adapted to the system, others are not.

In the perfected team work of the major leagues batters must hit to advance runners and score runs rather than to get base hits. They are compelled to permit the kind of ball they can hit to cut the plate unmolested and then hit at one which, perhaps, they are

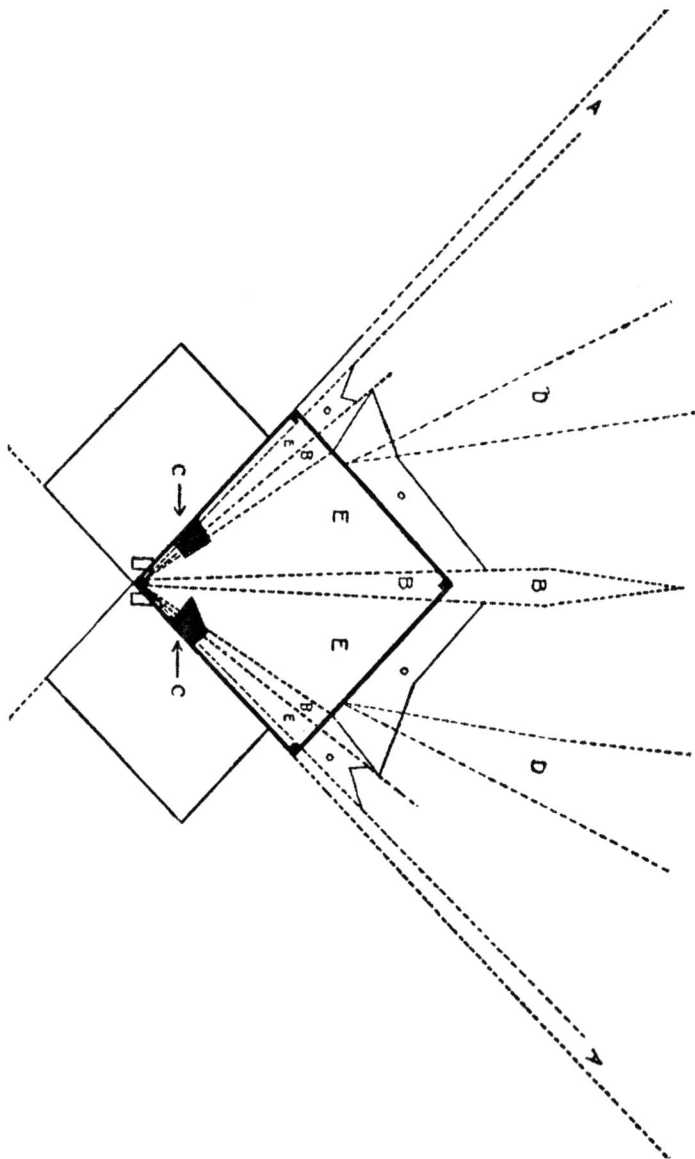

lucky to touch. Besides many times they are ordered to wait, and not to hit at all, in order to allow the pitcher to weary himself.

A few years ago the Chicago club purchased a player late in the season who was one of the great batters of the American Association. His hitting helped the team to win the pennant, yet Chance released him without even bringing him to Chicago to play the final games. The act surprised the followers of the Cubs and someone asked Chance why the man was released. "First ball hitter," explained Chance loquaciously (for him).

Chance was right. The player was worthless as a team hitter, but if permitted to hit the first ball pitched to him he batted heavily and if he could have been the first man up in every inning he probably would have led the league in hitting.

The reason for the improvement in scientific batting lies in practice, and the amount of batting practice indulged in during the season is astonishing. It is the one thing about the game of which the players never tire. Morning, afternoon and evening from March first until far into October players bat as long as any one will pitch to them, and on November first the bat feels as good in their hands when it meets a ball squarely as it did the day spring training started. The first thing in the spring is the selection of bats and when the season closes the players still are sawing up disgraced bats and buying new ones. Bats get to be a mania with some. Roger Connor used to oil, polish and rub down his substitute bats every night and hang them from his window while he took his favorite to bed with him.

Opposite: Diagram showing infield "grooves," home run "grooves" and safety zones for bunts. Hard hit balls following these "grooves" ought to go safe. A—The first and third base "grooves." B—The infield "grooves." C—Spots in which bunts are normally safe. D—The home run "grooves." E—Territory upon which grounders ought to be fielded.

Touching Second

There was a bat in the Boston club in 1909 which became famous. It belonged to Gessler, and a scorer one day jestingly marked upon it the symbols meaning a two base hit and a single. Gessler happened to make a double and a single that afternoon, and the players swarmed upon the scorer pleading with him to mark hits into the bat. He marked it full of hits; the Red Sox began a wonderful hitting spurt, all using the same bat, and before long the scorer was claiming part of the credit for their winning streak. Before the season ended Gessler hardly would have traded the bat for its weight in gold.

"Evelyn" the famous bat with which Isbell, of the Chicago White Sox, made four two base hits in one game and won the World's Championship for his team, "Big Betsy," Ed Delehanty's famous war club, "Nellie," used by Schulte, and a dozen other bats have become well known through being the favorites of good hitters and used by them during batting streaks.

There is a player on the Brooklyn club who has an odd habit of using in practice the bat he intends to use in a game to "fill it up with base hits." He tries bat after bat during practice, and if he happens to hit well with one, get "two or three hits into it," he uses that one during the game to get the hits out again.

The eagerness with which the batting practice is indulged in often is laughable. One evening two members of the Cleveland club broke training and returned to the hotel at two A. M., feeling jolly. They reached their own floor in the hotel without being caught by the manager and went to the room of a player who is a wonderful hitter. Banging on his door they urged him to get up.

"What do you want?" growled the awakened slugger.

"Get up, we're going to have batting practice," replied one of the jokers who knew the weakness of the inmate of the room.

"There in a minute," responded the player, and as they heard him scramble from bed the jokers fled. Ten minutes later the night clerk was startled to see the great player enter the lobby in his uniform, carrying his two favorite bats, nor did he see the joke until the clerk pointed into the darkness outside.

In the early days of the game batting practice was neglected. The heavy hitters practiced, but there was no system to their work, and very little time or thought was given to the scientific hitting, except by a few men who realized the possibilities of play. "Dickey" Pearce invented the bunt and the "fair foul" hit in 1866, but generations passed before the bunt was used intelligently by all classes of players. Indeed it was the theory of players, as it now is with many followers of the game, that "place hitting" was more or less of a myth. In fact it has been within the last decade that even the major league players have made intelligent efforts towards perfecting place hitting, and their successes in that line have been wonderful. Managers began to realize that the attacks could be directed at the vital spots of defending teams, and the attack has steadily become more resourceful, better calculated to bring results, and more adapted to cope with the improved pitching. Especially has it been made necessary in order to break up defensive team work.

Whether the modern game of "push, poke, shove and chop" is better than the old "swing and kill it" style may be judged by a comparison. The Philadelphia club from 1894 to 1898 always had from five to seven .300 hitters in the game. In one game in 1897 there were nine .300 batters. Yet the team never won a pennant. The games were spectacular, but even when hitting hardest it was a bad hitting ball club. The Chicago White Sox, "the Hitless Wonders," won the World's Championship in 1906 when ranking almost last in batting in the American league. The team excelled any team ever organized in concentrating every move toward making runs, one at a time, and while nearly weakest in batting, scored the greatest average number of runs per hit of any club in the history of the game.

Touching Second

There is a wide difference of opinion among players themselves as to the placing of balls hit hard, but the fact remains that some players can do it by holding their bats at certain angles, and the increase in skill in the last five years has been great. None denies that balls can be poked, or pushed easily in a given direction. Many of the old timers were skilful in "pulling" the ball foul in order to wear down pitchers, and by hitting late in fouling off. The skill of batters in that direction increased through steady practice until McGraw, Keeler, Roy Thomas, Slagle and others could prolong the games indefinitely and tire out any pitcher. The rule makers promptly legislated against foul balls, and opened the new era of batting science. Their object was to hurry the game and avoid unnecessary delays and they thought that batters penalized one strike for a foul, would hit harder, and oftener. The players discovered, however, that hard driving did not pay against improved infield work, and that the new rule aided both the pitchers and fielders when the ball was hit hard, as it went too straight towards second base, and allowed the infield to concentrate their defense. One of the first results of the new rule was the increase in bunting, with variations tending to upset the infield. The "force bunt" was brought into prominence by little Butler, of Columbus, who afterward blew one hand off with a fire cracker and retired. He pushed the ball slowly down the infield, striving to make it roll fast enough to pass the pitcher either to his right or left, yet so slowly that the short stop or second baseman playing deep, would have to take it while sprinting forward at top speed and make a perfect throw. The gain by the play was not to the batting averages. It did not produce many safe hits, but it was productive of wild throws, and fumbles, and it at once became popular as a method of destroying infield team work and breaking up games.

The Chicago Cubs used the force bunt during all their championship term, pushing the ball, instead of bunting it dead, a short distance in front of the plate. Their success with the ball was marvelous. In the fourth game of the World's Championship series in 1907 at Detroit, Sheckard pushed a force bunt past Donovan in the critical moment of the game, and before the panic in the Tiger ranks ended, Chicago had made three runs as a result of the bunt, and won easily thereafter, 6 to 1. In one game at Philadelphia in 1908 Tinker made the bunt with two men on bases, pushing a slow roller toward short stop. Doolan was running to cover second base and the ball rolled clear onto the grass behind short stop, Tinker taking two bases.

Men of the type of Speaker, Cobb, Clarke, left-handed-batters, and occasionally a right hander, Leach for instance, use the force bunt with great effect.

During the seasons of 1906 and 1907 Sheckard, of Chicago, used a bluff bunt which worked with great success. He bunted at the first ball pitched to him, and purposely missed it. The he bluffed that he intended bunting again and, as the third baseman tore forward, Sheckard poked the ball over his head. Leach, in the World's series of 1909, beat Detroit two games by the same play. Three times he drew Moriority forward to field expected bunts and then drove the ball past him like a rifle shot. Beaumont, a veteran of many teams, has for years been regarded as one of the most dangerous place hitters, either when hitting the ball hard or when pushing it on a short line fly over fielders coming forward. In the hit and run game his batting was remarkable, for whichever fielder the runners managed to draw away from position it was almost certain Beaumont would hit through the deserted post.

"Calling the turn" is a style of batting employed by some batsmen in trying to outguess the opposing pitcher. It means striving to guess what kind of a ball is about to be delivered. This style, while effective, is extremely dangerous for the batter, as to guess wrong is

Hans Wagner, the greatest "all-round" player in baseball.

to court serious injury. In one game at Cincinnati a few years ago, Coakley pitching, McGann tried to outguess him. He guessed a curve was coming, and his wrist was broken by a fast inshoot. Two innings later Bresnahan guessed wrong and was knocked senseless.

There are times when a play comes up to a batsman which compels him to try to outguess the pitcher. One of these times is when the hit and run play is ordered. With a runner on first or second base, and the batter giving the signal, he is compelled to attempt to guess

when the pitcher will put the ball over the plate. He guesses, signals
the runner, who is expected to start as if to steal the next base in
order to draw one or more infielders out of position, and strives to
hit through the deserted place. If the batter's guess is wrong, the
runner is the victim.

Selee, when manager of the Cubs, once secured a player from
the Coast League who was reputed to be a wonderful batter, who
had hit over .400 in his league and could call the turn every time.
Selee tried him in right field against Boston, and "Vic" Willis, one
of the best "guessers" in the business, and a pitcher with a marvelous
curve, both slow and fast, was on the slab. The recruit struck out
four times and when he returned to the bench after the fourth effort
some of the players sympathized with him.

"Tough to start against Willis," remarked one.

"Yes, and I'm calling the turn every time, too," mourned the
recruit.

"Well, old boy," said Chance, "I'd like to watch you when you
weren't."

But not all of batting is hitting the ball. There is method in the
jockeying of the batter. The moment a batter steps to the plate with
the bases clear the game becomes a duel between him and the pitcher,
and although the crowd may be calling for him to hit, his intention
may be not to hit until compelled so to do. His first effort is to "get
the pitcher in the hole;" that is, make him pitch enough balls so the
batter can be certain the next one will be over the plate. For, if the
batter knows the ball is coming straight the chances of making a base
hit are doubled.

Then too, the batter may be under orders to follow out a manager's plan of battle. Frequently a manager, feeling certain the game
will be close, orders his men to wait. The waiting may be either to
discover whether the pitcher is likely to become wild, or to wear him

out. Each batter then, instead of hitting, tries to make the pitcher throw as many balls as possible. If a batter can get three balls, foul off three, and then strike out, he may have accomplished far more toward the final result than he would have done had he made a base hit off the first ball pitched. The average number of balls pitched by one pitcher in a game of nine innings will run about 125, and every additional ball pitched wearies the pitcher. Many "ninth inning rallies" by which spectacular games are won, are the results of the waiting of the batters who struck out during the early innings.

Chance is a great believer in the waiting game, and insists upon his men trying out pitchers during the early innings of games, especially new and unfamiliar pitchers, believing that what each man discovers, will help the succeeding batters.

The practice of getting to first base by allowing the pitched ball to hit them, is more general with batters than usually is supposed. It is not indulged in as extensively as in former years when "Red" Galvin used to allow the ball to carrom off his head in order to reach first, but it still is used extensively, despite rules forbidding umpires to allow batters to take first when purposely hit. There is scarcely an important game between contenders for pennant honors, in which a dozen batters do not strive to make the ball hit them.

Batters who "crowd the plate" usually are good hitters. They have the courage to risk injury, the nerve to allow the ball to hit them, and the advantage in getting decisions because, knowing they crowd the plate habitually, the umpires decide that they tried to escape. Besides pitchers will pitch outside to them steadily through anxiety to avoid hitting them, if they know the men will let the ball break a rib in order to reach first.

The actual gain through allowing the ball to hit him is not so much for a player's team, as the moral effect upon the defending club. Nothing in baseball is so calculated to discourage a team, or destroy its confidence in a pitcher as to have him hit a batter in a crisis in the game.

Scores of batters each season make the ball hit them, and take first in spite of the rules. The umpires must judge from the actions of the men whether they tried to avoid the ball, and in most cases any contortion of the arms is construed as such an effort, especially when there is a large home crowd on the field. In the season of 1908, during the fierce struggles of New York, Chicago and Pittsburg for the pennant, New York won three games from Chicago because players allowed themselves to be hit, and they came near winning the game in which they played off the tie by the same method—the second batter up throwing his arms across the plate and making the ball hit him. McGraw's verbal orders to players to get hit were audible in the stands, and in one game Doyle made three attempts to get hit before he succeeded and then was allowed to walk.

Umpire O'Day unmasked one trick on the Polo Grounds that same season which was laughable. Bresnahan was batting and, while wiggling a là [*sic*] Salome, he kept pushing his knees out toward the ball. O'Day stopped the game, ordered Bresnahan to adjust his clothing. Bresnahan argued, but O'Day made him obey, while the crowd roared at the umpire. Bresnahan had stuffed his shirt front out six inches, and inflated his trouser legs three inches in order to give the ball more surface to hit.

Such tricks, however, are outside the real sphere of baseball and are the final resorts of desperate men in desperate situations. Only a quick eye, long practice, courage and accurate swinging of second growth ash will win steadily.

CHAPTER XI

Base Running

A player who can run fifty yards in six seconds ought, with a lead of eight feet off first base, run to second base, 82 feet away, in three and one-half seconds. A pitched ball will travel from the pitcher's slab 68 feet to the catcher's glove (fast ball with catcher standing nine feet back of the plate, timed from the start of the pitcher's motion), in seven-eights of a second. The catcher, if he handles the pitch perfectly and gets the ball away fast, will start the ball towards second in one and a quarter seconds after it hits his hands and his throw from nine feet back of the plate, if perfect, ought to reach the second baseman in one second, and be caught and the ball be ready to apply to the runner in one-quarter of a second additional. Perfectly handled in that time, the ball ought to beat the runner to second base by from one-eighth to one-quarter of a second, or by from 3⅓ to 6¼ feet and result in an easy out.

The calculations are based on the pitcher holding the runner within eight feet of first base, and preventing a flying start, upon perfect handling of the ball, and upon the throw being "on the runner" at second.

Hours spent in snapping split second watches have proved that every base runner, if properly held up at first base, ought to be caught stealing second base. Yet the same timing proves that not one pitched ball in ten, during actual play, is pitched, relayed by the catcher and handled by a second baseman in three seconds; and, while figures based on perfect play prove one thing, actual timing indicates that 62 (plus) out of 100 runners ought to reach second base if they can start and run 82 feet in 3½ seconds.

Shortening the catcher's throw to approximately 93 feet and figuring that the runner can gain fifteen to eighteen feet running start, instead of eight feet as at first base, and calculating on perfect playing in average time, a man who can run 90 feet in 4 seconds (including start) ought to beat the ball to third base by nine inches in every attempt perfectly made.

These are mathematical facts. Now for actual conditions as proved by what has been done. In one season (1896) a complete record was kept of Lange's base running. He stole exactly 100 bases, stealing second base 68 times, third 31 and home once. Eliminating hit-and-run plays entirely, or steals spoiled by hits, he made 141 efforts to steal, and was successful in 100, or about 70.2 per cent. of his trials. The returns (unofficial) for the season of 1909 show that Ty Cobb stole 76 bases out of 105 attempts, or 72.4 per cent. While Cobb's total attempts are unofficial, they are close enough to show that the first-class base-runners succeed in about seven out of ten efforts to steal second. The figures really reveal more than that. They show that, while the runners steal only about 64 out of every 100 times they try for second base, they succeed nearly eight of ten (78 plus out of 100) times they start for third.

The conclusion is clear that the pitchers do not hold up runners closely; that the ball is pitched wide a large percentage of times, and that the catcher, for various reasons, is lucky to handle the ball perfectly three times in ten in actual play.

If further proof is needed, here it is: Lee Tannehill, one of the slowest runners in the American League, in 1909 stole 12 bases out of 19 attempts, two of which were palpable failures of batters to hit on hit-and-run signals. Even at that, he stole over 63 per cent. of the bases for which he tried. With these facts in view, the insistent query of baseball lovers, "Why doesn't he steal?" becomes pertinent.

The truth is that base-running is fast becoming one of the lost arts of baseball. There is no possible doubt but that there are men today who could steal as many bases as Hamilton, Lange, Mike Kelly or any of the old-time star runners if they played the game the same way. There is not the slightest doubt but that Cobb today is as good a man as Hamilton, Lange, Keeler or Harry Stovey; that Chance, Fred Clarke, Wagner, Bush or Collins could run bases with the best of the old-timers. Yet Stovey stole 156 bases one season, Hamilton 115 in one year, 102 another and nearly 100 two other seasons, while Cobb stole 76 during 1909 and was considered wonderful.

There are reasons for the elimination of base-stealing from the run-getting tactics of modern teams; more reasons than one. In the old days the motto of every manager was "run and keep running; make the other fellow throw." It was a baseball adage in those times that any team that could keep the opposing team throwing the ball around would win. As a matter of fact, the modern manager recognizes the same thing. He knows that if he can make the other team throw, it is only a question of time until they throw away the game. Why, then, does he not carry out his theory?

The first and greatest cause for the degeneration of the art of "sprinting and hitting the dirt" is that in modern baseball, more and more every year, individual effort is being sacrificed to team work. Team work, in many respects, has been overdone, and there are scores of players today who will not do anything on their own initiative or attempt a steal unless signaled so to do from the bench or by the batter. The modern ball player has been so trained to team work that only a few with brain and daring pull off the brilliant individual feats that are necessary to win pennants, no matter how much team work there is.

A player reaches first base, looks at the batter for a hit-and-run signal, looks toward the third-base coacher to see if a signal to steal has been flashed from the bench, takes his lead, watches the batter, and anchors himself. Two balls and no strikes are pitched; he looks again for the signals. Failing to get them, he knows the batter is going to take a strike, and anchors himself again—afraid to risk the displeasure of the manager by stealing. Even should the pitcher carelessly permit him to get a big running start, he trots back to first base, perhaps slides back as hard as he would have had to slide to second. He catches a hit-and-run signal on the next ball, takes his lead, gets his start. The pitcher and catcher know as well as he does that the stage of the game calls for an attempt to run and hit; the pitcher pitches fast and out; the catcher takes the ball perfectly, throws, and even if the runner is a speedy man he is out by at least three feet. The pitcher and catcher did the thinking, the base runner used stereotyped "team ball" and was caught.

Another cause for the decline in base running is the vast improvement of pitchers in watching bases. The average pitcher of today holds the runners to the bases much more carefully than did those of fifteen years ago. There are exceptions on both sides. Kilroy, Griffith, O'Day, Red Ehret, Brietenstein and others of the old school held them close, while today there are some who allow a running start. The balk rule handicaps the modern pitcher somewhat but the chief improvement in watching runners is the result of constant training and practicing.

Still there are few pitchers who do not give the runner at least one good chance to steal. At least once in every five pitched balls, no matter how closely a pitcher may watch, his mind is diverted and he leaves an opening which a quick thinking runner may use to gain a flying start.

The hit-and-run and the bunt-and-run games, of course, reduce the number of opportunities to steal. Ty Cobb was on first base about 310 times in 1909 and stole only 76 bases. He had 310 chances to steal second, perhaps 200 chances to steal third and nearly 150 chances to steal home, as he scored 150 times. The records show he stole second 52 times, third 21 times and home three times. Yet he is the most daring base runner of modern times. How often attempted hit-and-run plays, or third outs prevented an effort to steal is not recorded.

Cobb is one of the rare players who can play "inside ball" and individual ball at the same time. He is brilliant, thinks for himself and is not much hampered by bench orders. He runs mainly on his own judgment (or lack of judgment) but still he RUNS and he wins pennants for Detroit by running. The pitchers try harder to hold him to the bases than they do any other player in the league; the catchers give more pitch-out signs to catch him, but they do not stop him. He is a living proof of the fact that modern ball players could run bases with as much effect as the old-timers could—if it were not for their lack of individual thinking.

The more one studies the situation, the more convinced he must become that, despite the vaunted advances of the game, there is less brain work exhibited on the bases than there was twenty years ago. This is not to claim that the players of today are not as intelligent, but that they have subordinated their intelligence to the brains of the manager, and allow one man, or, rather, insist upon one man, doing the thinking for the entire team, which is an impossibility.

It is so seldom that one who watches a couple of hundred games of baseball every season sees anything new in the base-running line that when he does it is refreshing. That the baseball-loving public

"The Chicago Slide." Lobert of Cincinnati sliding under Kling.

sees it the same way is proved by the wild applause that greets unexpected steals, and by the public admiration for Cobb, Wagner, Bush, Collins, Evers and Chance. Philadelphia went wild over Collins, who ran with execrable judgment, but got results. Billy Maloney set Chicago to talking by just such running, and led the National League one season in base-stealing. He ran wild, ran at the wrong time, ran all the time—and the showing that he and Collins made proves the wisdom of the old order to "keep the other fellows throwing." The other fellows tell "how lucky such runners are," and keep on making errors.

A few years ago, Frank Chance, always a base-runner of rare judgment, coupled with great daring, started his team working the delayed steal. His runners started, stopped, and when the catcher relaxed from his throwing attitude and the man covering second base started back to his position, the base-runner made a dash for second. Mathematically figured out, the runner will beat the ball to second by over two feet, on the bases of 3⅓ seconds to run the distance. Really, the runner gains more, as the baseman usually is slow getting up to cover the base, and a slide in front of him causes him to lose almost half a second diving forward to touch the player, after catching the ball.

One day in 1909 Chicago and Pittsburg were playing, and a run meant victory for either side. Evers was on second base, with one out. He made a bluff run towards third, putting down his head and sprinting at top speed. Gibson whirled to throw to third. Evers stopped dead still—and laughed. Gibson instantly made a perfect throw to second, and, like a flash, Evers dashed for third and slid safely. He scored on a fly ball and won the game. The play, magnificently executed as it was, set the crowd wild, and Evers deserved the tribute. The play had not been made in Chicago in five years, yet it was common in the old days, and the catcher had to watch every runner and calculate his distance between the bases before making a throw, else he would be trapped.

Figures prove positively that the runner can go 32 feet up the line towards third, and, if he starts back quickly enough, can beat the throw back to second. If he goes the other way, he has 58 feet to run and slide only 23 feet farther, and the ball must travel almost twice as far and be relayed perfectly to catch him. If he makes the play correctly, the fastest possible handling of the ball will only catch him by three feet, unless he is blocked off the base. That calculation allows for the second baseman coming ten feet inside the base to meet the catcher's throw.

The play can be made every time by a fast man if he can draw the throw to second, yet Evers was applauded as a hero because he thought it out.

XI. Base Running

One of the cleverest bits of base-running Ty Cobb ever did was in one of the games of the first World's series between Chicago and Detroit. Cobb was on first base, when Crawford drove a single to short right center, making Slagle cut in towards Shulte to reach the ball. When Cobb reached second base, Hofman had thrown and the ball was coming in to Evers, who had gone into the grass to meet it. Without hesitation, Cobb turned second and raced for third. He had figured the play in an instant. He knew that Slagle was a weak thrower; that Evers' back was to the diamond; that he would have to catch the ball and swing entirely around before he knew what was going on. He calculated that Evers would expect him to stop at second, and, therefore, look at second base first, and so lose enough time to allow him (Cobb) to reach third. Evers looked at second, looked at third, saw Cobb already within ten feet of the base, and he made a wild, hurried throw that went into the crowd and almost gave Detroit the game. No manager could have told Cobb to do that, and because 99 out of every 100 base-runners would have stopped at second to await orders, they would not have made the play.

Baseball has been reduced to a science, and is in danger of becoming mechanical unless a few base-runners like Cobb, Collins, Evers and Clarke, exponents of the unexpected, convince managers that base-running pays, and that remaining anchored to bases is a poor policy.

The two glaring examples of the different schools of baseball playing appeared in 1909, one in Boston on the American League grounds, and the other in St. Louis on Hedges' Park. The St. Louis Browns of 1909 was the historical stationary team of baseball. Never again will there be another. It could make fewer runs on more hits than any team extant. If a player reached the plate on less than four hits, his fellows accused him of showing them up.

The Boston team went to the other extreme. Fred Lake, a minor league manager, exploited the old theory of making the other fellows throw, and without first-class pitchers he made the teams in the American League fight to the finish to hold his "Speed Boys" out of pennant honors.

The entire theory of the Boston team was "run," and with the fleetest aggregation of runners in the circuit, perhaps in the country, the "Speed Boys" ran.

It is history that Frank Isbell, when he was on bases, never stopped until he broke a leg, went out or some one shut the gate on him. He could take wilder chances than any runner who ever landed on a base, and he kept running after his legs wore out and his speed left him—and running with excellent success because the opponents would be so surprised to see him going that they would throw wild. But Isbell, in his palmist days, would have been a second rater for "crazy" base running in the Boston team of 1909. "Get on and run" was their motto and they ran wild through the league. All the other players said they were "crazy," complained that they were not "playing the game," that they were ignoring all the science of the hit-and-run, sacrifice and bunt-and-run, but the "Speed Boys" kept on running and winning. Eventually, of course, the pitchers and catchers let them run and caught them by pitching out, but not until Boston had come near winning the pennant by persistent recklessness.

The kind of baseball played by the Red Sox would not win consistently, yet neither will the studied, systematic playing, exemplified by the Chicago Cubs, win always. That was proved by the way some of the National League clubs stopped Chance's team and kept them from winning their fourth straight pennant. Pittsburg blocked Chicago's system of attack, because in three seasons they had studied it and knew every move to expect. Gibson was chiefly responsible, but the pitchers did their part. The well developed plan of attack was becoming stereotyped, and this was proved by the fact that Chance was compelled to alter his campaign plans more frequently than ever before. Pittsburg, during the middle of the season of 1909, had the most varied and resourceful attack of any team in the league, and mixed up the base running style successfully, but before the finish the Pirates, too, became stereotyped.

Base running consists chiefly of doing the unexpected, and the team that refuses to run bases because a strong throwing catcher is pitted against it is beaten. The strong throwing catchers, paradoxical as it may seem, have the least throwing to do, proving some teams surrender before they are beaten, while the worse thrower a catcher is the more throws he has to make.

Myers, the Indian, with New York, won a game from Chicago in 1909 by pretending to have a sore arm. He complained that his arm was so bad he did not want to catch. The Chicago players heard his complaint and decided to run bases. They ran for three innings, until four men had been caught, then changed the style of game. If they had persisted in running during the entire game, they probably would have won, as they needed only one run to get ahead in the eighth inning, and had two chances to steal, either one of which would have meant victory. The team that stops running because one or two men are thrown out is on a par with a man who puts up three stock margins and then quits.

In thirty-two games in 1909 scores were kept to see how plays resulted with reference to stealing and hitting and running. In those games 66 efforts to steal were made and 41 were successful. Steals which were palpable efforts to make other plays, as well as failures of such steals were not counted. The average of successful stealing was .621. In the same games 72 plain hit-and-run signals were detected.

Eleven of the attempts (15.3 per cent.) resulted in clean hits, eight of which (11.1 per cent.) enabled the runner to take extra bases. Twenty-seven of the attempts (nearly 40 per cent.) advanced runners at the expense of retiring the batter at first base. Seven (09.6 per cent.) resulted in the batter striking out, and three of these strike-outs (04.2 per cent.) resulted in the runner being doubled with the batter, while two of the strike-outs (02.8 per cent.) resulted in the runner reaching second, anyhow. Seventeen runners (23.6 per cent.) were forced at second for no gain; three (04.2 per cent.) were doubled on line drives, and seven (09.6 per cent.) of the batters flied out.

The object of the hit-and-run being to advance runners, the result in these games shows that it succeeded in 50 out of 72 times, or 69.4 per cent. Yet, while the percentage of success was larger in the hit-and-run than in stealing, it is extremely doubtful if the figures do not show that plain stealing was more effective as a ground-gainer.

These figures were made while watching a slow team and one which is supposed to play the hit-and-run game perfectly. It would be interesting to study the same way, say, fifty games played by Detroit or Pittsburg. Figures accumulated that way ought to prove convincingly whether or not base-running should be neglected.

The game needs more dash, less mechanical work, more brains by individuals, and fewer orders from the bench. John McCloskey was the only manager who could signal runners whether to slide feet or head first while they were stealing second.

CHAPTER XII

Umpiring

Umpires, in spite of the theory upon which baseball is conducted, and the apparent belief of spectators, are human beings, endowed with sensibilities. They can feel such emotions as anger, resentment, and revenge; their systems are capable of suffering pain, surprise, regret, even acute mental torture. Umpires (the officials to the contrary) are likely to blunder, to be carried away by prejudice, by desire for revenge, and more than likely to become confused by the fierce heckling of players or spectators, and to blunder worse and worse. Umpires may even be dishonest. They are only human.

Yet baseball, as an institution, is more dependent upon the honesty, courage and fairness of umpires than upon any other element in the game. One incompetent or dishonest official, or one of violent passions who permits personal animosity, or his sense of wrong, to influence him, can mar an entire season, ruin the chances of one or more teams, and perhaps give the championship to a club not deserving the honor.

In spite of these facts, the rulers of baseball have adopted an extraordinary code; first, that the umpire always is right; second, that those who differ with him are "anarchists;" third, that all criticism of umpires should cease "for the good of the game." The rulers of baseball are striving and have striven for years to align all forces with the umpire, to extend his already dangerous power, and to deprive players and others of the right of criticism.

To a large extent this movement was caused by continual and senseless criticism of umpires, which served only to make the umpiring worse. The established principle of baseball has been that, in matters involving only judgment, the umpire's decision is final. The attempt to make his decisions on matter involving rules and their interpretation beyond appeal and extend their power to punish critics, is not of their seeking.

The danger lies not with the umpires, but with the powerful financial forces behind organized baseball and the establishment of a system which would muzzle all criticism and would place in the hands of these men absolute power to dictate the standing of clubs by directing the umpires. Those who have the good of the game at heart, and many of the players, who trust umpires, would not trust the club owners if it were within their power to make the pennant races close.

The honesty of umpires, as a class, never has been questioned. Some have been actuated by prejudices, some by dishonest motives, but as a body they are as honest and straight as any men that can be found. They are men of strength of mind and character, else they would not remain in the position a week. They are men of courage, quick decision, steady nerves and moral strength to face angry crowds for the sake of principle. But the honesty of club owners with fortunes involved has not escaped attack and there is ample evidence that some have attempted to influence umpiring.

Many persons, wearied by the senseless carping of some writers at the officials, have started a movement to have the umpire ignored in all sports. The danger would lie in leaving an opening for the introduction of dishonest methods. The financial temptation is great and should not be increased. The practice of presidents of leagues giving secret instructions to their umpires is considered a grave danger to the game.

The umpire, from being the abused, downtrodden victim of fanatical frenzy, as pictured in the comic supplements, has in the major leagues at least, become the Czar, armed with arbitrary power to use or misuse, and certain of the support of his league in any case. The only restraint placed upon them is the criticism of the crowd, or the in press, as the players cannot address them in argument, and to remove the restraint of publicity would make them a menace in case they either were prejudiced or revengeful. Umpiring now is a more important element in the game than pitching. It would be as bad reporting to ignore a bad decision that won or lost the game for fear of injuring the umpire's feelings as it would to fail to mention a home run hit because the pitcher might feel hurt.

Few persons understand the full extent of the umpire's power in, and effect upon, baseball. In fully one-third of the games played in major leagues during a season, the umpire can turn the result by one decision. He can make or mar a contest by his manner of handling the players. Games under competent and hard working umpires are played in an average of twenty minutes faster than when an incompetent man is handling the teams, and the best way in which to judge the qualifications of a man for the position is by comparing the playing time of games, taking into consideration the rapidity with which the pitchers work.

The popular conception of an umpire is that of an abused individual. This is the result of old time conditions, which still prevail in some minor leagues. In the old days an umpire, armed with a life insurance policy, took his life in his hands and walked between rows of ranting, raving athletes who, if they did not want to kill him themselves, urged the populace to do it. The education of players to the point where they realized that kicking and abusing the umpire would not win, but tended to turn the decisions against them, was slow. The education of spectators to a sense of fair play above partisanship has been slower. As conditions improved, however, higher and higher types of men entered the umpiring field, until now the salaries and the work attract many clean, decent men who command the confidence and respect of players and spectators.

The great mistake of the officials of the leagues has been upholding the goats as well as the sheep. To a great extent the reformation of the umpiring system, and the steady improvement in deportment of players and the work of the umpires has been due to President B. B. Johnson of the American League, who has either had the luck or the judgment and firmness, to revolutionize conditions existing ten years ago and set an example which all executives have been compelled to follow. His first move was suppression of rowdyism by stern methods, and the suppression of the rowdies at once resulted in better umpiring, and a large increase in the number of desirable men who wanted the positions.

The large majority of umpires are honest and mean to be fair, but, as Umpire Johnstone remarked: "Some umpires have one bad fault, and that is not being able to forget to-day to-morrow." The umpire who remembers is a bad umpire, and it is almost as bad for the player to remember. Tim Hurst had a bad day at Washington and Joe Cantillion thought he robbed his team of the game. The following day Hurst, willing to forget, walked over to the Washington bench and asked cordially: "Who is your pitcher today, Joe?"

"Guess, damn you," responded the retentive-memoried Cantillion. "That's all you did yesterday," and the trouble was renewed.

Heads of leagues make their serious mistakes in upholding umpires who are palpably wrong. They are compelled to uphold them on all questions of judgment, but to declare the umpire was right in some cases is laughable. There was a case in 1894 in Chicago with Moran umpiring. Corcoran, at short for Cincinnati, picked up a grounder batted by Tinker and threw the ball five feet over Pietz's head, Pietz playing first base. The ball went on to the bleachers, sixty feet away. Pietz jumped, pretended he had caught the ball and Moran called Tinker out. Other players were compelled to hold Tinker to keep him from assaulting the umpire who ordered him off the field, and ordered all players who talked to him out of the game. Pietz chased the ball around the bleachers, ran back to the bench and touched Tinker.

"Now, Tinker," said Moran, "you are out, anyway." And the decision stood.

In Brooklyn, in 1908, with the score 0 to 0, Brooklyn had runners on second and third bases and two out when the batter missed the third strike. The catcher dropped the ball, but recovered and threw the runner out at first. Two runners crossed the plate, and the umpire permitted both runs to count. But the Chicago club, in an exhibition game at Birmingham, met the worst on record. A runner trying to score with two out in the ninth, was thrown out so far from the plate that he did not slide, but turned and ran through the diamond to the bench. The umpire called him out, but when Manager Vaughan protested the runner had not been touched, the umpire lost his head. The runner, in the meantime, had gone into the dressing room, had his shirt off, and was starting to wash. When notified of the situation he put his shirt on, ran under the stand, climbed through a box, ran behind the catcher, after two balls had been pitched to the next batter, and when he touched the plate the umpire allowed the score and tied the game.

To uphold decisions of that sort is to put a premium either upon dishonesty or incompetence.

One of the greatest examples of individual heroism the game

has known was that of Henry O'Day in the historic game between New York and Chicago on September 23, 1908, when Merkle forgot to touch second base. Ten days previous to this game O'Day had been umpiring at Pittsburg and missed the same play, turning away to get a drink and failing to see Gill, the runner, who forgot to go to the base. In New York when the hit was made that sent home what seemed the winning run, the crowd surrounding the field, swarmed upon it. O'Day, remembering the Pittsburg play, raced nearly to second base, saw Merkle turn and go to the club house, saw Evers with the ball on the base. "The run doesn't count," he said—just as the crowd swarmed over him. For two hundred feet he walked through a raging mob, telling them the run did not count, while they shrieked, struck at him, pulled him and threatened his life.

Even after New York claimed the game and the entire country was aroused over the situation, O'Day could have ended the trouble with a word and given New York the pennant. He knew the National League wanted New York to win. He knew the Giants ought to have won, that the hit was clean and one that deserved to bring home the winning run. Even when officers, politicians, men big in baseball, urged him to say he had not seen the play, had not made a decision, he stood firm. It was said O'Day would be mobbed if ever he went onto the Polo grounds again, but when he next appeared he was greeted with cheers that showed the admiration of the fans for his courage.

There are weak umpires and strong ones. The weakest is the "Homer" who gives all close decisions to the home club. But the "Homer" is not as bad as his antithesis, the "bullhead" who gives all close decisions against the home club for fear he will be called a "Homer."

With all their mistakes, prejudices and human weaknesses, the umpires have a smaller percentage of errors than the players. As an experiment, Mr. I. E. Sanborn ("Cy") of the *Chicago Tribune*, kept accurate score of all decisions made in a number of games. When in doubt, he questioned umpires and players in regard to the decisions. He found that the umpires averaged about .970 per cent right and that even then some of the decisions scored against them might have been given either way without prejudice. The good umpire is not palpably wrong in more than 35 cases in a thousand, although, of course, he may have a bad day, just as a player does and pile up errors. "Silk" O'Loughlin had such a day at St. Louis once when he seemed to call everything wrong. Finally he called Wallace out. "What for, 'Silk'?" demanded Wallace.

"Well, you see," explained the umpire, "I really thought you were safe, but wanting to get one decision right, I called you out."

The phrase "senseless kicking" is widely used and is redundant because all kicking is senseless. It is different from "causeless." The "causeless" kicker always is a bad ball player. The "senseless" kicker may be one goaded to desperation by bad umpiring. In the modern game there is no (at least little) "kicking for effect," such as was indulged in by McGraw, Jennings, Tebeau and O'Connor. The players know they do not gain any advantage and are liable to arouse the retaliatory spirit of the umpire and be put out of the game. Strangely enough, kicking, when there is just cause for complaint, is the most dangerous kind. An umpire seldom expels a player for causeless kicking. He drives him out for objecting to decisions which he knows were wrong and is therefore angry with himself.

Some expulsions are laughable. In 1908, Pat Dougherty, goaded to a state of frenzy by Hurst's ball and strike decisions, turned upon the umpire and said, "You blank, blank, blankety blanked blank crook."

"Do you think I am that sort of a crook, Patrick?" asked Hurst.

"Yes, blank blank you, I do," spluttered the angry player.

"Then, Patrick," said Hurst in his softest voice, "If I were you I would not associate with such a person. Git on off the field."

Muzzling players completely is merely placing a premium on weak umpires because the modern player does not kick against good umpires who have their confidence and respect. Some umpires attempt to rule by bullying players and misusing their power. The worst scenes in modern baseball have resulted from the aggressiveness of the umpire. The good umpires, who have tact, usually admit to the angry players that they might have been wrong, and in almost every case the player retires satisfied.

Clean aggressiveness must remain a part of the game, for it is necessary to keep a team fighting for every point and the spectators demand it. Modern major league players outside the "bonehead" class, understand the difficulties of the umpire's position and sympathize with him as long as he appears to be trying. Minor league players will assure you that the umpires in their leagues do not get half what is coming to them, and in many leagues the same process of suppressing rowdyism that the major leagues went through is going on. What some of the "bush league" umpires will decide really is astounding, and what they must endure from the players would rejoice the heart of the old time "fan" of the "kill him," "take him out" epoch.

There was an umpire at Evansville, Ind., in 1908, who called a game on account of darkness at 3:26 p.m., the moment the Evansville team scored a run and went ahead. Schmidt, when managing the Meridian, Miss., team passed himself off as an umpire and was caught stealing the opposing catcher's signals, signaling his own batters and base runners, and then miscalling balls and strikes as fast as they were pitched in a vain effort to make his minor leaguers beat a major league club.

XII. Umpiring

One of the best comparisons between the umpiring in major and minor leagues was given unconsciously by "Ducky" Holmes, who, after years of service in major leagues, retired to manage the Lincoln, Neb., club. After the third game, he pleaded with "Bill" Rourke, with tears in his eyes, to lend him a revolver, with which to kill an umpire.

Years ago there was an umpire who, in a game at Quincy, Ill., called a runner out at the plate in the ninth inning, ending the game and giving the visiting club the victory. The crowd, angered by the decision, made a rush but he escaped, and fleeing with a hundred men and boys pursuing, leaped into a passing delivery wagon, implored the driver to save him, and escaped to the hotel. Before he could dress and flee, the angry crowd surrounded the hotel threatening lynching. He hid in a room on the top floor. Night came and still the crowd, muttering threateningly, remained on guard. At eleven o'clock the umpire raised the window of his room and cautiously stuck out his head.

"Ladies and gentlemen," he yelled, "I reverse my decision. The run counts."

The crowd dispersed and his life was saved.

Abe Pollock, who umpired a few frenzied games in the Central League, quit abruptly and tells the following story in explanation—President Carson entering strenuous denial.

"I stood everything," Pollock groaned. "They spiked my feet, hit me in the eye, waylaid me after games, kicked me on the shins, pulled my hair, abused and cursed me. Still I stuck until one day at Fort Wayne when a big fellow walked down to the front of the stand, dropped a big bull dog over into the field and yelled, 'Sic him,' then I resigned."

The worst feature of an umpire's life, perhaps, is the necessity of avoiding everyone and concealing one's identity as far as possible.

During the season the umpires travel incognito, if possible, and keep their hotels secret except to the presidents of their leagues; avoid players and all conversation with outsiders, practically exiling themselves. These precautions are necessary because irresponsible persons are likely to start false stories. O'Day met McGraw on Broadway one morning and walked two blocks with him. Before the game started, the "tin horn" element along Broadway was betting on New York on the report that "McGraw had it fixed," which was started by someone who saw the umpire and player speak to each other. In St. Louis an umpire was accosted in his hotel by a stranger, who seemed to know him.

"What do you think of the race?" asked the stranger.

"Pretty close," replied the umpire.

"Think New York will win?"

"They have a good chance."

"Is New York a good bet?"

"As good as any in baseball."

Three days later the president of the league received a letter stating that the umpire was betting heavily that New York would win the pennant.

On the afternoon that New York and Chicago played off their tie for the National League Championship of 1908, the rumor ran all over New York that the game was fixed for New York to win. Tinker was called from the Chicago bench an hour before the game and advised to save himself by betting on New York because the umpires were fixed, and offers to bet large sums were made at all saloons, and in the Polo Grounds itself on the strength of the rumor. When the Kreamer case was exposed, months later, the probable origin of the rumor was revealed.

The umpires are compelled to avoid the slightest appearance of evil or accusations will arise. Still an umpire may have friends,

Comiskey to the contrary notwithstanding. Once Comiskey was angry with Cantillion, who then was an umpire. The previous day Cantillion's decisions had aroused the crowd against him and when the umpire came to the gate with two other men, the gate keeper, a bitter Chicago partisan, refused to admit the men Cantillion had invited to attend the game. Comiskey appeared.

"Umpire is here with two friends," said the gateman. "Shall I let them in?"

"Any umpire who has two friends ought to bring them," snorted Comiskey, "they are all he has."

The life of an umpire is graphically described in J. Peck Sharp's version of the manner in which Jack Sheridan entered the profession.

"Jack had been playing in the Southern League," relates Sharp, "and Oakland purchased him. Great stories had been told of his ability to field, and before the season opened the Oakland papers were printing two columns a day telling how good he was. The season opened; Sheridan did not come. Urgent telegrams were sent. The team lost steadily. The people cried: 'Give us Sheridan.' More telegrams, money, tickets, still more telegrams, and finally Sheridan came rushing to the rescue. The papers printed seven column headlines announcing his arrival, and all the people in the city poured out to see Oakland start to win the pennant. The first afternoon Sheridan made four errors, the next day six, the next seven, and when the game ended the crowd chased him for miles. He fled on and on until at last he came to a dense forest and in that he hid by day and fled by night.

"On the third day he came to the great redwood groves and stumbled upon a lumber camp. The foreman fed him and gave his a job. The next morning he was given an ax and a team of oxen, and the foreman, taking him into the forest, marked two redwoods for him to chop down. Sheridan set to work, hacking around and around the giant tree like an Indian with a tomahawk. At dusk when the foreman came to help him haul the trees Sheridan had not chopped through the first one. The foreman accused him of loafing. Sheridan, with blistered hands and aching muscles, retorted angrily. While they quarreled the tree fell, killing both oxen. The foreman, seizing an ax, leaped toward Sheridan to kill him. Again Sheridan turned and fled. For days he fled on and on, deeper and deeper into the forest. Hiding by day for fear of being seen by some watchful Native Son, and slinking through the forest by night, he lived on roots, barks and berries. Twelve days he wandered. One afternoon he threw himself exhausted upon the ground, his mind filled with bitter thoughts.

"'What is left for me?' he soliloquized mournfully, 'driven from the haunts of man, forced to hide and skulk through the bushes like a hunted animal. Scorned, beaten, despised by my fellow man; hated; an Ishmael and out-cast. Why shouldn't I make a good umpire?'"

One night a few years ago "Silk" O'Loughlin had the blues and was descanting upon the bitterness of an umpire's life.

"It is a dog's life," he said. "Worse than that, for sometimes persons speak kindly to dogs. Even a criminal, a murderer, is more respected and better treated. We are outcasts, pariahs, things to be abused and insulted. Why, from three o'clock every afternoon until after five, we stand out there with ten thousand persons abusing, insulting—"

"Yis," remarked Hurst, "But can yez beat thim hours?"

CHAPTER XIII

Developing New Plays

Once there was a mathematician who calculated that there are 7,226,433 plays possible in baseball and the next day someone made one he had not included in his figures. It is a game of surprises, freaks and accidents. Almost every day some new play, some new way of making an old play, or some startling innovation is recorded somewhere. Of the many things that go to make the game interesting to spectators, the greatest is the new plays that are developed day by day, tried, discarded, or added to the team's repertoire. There is scarcely a morning practice that passes without a new play being proposed by someone, and accepted for trial or rejected by his fellows.

The game has developed toward exact science steadily for the last fifteen years and while the freaks and the accidents continue to add to interest and excitement, the discoveries of real value are becoming fewer and fewer. This is not because the players are any less resourceful, but because there is so much less to be discovered.

Players even of a few years schooling in the minor leagues today, know more about the game, how plays should be made, and what not to do than did Mike Kelly or the other famous inventers and originators who were the pioneers of scientific baseball. The modern player has the benefit of the accumulated experience of a dozen baseball generations to study before he even starts to play.

If there is a serious menace to the popularity of the national game it is that the playing will become mechanical, if not monotonous. It is the history of every great team that has remained together long that patrons ceased attending games because they were lacking in sensations. Many lovers of the game declare major league baseball is less exciting, less spectacular and therefore less interesting than in the minor leagues. It is certain that hustling, aggressive tail-end teams in the major leagues frequently furnish better average sport than do the clubs contending for the pennant.

There is danger that the game may become machine-like. There is a tendency in that direction with all championship teams, except that in their ranks usually is found some fighting, aggressive player who, refusing to stop at the set rules, thinks out and tries out new plays or new ways of making plays, tests his theories and keeps all the others stirred up. It is these men who discover the new plays.

History has its records of the inventors, but baseball history is tradition passed down from generation to generation until even the discoverer of the curve ball is in doubt.

One of the odd things of baseball is that many of the pioneers made plays repeatedly and won games by them without being imitated. Many plays, such as the "push bunt," the "bluff bunt," the "delayed steal," have been "discovered" about once a decade, and then neglected, if not forgotten, until some other genius brought them into action. In the pioneer days of the game, it seemed that if a player invented or evolved a play, the others, instead of seizing upon it to use, gave him a kind of patent-right to it. Indeed it was not until 1885 that any systematization of plays was begun.

When Dickey Pearce invented the bunt, and used it as a means of reaching first base, he was scorned and his fellows thought it rather a baby trick. It never occurred to them that it might be more effective as a run-getting device than trying to beat the cover off the ball. F. R. Boerum caught pitched balls behind the bat without waiting for the bound as early as 1859, yet as late as 1897 catchers played back except on third strikes or when runners were on the bases, little dreaming the assistance they gave the pitcher by remaining close. Ross Barnes, in a game between the Chicago and Rockford teams in 1870, stole home twice while the pitcher was in the act of delivering the ball without finding imitators for many years. Comiskey used the "delayed steal" when he was playing at Des Moines as a boy. Ted Sullivan records that the St. Mary's college (Kansas) team played off bases to draw throws and then advanced a base by beating the relayed throw, when he was at school in the sixties.

In the days of the "New York" and "Massachusetts" games, the first bound was out, and often games were played in which the batter was out if the ball was caught on the second and even the third bound. When the Knickerbocker team proposed that the ball should be caught on the fly to make an out, it was ridiculed. Tyng, the Harvard catcher, who arranged the famous demonstration before the faculty to prove that a ball could be curved, wore the first mask in 1876 and was received with scorn. It was not until 1886 that the left hand glove came into use, and then many teams refused to play if their opponents wore gloves, and for a long time after that there was a deep prejudice against the hand armor. Anson, during all his career, refused to wear a mitt, playing first base with a light glove against the terrific throwing of Williamson and Pfeffer. He was converted two years before his retirement.

The adoption of the glove in catching was the result of the change in the rules in 1884 which allowed overhand pitching and made more protection necessary, and in 1886, with the abolition of the high-low ball rule, the game entered into its best period of development, with more rapid progress.

During the early eighties, there came into the game two of the greatest inventive geniuses it has known: Mike Kelly, of Chicago, and Charles A. Comiskey, leader of the St. Louis Browns. According to James A. Hart, who was for years head of the rules committee, fully one-half of the restrictive rules enacted were the direct results of the activities of Kelly and Comiskey to find ways of beating existing rules and winning games. Whether they invented them or not, both used the "bluff bunt," the "delayed steal," the "double steal" with runners on first and third and many other plays used today by the best teams.

Kelly's greatest invention, however, was the famous "Chicago slide," now used by every good base runner. The slide, it is conceded by the veterans of Anson's famous White Stocking infield, was the invention of Kelly, although every man on the team used it with great success until it became the trademark of the White Stockings. The slide consists of throwing the body either to the right or to the left while at full speed, and sliding upon the hip, with the leg doubled under, and the foot extended so as to hook around the bag. The runner throws his body away from the baseman to avoid being blocked or touched, pivots on the foot that hooks the bag, and prevents oversliding.

The Chicago team of 1880, which reached its fullest development five years later, was the pioneer of "inside baseball," and from that team came more original plays, now in common use, than from any other source. Those were the formative days of the modern game, and the players, Quest, Anson, Kelly, Burns, Williamson, Gore, Flint and Corcoran, were learning from each other while teaching others. But it really was with the coming of Pfeffer in 1885 that the team began to play "inside baseball" coherently, both at bat and on the

Chris Speaker, one of the sensational "finds" of the season of 1909.

infield. A system of signaling, involving the catcher, third and second baseman and pitcher, was invented, Anson for some reason being excluded from the team play. The marvelous success of the team was due more to intelligent team work, and the protecting of base runners by the batters than to the individual skill of the players, although that was great.

During the same evolutionary period another leader was coming forward in the rival American association. Oddly enough, Comiskey, leading the St. Louis Browns, was working along the same lines of development of team plays as was the Chicago team, inventing plays, teaching them to his men, learning from others and winning pennants.

Comiskey was and is one of the great constructive geniuses of baseball and the only one who kept abreast of the progress of the scientific part of the game, and usually ahead of it. He was one of the first to use the hit-and-run play effectively, but his great improvement in defensive work was his style of playing first base, which was revolutionary in its effect upon the infield game. Comiskey not only invented plays, but seized and improved upon plays learned from his men and his opponents.

In the contests between St. Louis and Chicago for the World's Championship in 1885 and 1886, the difference in style of infield play between the League and Association forced itself upon the attention of students of the game. The Chicago infield played close, St. Louis deep, and the chief advantage of the Browns was in the fielding of the pitcher and first baseman. The fielding of the pitchers of the St. Louis team was an innovation in baseball, and their covering of first base at a dead run, and backing up on plays was wonderful. They enabled Comiskey to play a deep first base and he, playing deep, gave the second baseman a chance to play deeper and closer to the base, which helped the short stop by many feet.

XIII. Developing New Plays

Comiskey thus was the first manager to use the two weakest defensive parts of the infield, the pitcher and first baseman. Up to his time, both had been useless as far as fielding went. Comiskey won pennants at St. Louis by his inventiveness, and it is a remarkable thing that every team he ever has handled has had great fielding pitchers. If they were not good fielders when they joined the team, they had to learn.

The World's Championship series between Chicago and St. Louis marked an era in the development of plays. Each team learned from the other, and the National League took the best of the Association's style of play, while the younger organization improved from experience. Baseball developed rapidly up to the time of the players' rebellion, many new plays being invented, and the education of the public and the players to the game was rapid. The war, however, arrested development, and with the organization of the twelve club league it was found there were not enough first-class players to fill the dozen teams, and improvement was slow, except in the cases of the Baltimore and Boston teams.

Possibly the best period of developing plays baseball has known was during the period following the reduction of the National League to eight clubs, when all the great players of the country were concentrated in one eight club league. Another set-back came when the American League started war and scattered the players through sixteen clubs, but the supply of players increased until both leagues were able to continue the development.

Today knowledge of the science of baseball is so widespread that school boys on the lots and playgrounds, and lads around the country school houses, know how to make the plays Kelly, Comiskey, Latham and Ward, Ewing, O'Neill, Fogarty and Sullivan invented and perfected. They have the theory whether they can execute the play or not.

There is scarcely a doubt that almost every play made today was made by some pioneer. Kelly, Tom McCarthy, Pfeffer and others made plays their own team mates did not comprehend, so if a play is called a "new" play it is in the sense that it probably has been rediscovered. Frank Chance, in 1906, commenced to work the "delayed steal" persistently and was proclaimed the discoverer of the play. Yet Kelly, Hamilton, Lange, O'Neill, Comiskey, Duffy and many others used the play, and "Sadie" Houck stole in that way with much success. Maloney once was on second base, another runner at third and the ball was hit to the short stop, who threw home. The runner trying to score from third was thrown out at the plate, but Maloney, following him ten feet behind, slid in front of the plate and scored before the catcher could recover and touch him after touching out the other runner. It was proclaimed as a new play, but Kelly and Lange had made it several times.

Jimmy Callahan, former manager of the White Sox, was watching a crowd of small boys playing on a vacant lot. Runners were on first and third bases, and it was evident they intended a double steal. Callahan watched the play, feeling certain the diminutive catcher could not make the throw. The pitcher made as if to start his pitching motion, but instead stepped directly toward third base and threw to the baseman. The base runner dived back to third, but the third baseman threw to the second baseman and the runner going from first to second was caught twenty feet.

"Well, by George," ejaculated Callahan and went on his way thinking.

That afternoon Callahan worked the boy's trick against a pair of experienced base runners, and within a week half the teams in America were using it, and driving umpires to distraction trying to decide whether the motion was a balk or not.

Pittsburg, about 1894, used a play something like that to stop the double steal, and also with runners on second and third bases. The pitcher delivered the ball to the catcher who apparently tried to catch the runner off third by throwing sharply to Leach, who in turn would relay the ball to Ritchey at second as soon as it touched his hands. Many times the unsuspecting runner was caught at second, standing still, intently watching the play at third. The play has been made from the catcher to the first baseman to the short stop with some success.

In 1895 clubs worked the double steal against the Chicago Nationals so often that a meeting of the infielders was held to devise a scheme to stop it. So, when runners were on first and second, and a steal was suspected, Kling threw to second instead of to third, and half the time the runner who was trailing was caught watching the play at third.

Tinker and Evers plotted a play a few years ago that caught many men and furnished the spectators much joy. When a hit-and-run play is attempted and the batter hits a fly to the outfield, the base runner hearing the crack of the bat, must judge from actions of the fielder in front of him what has happened. When such a situation came up Tinker and Evers went through all the motions of trying to stop a grounder, or diving after a hit. The runner would fear being forced out at second and tear along under the impression the ball had gone through the infield. Sometimes he would be nearly to third base before the outfielder, catching the ball, would toss it to the first baseman and complete the double play. Sherwood Magee was caught three times in one season on the play, and finally in Philadelphia, the Cubs tried it again. Magee, not to be caught again, gave them the laugh and jogged back to first, whereupon Schulte dropped the ball, threw it to second, and Tinker fired it back to first, completing the double play.

The "bluff bunt," aimed to pull defensive infielders out of

position, has resulted in a variety of plays, all based on the same principle. Possibly the cleverest variation is the "bluff bunt" used as a substitute for the sacrifice hit to advance runners, especially from second to third base. The play was used sporadically for a number of seasons, but it remained for the Chicago Cubs to add it to their repertoire and use it scientifically. After they had demonstrated its possibilities it suddenly came into general use. The most successful use of the play is when the situation seems to call for a sacrifice bunt under all the accepted rules of the game. With runners on second and first, or on second with none out, the best play, according to all baseball authorities, is to sacrifice. Chance, however, figured he could advance the runners without the loss of a man, and at the expense of only one strike. By close calculations he concluded the danger of having the runner thrown out at third was only a little greater than having him caught by a failure to bunt, or forced out at third. The batter was ordered to pretend to bunt, miss the ball purposely and shove his body over the plate so as to interfere slightly with the catcher's vision. The third baseman, expecting a bunt, comes forward rapidly, leaving the base unguarded. The runners, who have been signaled, start to run as the pitcher winds up, and the leading runner is expected to slide safe back of third base before the third baseman can get back to the base and catch the throw. As the third baseman is compelled to run backwards, in order to watch the catcher's throw, he must touch blindly at the runner, and the chances of a muff are largely increased. The best way to defeat the play, it soon was learned, is for the short stop to cover third base and take the throw.

The "bluff bunt" also is used to assist the "delayed steal," but the assistance is unfair, as it consists of hampering the activities of the catcher. How much the batters can help base runners in that way without being censured or punished by the umpire is a matter of much study. A slight motion of the batter's body may interfere with the catcher's throw just enough to cause it to go wild, interfere with the view of the catcher or umpire and prevent the catcher from touching base runners who are scoring in close plays at the plate. The umpire has great difficulty in deciding whether the interference was enough to warrant punishment, as the batter all the time is pretending to be striving desperately to avoid doing the thing he is trying to accomplish.

There was an odd play introduced on the Polo Grounds in 1908 which was the result of a "fanning match" the previous evening. Bresnahan and several of the Chicago players were discussing plays and arguing the chances of one umpire seeing everything that takes place, all conceding it to be impossible. A reporter who was present suggested that, when the one umpire was behind the plate and either a bunt or hit-and-run was attempted, the umpire always ran down into the diamond, in front of the play in order to see a play either at first or second base, and that the catcher could, therefore, stop, trip or interfere with the batter without the slightest danger of being seen. Later in the evening the reporter, meeting Kling, asked his opinion of the possibility of such a play.

The following day, early in the game, Chicago had a runner on first base and the batter tried to sacrifice. Bresnahan cut in ahead of the runner, bumped him off his feet, and after the other runner had been forced at second the luckless batter was doubled at first base. Two innings later Kling did the same thing to a New York batter, tripping him so he was thrown out on a hit that probably would have been safe. Twice after that the catchers took advantage of the umpire and interfered with batters until the crowd was roaring with indignation. The play had one result—there were two umpires on the field the following day.

CHAPTER XIV

Combination Plays

The plays in which quick thinking counts most, and is absolutely necessary if the club is to win, are the combination plays in which the success of the man who is executing the mechanical part of the work depends largely upon what is done by one or more of the other players.

There are hundreds of plays executed every week during the season by the major league players in which perhaps only one man touches the ball and yet in which the others may have some part. If the assistants in such a play fail, either by action or by neglect, to act or move, they may give the opponent a clew as to what is to be attempted and enable them to foil the attack or turn it against the attackers. If each man does his allotted part, and then the play fails, the one who handles the ball receives the censure, as he would have received the praise had it succeeded.

The player who is the assistant in combination plays has one principal duty and that is to go to the right spot at the right time. He may have no part whatever in the play except to be there, ready to take part in it if it should miscarry in any way, or if the attacking player should make an unexpected move in countering the attack. The unexpected is what wins games between teams closely matched, and combination plays afford the greatest chance for such happenings. It is the duty of each man to guard every possible avenue of escape in case a base runner is trapped by some clever combination, and resorts to quick use of his wits to escape before actually being touched out.

A play which happened when Malachi Jeddidah Kittridge was catching for Washington illustrates the necessity of every man taking part in the combination formations. Runners were on second and third bases when the ball was hit sharply to the short stop, who threw to Kittridge, cutting Keeler off from the plate. The runner on second, of course, ran up to within a step of third base while Kittridge chased Keeler back toward the same bag, making motions as if to throw the ball. Keeler dodged, waiting for Kittridge to throw, intending then to make a dash for the plate. Keeler was within a few feet of third base when Kittredge, seeing the other runner standing flat footed on the other side of the bag, dived past Keeler, intent on touching the other runner first, then whirling and either touching out or throwing out Keeler, and making a double play. The other runner, however, happened to be thinking and he dived for the bag and reached it before Kittridge could tag him with the ball. Kittridge whirling, saw Keeler flying towards the plate. He threw and as the ball left his hand he saw the pitcher standing on the slab, the first baseman anchored to the bag, and no fielder near the plate. The ball went to the stand, two runs scored, and Washington was beaten because the first baseman and pitcher had taken too much for granted and failed to get into the combination.

The story of combination plays is best illustrated by the ones that went wrong. The necessity of keeping thinking all the time, not only of what is being done, but of what possibly may be done, is illustrated by a play that cost the Chicago Cubs a game at St. Louis in 1908. In that play half the men on the two teams, and the umpire himself, were caught napping. If there had been two umpires instead of one on the field that day, Chicago probably would have won the game and ultimately the pennant, without the bitter struggle they had to do it.

Runners were on first and third bases, one out, and St. Louis needed a run to win, it being in the ninth inning. Chance called the infield close in order to cut Hoelskoetter off from the plate. Billy Gilbert, who was the runner on first base, is a quick thinker and one who is likely to do unexpected and unusual things in a ball game. Fromme, the batter, hit sharply to Evers who scooped the ball on the first bound, and made a motion as if to hurl it to the plate. The play was made so rapidly Hoelskoetter turned tail and slid back to third base, seeing it was impossible for him to reach the plate. Evers, realizing instantly that a double play and the end of the inning was possible, leaped backward, touched Gilbert as he was racing from first to second, and started for first base to complete the double play, pleased at having outwitted Gilbert and made a brilliant move. Gilbert, however, was doing some rapid fire thinking and seeing for himself and his team. Leaping after Evers he threw out a foot and tripped him, sending him sprawling. Evers, still clutching the ball, rolled and crawled, then dived to first base and put his hand on it before Fromme was within ten feet of the bag.

Hoelskoetter, meantime, seeing the mixup, dashed for the plate. Imagine the surprise of the Chicago team when Umpire O'Day was discovered stooping and intently watching the plate, expecting all the time Evers would throw the ball there. O'Day did not see Evers touch Gilbert, nor did he see Gilbert trip the fielder, but when the play to the plate was delayed, he whirled in time to see Evers roll to the base and beat Fromme, so he called Fromme out but allowed the winning run to score. It was not O'Day's fault, except in that he did not think rapidly enough. The fault lay with the league for furnishing only one umpire.

XIV. Combination Plays

How often the best laid plans to work a combination play gang aglee is known only to the players themselves, and perhaps no miscarriage of a play is so glaring as that when some slow thinker forgets to cover the base. Billy Bergen, catcher, of the Brooklyn club, is an excellent thrower to bases and he is fond of throwing, which is a bad fault, particularly when the combination is not in working order. Chicago was playing Brooklyn late in the season of 1908 when games were precious. The score was tied 2 to 2 with one man out and Hofman on second base when Bergen signaled for a pitch out, intending to try to catch Hofman off second base. The sign was so apparent and the intent so plain that the Chicago coachers called a warning to Hofman. The pitcher pitched out, Bergen threw. Neither the second baseman nor the short stop moved and the ball went on to the center fielder, allowing Hofman to score and win a game that enabled the Cubs to tie New York for the pennant, which perhaps was the costliest piece of miscarrying combination in years.

A play went wrong in New York in 1909 because one man in the combination napped, his nap eventually costing the game. With a runner on second base the batsman hit to the right of short stop. Bridwell, seeing he could not throw the batter out at first, shot the ball to third figuring on the man overrunning that base. The runner made the turn and should have been out by ten feet, but the third baseman failed to get into the play, and the run scored. Often with men on bases, a quick thinking infielder can fumble ground balls and still catch the runner who was on the bases if three men are in the combination and all thinking. In seven cases out of ten the runner will be expecting or turning to look at the play at first base, and can be trapped by a fast throw.

Perhaps the grandest exhibition of combination playing ever seen in one game was in an eighteen inning pitchers' duel between Ed Reulbach, of Chicago, and Jack Taylor, of St. Louis in 1907. In the extra innings of that game Reulbach was saved again and again by wonderful work and some wonderful combination playing. No fewer than six double plays were executed at all corners of the infield, and in critical moments when a tenth of a second's forgetfulness or loitering would have meant the loss of the game.

The remarkable feature of the game was that not one of Chicago's double plays was made until the tenth inning, and the score of that game shows the way the Cub combination was working on that afternoon, and how far the men had to go to get into the plays. The record follows:—

Tinker to Evers to Chance. Chance to Kling to Chance. Tinker to Chance. Tinker to Evers. Casey to Kling to Chance. Chance to Tinker to Chance.

"The Old Gag," a play christened and used by Anson's infield when Pfeffer and Burns and Williamson were helping invent plays, was one which taught the succeeding generations of players how a man caught between bases should be run down. With the White Stockings never more than three men were allowed in the play, and to the present time all managers direct their men to play it that way, one man chasing the runner down near the man guarding the base, and then tossing the ball to him and, when the basemen turns the runner back, the one who has been pursuing him, falls in to guard the base. Thus both avenues of escape are closed, and a fresh runner is always ready to pursue the tiring man. The White Stocking infield worked "the Old Gag" to tire out pitchers of the opposing team and won many games through that alone. They would play to let the pitcher get a good start, and when they caught him between bases they ran him to a state of exhaustion, refusing to touch him until he surrendered from sheer weariness. They caught Rusie once— but the big pitcher refused to run and throwing both hands above his head, trotted to the bench without waiting to be touched.

XIV. Combination Plays

Combination plays made with the intent to catch runners off the bases require the greatest amount of exact moving and timing of both the ball and the runner. The short stop and second baseman, in order to catch a runner off second base, either from the pitcher or catcher, must assist each other and at the same time have the cooperation of the center fielder. The play to catch a runner at second base, after he has reached the bag, is made by the use of psychology as well as the hands and feet, and the infielders who study human nature are the most successful. The short stop and second baseman, as soon as they decide upon an attempt to catch the runner, communicate with each other by signals and commence a persistent campaign to stir up the runner. While their object is to get the runner two feet further from the base than he can go in safety, their first move is to pretend to be striving to "hold him up," which means keep him from getting a lead away from the base. This is a species of flattery by which they mislead the runner into thinking they are afraid he will steal third base. The fielders strive to arouse the runner's natural combativeness so that, when they appear to be trying to keep him from getting a lead, he naturally will strive to get as far as he can in safety. It is a paradox in baseball that it is much easier to catch a good base runner than to catch a bad one. The bad base runner cannot be tempted far enough away from the bag to be caught.

All the time the short stop and second baseman know which is to take the real throw when it comes and the one who is to make the real effort is the lest active of the two in the preliminary jockeying. The base runner is worked up to a pitch of combativeness and determination to gain a few more inches of distance from the base by the threats of catcher or pitcher to throw, and by the efforts of the short stop and second baseman to get behind him and beat him to the base. Finally one of the fielders, pretending to abandon the effort, does something to distract the attention of the runner and gives him an opening to take a longer lead from the base. If the runner still is wary, the fielder makes another move towards the bag, but laughingly stops and seems to give up the attempt. At that instant the pitcher or catcher makes the throw and the fielder who has been least active in the maneuvering covers second base, meets the throw and, unless the base runner is alert and thinking every instant, he will be blocked off the base and caught.

Bill Lange, Dahlen and Egan made the play in a strange way. Egan and Dahlen jockeyed with the runner and then both appeared to cease the effort and returned to their natural positions, drawing the runner further away from the plate while Lange, creeping closer and closer, finally came with a terrific burst of speed from center field and met the throw at the base.

The play to catch runners off first or third bases is much simpler, depending entirely upon its unexpectedness. The first baseman usually makes no effort to mislead the runner, holding steadily to his natural position and when the signal for the throw is made he makes no move, depending upon a quick dash to reach the base just as the ball does, and in time to block off the runner. The play must be executed in perfect timing. If the baseman starts even a fraction of a second too soon his move warns the runner what to expect, and if he is a fraction of a second late in reaching the bag, the ball will go on to right field.

The beauty of these combination plays to catch runners on the bases lies chiefly in executing them in the crises when some brilliant coup is necessary to break a winning rally of the attacking team. The plays are much easier to execute in such situations, as the attacking team always is over-eager and flushed with excitement and expectation, and therefore likely to be daring to the point of recklessness. The team which, either because of long experience in playing together,

or by the power of a cool headed leader, maintains its self-posses-
sion and keeps thinking instead of falling into panic, frequently can
stop the rallies of opponents, and save the pitcher and the game.
There is nothing that steadies a pitcher and a defensive team, or
stops an attacking club quicker than to catch a runner asleep on the
bases in a critical moment.

In this particular of catching runners in the crucial moments
of games John Kling was the greatest in the business. His ability
and his coolness in that style of play alone was enough to stamp him
the best of catchers. Kling probably did not catch as many runners
in a season as some other catchers did, but he caught them always
at the right moments, when they counted, and scores of games won
by the Cubs during their championship career was due to that alone.
Kling had a great advantage in having such an infield to throw to,
but when Kling signaled his intention of throwing the others were
so full of confidence that they executed the play with absolute certainty.

Unless the infielders think quickly, follow signals closely and
above all, possess the faculty of meeting a thrown ball at the right
spot, the combination plays of the team fall to pieces. Some of the
best players in the country have failed wretchedly with certain teams,
not because they were bad ball players, but because the men with
whom they were trying to work in combinations failed at their end
of the play. Spectators cannot tell, when a play at second base mis-
carries, which player was at fault. When there is a bad ball player
and a good one working together, especially around second base, the
better ball player looks worse than the bad one. This is because the
good player always is trying to do something and because the other
man fails to get into the play properly, the man who tried it is made
to appear a blunderer.

Perhaps the worst fault, as far as team work goes, an infielder may possess, is coming late to meet thrown balls from any direction, as his delay is fatal to combination plays. There is one of the finest ball players in the country today, who has been sent back to the minor leagues; a fast man, clever, "game," who throws well from any position, who is aggressive and thinks quickly, yet is a second rate player because he lets the throw come to him instead of coming quickly to meet it. The throw from other infielders goes over the base before he arrives, and he steps onto the bag after catching the ball, instead of being on the bag, stretching to meet the throw. The distance he loses is the difference between "safe" and "out." Throws from the catcher he meets back of the line. To catch the ball he must slack his speed, and before he can recover from the shock of the catch and make a new motion to touch the runner, he has lost the vital trice. The man is just one step short of being a great ball player. He knows his own fault as well as anyone, but is unable to correct it. The nine inches or a foot he loses by the habit, sent him back to the minor leagues, which shows how vital the element of time is in combination plays.

CHAPTER XV

Spring Training*

Lost river had found itself, flooded the "Valley of Vapors" and lost itself again, leaving the grounds around West Baden, Ind., plastered with two inches of alluvial mud. Sawdust poured upon the mud made paths by which the guests could pass dry-shod from the hotels to the bubbling springs scattered through the valley.

Along one of those paths a man, lithe, active and graceful, swathed in heavy flannels, sweaters and a blanket coat, was pirouetting wildly. Three long, gliding leaps, a rapid waltz turn, a triple reverse, a gyroscopic spin, three more long, gliding steps, a series of reversing revolutions so rapidly executed it looked as if the man's legs would become tangled, three more steps—and so on until the human top came spinning up to where some spectators were sitting on a fence.

"What the dickens are you up to now, Brownie?" called one.

Mordecai Brown, premier pitcher of the baseball world, panting and flushed, stopped spinning, leaned against the fence, laughed and said: "Learning to field bunts."

*Reprinted from *The American Magazine* and copyrighted by it. Additions and corrections by Evers.

Then he flashed off down a side path, keeping up his imitation of a gyroscope which had slipped an eccentric. The crowd watched him waltz far across the mud-crusted valley, spin along another path, and finally sprint to the hotel.

Six months afterward the reason for his eccentric dance was made plain. The Chicago and Pittsburg baseball clubs were fighting for the pennant of the National League. Tommy Leach was on second base and Fred Clarke at bat. Clarke bunted down the third base line. Brown, who was pitching, leaped forward, seized the ball and, while seemingly spinning like a top on his feet, threw with terrific force to Steinfeldt, and Leach was caught sliding into third base. The play was magnificently executed and the Chicago crowd that saw it went wild over the marvelous fielding of Brown. But that play, which came near giving Chicago its fourth straight pennant, was prepared for on the mud-plastered field at West Baden early in March at the start of the training season.

In the spring, when the sap in the trees and the enthusiasm in the baseball fans begin to flow, about five hundred ball players belonging to the eighteen major league clubs move below the frost belt, scattering from California to Florida, to train for the season. Ten days to two weeks later the Northern minor league clubs follow their example, and by March 20 more than fifteen hundred professional baseball players are training in perhaps fifty Southern towns and cities.

Correspondents with vivid imaginations and even more vivid lack of experience begin to telegraph home the "news" from the team and to stir the enthusiasm of the fans. They tell of Johnson "showing midseason form," of the marvelous work of the new infielders and the promising showing of the young pitchers. The sporting page blossoms from the evergreen of billiards and bowling and the first box score of the year buds out.

XV. Spring Training

Most of the followers of baseball imagine that the spring trip of the teams is a pleasure junket. They have no idea of the hard work, the pains, aches, strenuous self-denial, and hours of thought involved. Most fans think baseball is merely a question of natural speed of foot, quickness of eye, strength of arm, accuracy of throwing. To that class of fans is due the perennial hope of every town that the local team will "win the pennant this year, sure." And to them the training season is one long, jubilant period of hopefulness. They base their hopes on the theory that a youngster who can throw, hit and field well, and is fast of foot, is a good ball player.

It seems useless iconoclasm to refute the idea, but the fact is that baseball, like every other trade or profession, consists more of experience and hard work than of natural ability, and it is hard work that counts for most. An average boy, with average brain, average legs, arms, and health, can in time become a great baseball player if he will work hard, work long and work faithfully. The more natural ability to run, throw and hit he possesses, the greater his success will be, which applies to every other line of endeavor as well.

On April 15, or thereabout, the annual cataclysm known as "opening the season" strikes the United States, but the real start is six weeks earlier. All winter the owners and managers have been busy striving to strengthen their teams. A club finished fifth, perhaps, with eighteen men on the pay roll. Of these Casey and Wiegman were failures and were relegated to the minors. Dorsey and Grant were traded for Bjones. Seven new men were drafted from minor leagues and five were purchased. Three youngsters from independent clubs are to be given a trial and two of last year's tryout squad, "planted" with a friendly minor league club, have been recalled. Of the eighteen new men the manager hopes one will develop enough strength to replace Jenkins at short stop or Yoder in the outfield; that one of his eight trial pitchers will prove good enough to win a regular berth, and his wildest dream is that two will be so promising as to warrant keeping them as utility men to be broken into the team work of his club. With the trainer, secretary, correspondents, wives of players, the training party of a major league club frequently numbers fifty persons, and on his spring tours to California Comiskey usually takes about one hundred on a special train.

Major league teams are scattered from Los Angeles to Jacksonville, and there is scarcely a city or town in the South or West that will not receive a visit from some team before the season opens. The movement, however, is more and more toward permanent training camps, and against exhibition tours. Some of the teams already have purchased grounds or secured long term leases, and are preparing to build baths and gymnasiums. Some purpose operating their training plants all winter and sending the young players drafted or purchased from minor leagues there early in the winter to develop under the eye of an experienced coach, who will turn them over to the manager ready for play.

The scarcity of really good players has compelled the movement toward these permanent schools for educating and developing players, and the business as an amusement enterprise has become so remunerative that the returns justify the expense.

The sun is shining brightly, the air soft and redolent of the scent of growing things, spikes sink into warm earth. Before ten o'clock thirty or more men, let loose from the snow drifts of the North and a long winter of inactivity, race out onto the open field for the first time and begin throwing a dozen balls around.

The veterans, chary regarding their arms, throw with slow, long-arm swings, while the youngsters, proud possessors of "strong whips," begin to throw harder and harder. The crack of the ball against gloves beats a steady tattoo above which the warning shouts of the manager rise:

XV. Spring Training

"Save some of that ginger—you'll need it in a couple of days."

For an hour the players warm up, throwing, running easily, scooping balls. The warmth tempts them to greater efforts, but experience warns them to resist. Suddenly the "high-low" game starts.

"High-low" isn't a game, properly speaking; it is a torture. It is the ball player's invention for tormenting the body and limbering the muscles. It looks simple, almost childish, but it is one of the greatest conditioning exercises ever invented. The game consists in throwing the ball short distances either just too high, just too low, or just too far to the right or left for the victim to reach it without a sudden movement, leap or dive. Half a dozen men play at once, and the principal skill lies in looking at the top of Jones' head and throwing the ball at Smith's feet. It looks easy, but outsiders who attempt to stay in the circle fall exhausted in five minutes trying to hold the pace.

By noon the individual players are beginning to drop out of the groups, and start some form of exercise designed to fit their own needs, slow running, gymnastic exercises, or some like hobby. One o'clock comes. The players, dripping with perspiration in heavy flannels and sweaters, have forgotten time, and some of them have forgotten caution. The ball cracks harder against the gloves. They are hard at work—playing.

"Everyone run in" orders the manager, and before the words are out of his mouth a line wheels across the field, straggles out the gate, and starts on the long jog through town to the bath house, perhaps two miles away. For half an hour they jostle, slap, and scramble around under the showers, throw themselves down, one after another, for a hurried massage by the over-worked trainer, dress rapidly and are off to dinner.

"Nothing doing this afternoon," says the manager—and the first day's training is over.

Touching Second

After dinner that evening Jenks, the star pitcher, cautiously flexes his "salary wing" and remarks to Bjornsen: "I don't think she's going to be so *very* sore." By ten o'clock all the players except the interested recruit from a country town are in bed, and insistent calls for the trainer from half a dozen rooms prove that the athletes already are feeling the effects of the first day.

If ever waiters suffered for their sins those who attempt to serve a ball club on the morning of the second day of training are the ones. The breakfast room at ten o'clock is like a cage of sore-headed bears, each suffering with rheumatism. The athletes limp downstairs, hobble around the lobby, nurse sore arms and strive to revive quarrels two years old. The wretched trainer confesses to a sympathizer that thirty ball players wanted to whip him because he could not rub them all at the same time. By eleven o'clock a thin red line of cripples hobbles into the park, limps onto the diamond like a G. A. R. parade, and the sound of creaking muscles and groaning swear words arises. The manager, who has been waiting an hour, grins and says nothing. He understands.

There is no flinching. Every man knows he must work the soreness out of his muscles as quickly as possible. With much grunting and many facial contortions the players throw and run, stiffly at first, but as the muscles warm up the aches disappear and by noon the squad is going faster than ever. At one o'clock the manager again calls off work for the day. The third day they are stiffer than ever, but not so sore, and on the fourth day they have so far recovered that morning and afternoon practice is inaugurated and the bats, forbidden up to that time, are produced.

The collective work of a team, which is here described typically, is only part of the real process of conditioning. Massage, baths, and the use of every conceivable device, goes on steadily fourteen hours a day during the preparatory season. The players are working for individual condition and effectiveness in their own way. Those persons who imagine that baseball is a "snap" or some special gift of nature should have been in the training camp of the New York Giants a few years ago, and their ideas would have changed. Early in the training season the word had flashed around the circuit: "Matty's arm is gone."

Translated, that meant a revision of all the pennant calculations of all the clubs in the National League. If Mathewson's arm really was permanently injured the New York club ceased to be a championship factor.

On the training field a few days later nearly forty men were hard at work. Over at one side a graceful, handsome, boyish-looking man was throwing slowly and with evident caution to a young catcher. Slowly, and studying every move in order to avoid jerking or twisting a damaged shoulder, he kept pitching, trying to "throw the soreness out." He had drawn a little cross in the dirt upon which he pivoted his right foot, and two feet in front of that and a foot to the left was a hole in the sand. As he threw he swung "off his stride," and instead of planting his left foot straight in front he swung it into the hold to the left. He had changed his pitching motion to accommodate the sore shoulder and prevent adding to the strain. Presently he swung his arm slowly overhand. The ball floated away, seemed to hesitate in midair, dropped downward and to the right with a slow, twisting curve motion.

"Here, what's that, Matty?" a spectator called to him.

"That's the fader," he replied, smiling.

We all had read of the "fadeaway" and believed it one of the spring nature fakes evolved by imaginative reporters. But it was true. Mathewson, realizing that he might never again be strong enough to pitch the fast "jump" ball or the wonderful fast curve that had made him the greatest pitching sensation of years, had deliberately set to work and by steady persistent practice had evolved a new "system of slants" by which he came near revolutionizing pitching. Hour after hour, despite the deadening pain in his shoulder, he kept at it, pitching, pitching, twisting his hand a little less, a little more, stepping ten times to one spot as he pitched, then ten times to a spot two inches to the left or the right, to find how the change in stride would affect the ball, he worked until he developed one of the most puzzling curves ever pitched. How many hours of suffering and hard work were required to perfect his "fadeaway" and make him again one of the greatest of pitchers, no one knows.

Players of the present day are prone to scoff at the tales of the prowess of "Matty" Kilroy, better known as "Bazzazaz," a left-handed pitcher who performed marvels. Most modern pitchers declare that under present conditions Kilroy would have been a failure. The little left-hander, after years of triumph, retired because his arm was hopelessly worn out. In spite of that fact Tom Burns, when he assumed charge of the Chicago Club in 1898, resurrected Kilroy, whose arm was so weak, according to his own admission, he "couldn't break a pane of glass at fifty feet."

Yet for one season and part of another he pitched against the strongest clubs and beat them regularly.

Kilroy's success was due almost entirely to his "Bazzazaz" balk, which he evolved by persistent training. He was the only pitcher who ever balked without balking—if such a thing is possible. In the first four innings of the first game he pitched against Baltimore after Burns resurrected him, nine men reached first base. He caught six of them off the base and, although two umpires watched every move he made, they declared that under the rules he did not balk.

Kilroy explained after his permanent retirement, his system of training by which he acquired the "bazzazaz balk."

"I see the old soup bone was ready for the undertaker," he said.

Christy Mathewson. He has just released his famous "fadeaway."

"So I goes to work on the balk. I always had a good balk motion, but wanted a better one. I spent half the winter in the side yard at home with a chalk mark on the wall for first base and another on the fence for the home plate. I practiced morning and afternoon, making from two hundred and fifty to four hundred throws a day with my wrist and forearm trying to hit the first base line while looking at the other one and without moving either my feet or body.

"By practicing I got so I could shoot the ball faster to first base with wrist and forearm than I could pitch it to the plate with a full swing. That's all there was to it. Just look straight at the plate, pull your hands up against your breast, raise your left one to the level of your ear, then drive the ball to first without looking until after it starts, and you've got him. The umpire can't see whether you look before you throw or not."

He did get them. Probably he made twenty thousand practice throws at the chalk mark, but he perfected the motion that enabled him to pitch two years after his arm was "dead."

Ed Walsh damaged his shoulder in the strenuous American League campaign of 1908, and reported in 1909 unable to pitch the spit ball which had made him one of the wonders of the baseball world. His shoulder was so "bound" he could not swing his arm straight overhand to get the sharp drop to the ball. Robbed of his chief asset, Walsh set to work and within a few weeks, by steady, slow work, developed another spit ball, pitched slightly sidearm and curving outward, that proved almost as effective as the other had been.

The three most remarkable instances of training, perhaps, are found in the cases of Radbourne, who pitched practically two thirds of all the games played by Providence one season, and pitched the last third of the season alone; Jimmy Ryan, the famous old outfielder, who, after thirty years, still throws well; and Theodore Breitenstein, who pitched for St. Louis twenty years ago, and now is one of the star pitchers of the Southern League. The odd coincidence (if such it is) is that these three men all had the same hobby, and both Ryan and Breitenstein adopted it from Radbourne. They treated their arms through their stomachs. During the spring training season they resorted to the old-fashioned treacle (sulphur and molasses), taking large doses night and morning. Ryan says he started using treacle on Radbourne's advice, and believes that his long service in baseball was due in large proportion to the spring tonic.

Perfect condition is the aim of spring training, condition of blood and digestion being held as important as condition of arms and legs. Condition is the biggest asset of any club during the first six weeks of a season and counts more than "class," as one team is about as good as another mechanically during that period. The manager of a weak team who can bring it North to open the season in better physical condition than his rivals wins many games from stronger clubs because his men are further advanced toward playing form. This fact accounts for the early season strength of the Southernmost clubs of the major leagues, who usually have better weather at home than Boston, Cleveland, Detroit and Chicago, and condition more rapidly, while the Northern clubs are set back by bad weather.

Comiskey, owner of the Chicago White Stockings, usually has the best trained and conditioned team in the major leagues, and not only starts the season that way but continues the training throughout the year. He has won championships on condition alone, his team outlasting stronger clubs that have neglected to keep in condition.

Yet Comiskey has little system in training men beyond requiring steady work. His great success lies in his judgment in picking ball players who have brains enough and ambition enough to keep in good condition all the time.

Conditioning for baseball is unlike training for any other sport, and many college boys, accustomed to training for short football seasons or for the crew, reach an "edge" within a few weeks and break down before the season is a month old. The ball player must begin March 1 to work for the maximum speed, agility and strength, yet store up enough reserve power to carry him to October 15.

A layman unaccustomed to the idea of the possibilities of remaking the body by exercising would be amazed at what can be accomplished. A team of thirty men arriving at the spring camp usually is between five and six hundred pounds heavier than it will be at mid-season. The ordinary man would imagine amputation to be about the only method of reducing six hundred pounds in thirty days. How a man, who looks hard, feels hard, does not seem fat, and is in better physical shape than ninety-nine out of a hundred men, is going to take off twenty-five pounds is a mystery to an outsider, yet they do it without great trouble. Frank Chance lost fourteen pounds in one afternoon at Philadelphia in two games during his debut as a major league catcher.

Overall and Hofman met at the training camp in March, 1909.

"I've got to take off twenty-five pounds," said the giant pitcher.

"What are you going to pitch at, this year?"

"One hundred and ninety-four—I think I carried too much weight last year. What are you going to do?

"I'm going to put on five more pounds. I'll be stronger with more weight."

Overall kept his record of weight as follows:

March 5, 219; March 22, 206; March 29, 202; April 5, 199; April 10, 192; April 14 (opening season), 194?; July 4 (midseason) 193; October 15 (close), 195.

Hofman, playing just as hard, reported nine pounds heavier than he was the previous season, and added five more pounds before the season opened, and both were in almost perfect condition during the entire season.

Every player seems to have his own system, and some of the methods used are laughable, and few are of any practical value. One young catcher who joined a National League club two years ago brought five gallons of iron, beef and wine in jugs in his trunk to make him strong. Cannon balls that weigh twenty pounds are used to roll over the abdomen, iron rolling pins, special bandages, a thousand kinds of rubbing oils and lotions, ranging from patent medicines to horse liniments and oil made by boiling down fishing worms; vibrators of all sizes and shapes, bandages, arm bakers to be superheated with electricity, and rubber bands are employed.

Hotel rooms are turned into gymnasia, and one of the funniest sights of a year is to sit in a card game with half a dozen players swathed like puffy mummies in blankets, sweaters and flannels until they look as if they were starting on an Arctic journey.

One spring a cold rain fell upon the Chicago Cubs training camp, and continued to fall incessantly, dismally putting an end to practice just as the players were working off the first soreness.

The dejected athletes, knowing they would have to undergo the soreness and stiffness all over again, moped in the hotel. Toward the middle of the gloomy, cold afternoon some one proposed to turn a bath room into a Turkish bath establishment. The steam was turned on, cracks stuffed and the hot water was allowed to pour into the tub until the room was superheated and filled with steam. Four husky players, in Adamic condition, proceeded to swath themselves in blankets and take off weight. Half a dozen bath towels, folded, were placed on the steam radiator, and the players took turns sitting on the radiator with half a dozen blankets wrapped around them. Chance's turn came. He adjusted the blankets, parted them carefully, and sat down. Steinfeldt had a narrow escape from being killed, and

Chance to this day thinks it was Steinfeldt who took the towels off the radiator.

Brown, the three-fingered wonder, has a system of exercising that would make his fortune and banish corpulency as a human ailment if ordinary beings could endure it. Brown invented the system himself and uses it night and morning when desiring to reduce flesh or strengthen the muscles of abdomen or legs without running. Every spring he organizes a class in calisthenics, from which no one, not even the poor correspondent, is exempted if his room happens to connect with Brown's. It is a common sight during the spring training to see six or seven men, a la natural, each with the coverlet from his bed spread upon the floor, trying to follow the movements and orders of the premier pitcher.

Brown counts slowly—one, two—up to thirteen, and at every number the class struggles to follow his movements. The pauses between counts are more painful than the movements themselves. After two minutes the novices are doubled up like small boys who have eaten too many green apples; in three minutes the fat men weaken, and in four Brown usually is left to continue the exercise alone until he stops to assess fines on the delinquents.

Anyone can try Brown's exercise. It looks easy.

Brown lies on his back full length upon the floor, his heels together and thumbs touching each other on the floor back of his head, with palms up. He counts one, raises his feet six inches, ankles tight together, and holds them there an instant. At the count of two he raises the legs to an angle of 45 degrees, and stops them again; three, the legs are raised slowly until perpendicular with the body; four, the feet are lowered until over his face; five he drops them until the toes touch the floor above his head; six, the feet are raised halfway up again; seven, they are again perpendicular; eight, they drop to 45 degrees; nine, to six inches from the floor; ten, the heels touch the

Brown, Chicago Cubs, just after releasing his "hook curve." Note position of pitching hand.

floor; eleven, the arms are raised slowly until perpendicular; twelve, they are dropped outward until the backs touch the floor; thirteen (and worst), the body is raised slowly to a sitting position without the aid of the hands. Then he rolls back and starts over again.

Brown can go through the exercise a dozen times without breathing hard when in perfect condition, and he does it morning and night during the training season. Some of his students have gone through the exercise four times.

With five hours of running, throwing and fielding, several miles of jogging back and forth from the bath houses to grounds, and hot baths, rub downs, boxing, wrestling and walking, combined with individual exercises in rooms and massage at least once a day, the player's day is fairly busy during the training trip.

The first week is a constant fight on the part of the manager to keep the men from injuring themselves by overwork, especially if the weather be fine. After two weeks it is a fight to make them work at all, for the moment a player begins to get near to what he thinks is playing condition he begins to shirk the routine work, and strives to save all his strength for the playing season. About all he wants to do during that period is to bat. A ball player would get up at two o'clock any morning to bat. During the second stage the pitchers, who must condition their arms more slowly, do most of the work, and the others practice batting.

Batting is the bane of a manager's existence. One spring, while moving southward with his team, Fred Clarke conspired with a baggage master to send the bats astray. That kept the Pirates from batting for two days. Then Wagner showed up at the grounds with a five-cent bat he had purchased from a small boy and started batting practice. The manager cannot keep the players from hitting, so he turns their batting to his own purposes, and whenever they hit a fair ball he orders them to "run it out" hard to first base and jog all the way around the bases. Even that fails to cure their insatiable desire to hit.

As Frank Schulte remarked to Harry Lumley one day: "Lum, if you had a million dollars, you'd hire the best pitchers in the country and make them take turns pitching to you."

Occasionally a manager is as eager as his men during the early days of training, and the result usually is disastrous. Frank Bowerman, who managed the Boston club one season, was the victim of his own over-anxiety to get the team into condition. Knowing that his team could not compare in strength with some of the other clubs in the league, he had a theory that, with his fine squad of young pitchers, he could get the start on the other clubs by more rapid conditioning, "spread eagle" the field during the early part of the season at least, and make a good showing. Before the club had been in training three days he began to coach his young pitchers in fielding bunts, and for three weeks he kept the youngsters working desperately. They started the season in finer condition than any team in the league; finer, but not better—and, after a brief flash of winning form the entire pitching staff went to pieces and never was in good condition again during the season. They were overtrained before they started.

"Cap" Anson, leader of the famous old White Stockings, was one of the hardest and most faithful trainers ever at the head of a ball club. His system of conditioning consisted largely of running. Ned Hanlon also was a believer in running to reduce weight, strengthen the legs and add speed. Both of them blundered sadly because they seldom adapted the training to the individual, and gave the one-hundred-and-forty-pound athlete the same prescription they forced upon the two-hundred-pound fat men. Hanlon, when managing the Cincinnati club, came near ruining one of the greatest of pitchers—Ovral Overall—by ordering him to run around the ball park ten times every morning. Overall was big, but not fat, and the running so weakened him he never pitched good ball for that club.

Anson was one of the most tireless runners in the world, and training under him was a nightmare to his players. "Anse" would drive his men for three hours in practice, then lead them in long runs, placing himself at the head of the procession and setting a steady, jogging pace. If he felt well the morning training was a Marathon route.

One afternoon in New Orleans years ago Anson ordered ten laps around the field after practice, which on the old grounds was nearly ten miles. The afternoon was hot, one of those wilting Southern spring days that sap the life out of men fresh from the rigors of Northern winter. The players fell into line grumbling and scowling. Back of left field a high board fence separated the ball grounds from one of the old cemeteries and near the foul line a board was off the fence. The first time the panting athletes passed the hole in the fence Dahlen gave a quick glance to see if Anson was looking and dived head first through the gap into the cemetery. The others continued on around the lot, but on the second round Lange, Ryan, Kittridge and Decker dived after Dahlen and joined him in the cemetery. The third trip saw the line dwindle to four followers, with Anson still leading. The fourth found only Anson and poor Bill Schriver, who had the bad luck to be directly behind his captain, plodding on, and on the next trip Shriver made the leap for life.

Majestically alone, Anson toiled on while the onlookers writhed with delight. Perhaps their behavior aroused suspicion, or the absence of following footsteps attracted "Cap's" attention. He stopped, looked at the vacant field, a grim grin overspread his red face, and he resumed the jogging. Straight to that fence he plodded, and sticking his head through the hole, he beheld his team leaning against the above-ground tombs, smoking and laughing. Just for that he marshaled them into line again and, sitting in the stand, watched them grimly until every man had completed ten rounds.

It is compulsory training such as that which makes the players dread training trips, especially those who believe running long distances injures their speed. They are willing enough workers along their own lines of conditioning.

Arms and legs, to the present-day ball player, are what complexion is to a woman, and they devote more time and care to them. The attention bestowed upon a throwing arm by a player after his second or third year of training passes belief, and one who has suffered an attack of "Charley Horse" divides half this leisure time between his arm and his legs.

"Charley Horse" is peculiarly a baseball ailment, consisting of displacement and stricture of leg muscles, most commonly the Sartorial. It is the indication of "muscle binding" or hardening of the muscles. Commonly the ailment is brought about, not by running, but by quick stopping at bases. The player who "stops up on his feet," instead of "hitting the dirt," is certain to acquire the injury within a short time. The over-worked muscle, slipping out of place, knots itself into a great lump and exerts pressure on all surrounding muscles, producing lameness. Rubbing with volatile oils and steady massaging serve to press the muscle back into position, but the "horse" returns at the next serious strain. When you see a player make a long slide which appears unnecessary, the reason is that he would rather rip six inches of skin off his thigh than stop standing up and take chances of "horsing" himself.

The frequency of such injuries is a source of surprise to non-players, and explains the extreme attention bestowed upon legs during the spring training by players, manager and trainer. For each modern team carries a trainer, and, usually, during the spring trip, an assistant. The trainer is an expert masseur, something of a medical practitioner, surgeon, nurse, osteopath, bat boy, assistant ticket taker, general all-around man, and the object of the wrath of every player who happens to have a grievance.

To judge the "snap" a trainer has, Bert Semmons, trainer of the Chicago club, kept a record of his work one season. He massaged an average of eleven men a day from March 1 to October 16, some of them morning, afternoon and evening, treated 181 cuts, wounds, abrasions, "sliders" (which means patches of skin torn off in sliding), sprains and broken bones, including 42 spike cuts, and his record shows he used nearly forty quarts of aseptic lotion.

At the end of the first ten days of training, the soreness and stiffness has disappeared and the men are beginning to enjoy their work. Perhaps a couple of young pitchers are disabled because they worked too hard. Every pitcher in the squad has a sore arm, but unless the soreness is high in the shoulder it is natural and must be worked out. Thus far no pitcher has tried to curve a ball, and the batters are hitting viciously and longing to see some "real pitching," which testifies that the pitchers are using only speed.

About the tenth day, under ordinary weather conditions, the manager selects a "regular" team, makes up a club of youngsters, and orders a five-inning game. From the moment the teams are announced, the hottest kind of friendly rivalry divides the club and the series of fierce battles between the "Regulars" and the "Yanigans," who are trying to win their spurs, begins. The youngsters usually win, because they work harder, hoping to secure positions, while the veterans would lose a game rather than take a chance on damaging themselves.

After that games are played every fair day, and there is enough squabbling and fighting and noise to fill a championship season.

The manager pays little or no attention to the results of the games, but they give him the opportunity to study the movements of his young fellows in action. He judges them more by the way they try to do anything, and by what they try to do, than by what they actually accomplish. "Toots" Hofman, a youthful player now moving up rapidly, won the applause of one of the most astute baseball judges by the way he made four errors. He tried for the ball in a way that showed what he could do when he rounded into condition.

Up to a few years ago March 17 was a great day in the training camps of all major league clubs, for on that day the Irish and the Dutch met in the fiercest struggle of the season. But baseball has become too cosmopolitan. No longer can the Harp and the Carp monopolize the "great American game," and the St. Patrick's day contest has been generally abandoned because the Irish were forced to line up something like this: Dmitrius, 1 f, Mike c f, Ole ss, Pierre 3 b, Kzysxzki, 1 b, Kicking Mule, 2 b, Israel, r f, Colorado Madura, c, MacGregor, p.

By March 25 the permanent training grounds are deserted and the movement Northward begins, the teams marching homeward by easy stages, playing exhibition games with the minor league clubs along a zig-zag route. The first real opponents are encountered, and at last the batters, who have been longing for an opportunity to hit against real pitching, have their desire satisfied. The minor leaguers, primed to trounce their noted foes, work desperately. Young pitchers with wonderful curves, and weird control, shoot the ball recklessly around heads worth $25,000 cash to the big league clubs, and keep the timid and self-careful stars dodging and running.

The stars see curves for the first time and the results are laughable. The big league sluggers, who hit any kind of pitching in the season, swing wildly at the garden variety of "round house curve," and miss spit balls two feet. The major league club usually wins on its experience, seldom on its hitting, for it requires about two weeks for them to begin to hit the curves.

But the team is beginning to shape into condition. The men hit better, run faster, and throw with more confidence. Some pitcher, more daring than the others, pitches a few curves when defeat threatens his club instead of using all speed and slow ones. The manager grumbles at it, but secretly is pleased at the advanced condition of the pitcher. The weaknesses of the young recruits have become glaringly apparent and each team leaves a trail of discards along the route.

About April 1 the athletes, sunburned, hardened, almost down to weight, escape from the hot bread and cottonseed-oil belt and cross the line cheering at the prospect of real hotels and real food. Before them are the stronger minor league clubs which will give them real practice and perhaps a few beatings.

The managers discard all the men they do not intend to keep and the regular team settles down to perfect its team work. The training season is over for most of the youngsters. They are sold, released conditionally to minor leagues, or released outright. They are not yet ready for "fast company." With the squad trimmed down to twenty-two players, the real work starts. The veteran infielders and the manager begin to break in the new player to the inside work of the team. Hours and hours are spent devising signals and planning the batting order, and the team lines up as it will at the start of the season.

There is no need for the manager to spur his men now. The players are working desperately, and those who have shirked do double work to be ready. They are as excited as actors on the eve of producing a new piece.

Eight days before the date for opening the season the manager sends one pitcher "the full route"—nine innings—and studies carefully the condition of the man. His shows well. It is a certainty he will pitch the opening game. After that three pitchers in succession work the full game. The men chosen rejoice. They are the "regulars" for that season. The remaining games of the practice season the pitchers work only a few innings as a sort of preparation for the coming games—the ones that count.

The new uniforms are donned for the first time; a brass band blares; a great crowd roars its welcome; the mayor throws out a new white ball and a gentleman with a full-dog visage, garbed in new navy blue, doffs his cap and howls:

"La-deez an' gen-mn. Bat-trees for today's game will be Blup-Blup blup for Blup, Blup-blup, an' Blup for Blup. Play."

The training season is over.

CHAPTER XVI

Fine Points of
the Game*

Almost any spectator at a major league game will tell you: "Oh, I understand baseball," yet in every game hundreds of moves are made and orders issued and obeyed, each with exact purpose and scientific intent, that not one in a thousand of the onlookers sees or recognizes. The game has made such wonderful advances scientifically and the generalship and team work has become so involved and complicated, that the lover of the game, even one who attends scores of games each season, rarely sees or understands its fine points or knows how, or why a play is made even after it is successfully completed.

Every catcher and pitcher in the big leagues knows to an inch how far each base runner may leave any base and get back safely. Every infielder knows just how certain men will make a play, and they turn their play accordingly. For instance, each man must know whether Mike Mitchell "pulls" a fast ball or not, and whether he hits

*Reprinted from *The American Magazine* and copyrighted by it. Additions and corrections by Evers.

a curve to right or to center. He must know how hard Fred Clarke will hit a left-handers' curve, and a thousand other points of similar nature, of which the spectator never thinks. Besides knowing all those things the team must play, as a whole, so as to cover every inch of ground possible, and, by moving away and vacating parts of the field where a batter is unlikely to hit, they can defend the remainder with much greater success. A "rightfield hitter"—one who swings late at the ball, or pulls his body away from the plate, seldom is a good batter. He may hit the ball just as squarely and just as hard as a "free hitter," but the field into which he hits the ball is much better covered and the likelihood of the ball falling safe much lessened.

Do you remember the now famous game between the New York and Chicago teams when the season ended with the teams tied, and they played off one game at the Polo Grounds to decide the championship of the National League? Who lost that game? It was "Cy" Seymour, but perhaps not a dozen of the 30,000 persons who witnessed the struggle know he did. New York had the game won until the third inning in which Tinker was Chicago's first batter. During the entire season Tinker had been hitting Mathewson hard, and the psychologic effect of past performances has much to do with pitching and batting. Mathewson feared Tinker, and he signaled Seymour to play deep in center field. He was afraid that a long drive by Tinker might turn the tide of battle. Seymour saw the signal, but disregarded it, having an idea that Tinker would hit a low line fly, so he crept a few steps closer to the infield, instead of moving back. Matty dropped his famous "fade away" over the plate, and Tinker drove a long, high, line fly to left center. Seymour made a desperate effort to reach the ball, but fell a few feet short, and the ball rolled to the crowd in the outfield for a three-base hit, and started a rally that gave Chicago the victory. If Seymour had played a deep field, as he was commanded to do, the probabilities are that New York would have won the pennant.

Each man in a major league must know not only the strength but the weakness of every opponent, and the array of facts and information concerning players that each pitcher can muster up is amazing to the layman. Late in 1908 Boston presented a new outfielder who never had played in a major league before, and no one on the Chicago club knew him or ever had seen him play ball, yet they were perfectly familiar with him, his peculiarities, batting habits, and disposition. On the way to the grounds Brown and Reulbach, one of whom was to pitch, went minutely over that new man, analyzing his position at bat, the way he swung at a ball, the kind of ball he could hit, and what he could not, and exactly how fast he could reach first base. Steinfeldt was warned that the man was dangerous and a tricky bunter, and that he always bunted toward third. When the pitchers got through discussing the newcomer, Kling and Chance analyzed him as a base runner.

"I think," Kling remarked, "we can catch that fellow a couple of times if he gets on bases to-day. If he reaches second I'll pull off that delayed throw. Let Joe cover and Johnny stall."

In the third inning of the game the unfortunate youngster reached second base on a hit and a sacrifice. On the first ball pitched to the next batter he raced up toward third. Kling motioned as if to throw, Tinker covered second base like a flash, and Evers stood still. The recruit at first made a jump toward second base, then seeing Kling had not thrown, he slowed down. Tinker, walking back past him, remarked: "We'd have caught you that time, old pal, if the Jew had thrown." For just one fatal trice the youngster turned his face to retort to Tinker's remark, and in that instant Kling threw. Evers met the ball at second base, jabbed it against the runner, and before he knew what had happened he was out. That man really was caught in the 'bus on the way to the ball grounds, for the play was executed exactly as Kling planned.

SECOND BASE

PITCHERS BOX

FIRST BASE

Diagram showing ground between first and second bases covered by Collins of the Athletics in the game of August 30, 1909. Only the ground which he covered in fielding balls or getting into plays is shown.

First inning	Estimated distances covered in	
Second inning	plays ....1240 ft.	
Third inning	Returning to position.... ......1240 ft.	
Fourth inning	Running and walking in bluff	
Fifth inning	plays ....4000 ft.	
Sixth inning	To and from bench nine times..3600 ft.	
Ninth inning		

No play in seventh or eighth inning

Total, 10,080 ft.

Touching Second

Quick thinking by individuals, as well as by the directing heads of the team, is absolutely necessary, and unless a player's brain acts quickly enough to follow every move he is not of major league caliber. Professor Munsterberg could save managers and club owners much time, trouble and money, as well as many disappointments, by testing the brain action of players psychologically and discovering their brain speed before a season opens. Chance never has dabbled in psychological experimentation on a scientific basis, but he can discover how rapidly a ball player thinks more quickly in a poker game than in any other way and thus saves the expense of carrying some player for months only to have him lose a game because his convolutions fail to revolve fast enough.

"Bad Bill" Egan was playing second base, "Bull" Dahlen third and "Cap" Anson first. Chicago and New York were fighting desperately for victory. The score was tied. A New York runner was on second base, one man was out and George Van Haltren at bat. Van Haltren hit a sharp ground ball five feet to the right of Egan. The ball struck his hands, he fumbled and the ball rolled five feet away. Like a flash Egan pounced after the ball, recovered it, and without stopping or looking, hurled it toward Dahlen. The third baseman, intent on making the runner "turn wide" looked up just in time to dodge as the sphere flashed by his head and bounded into the stands. One run scored. Val Haltren raced around to third, scored on a fly, and Chicago was beaten 4 to 3.

"You're rotten," "Release him," "Get a second baseman," yelled the crowd. Within a week Anson released Egan.

That play shows how little the millions of fans who watch games know about baseball. Also it shows the relative speed with which the brain cells of the players involved worked. Egan thought too

Opposite: **Collins, Philadelphia Athletics, retrieving a wild throw.**

rapidly for Dahlen whose mind, intent on something else, moved an eighth of a second too late and Anson, by releasing Egan for making a brilliant play, showed that he never grasped the situation at all.

The speed with which Egan's brain convolutions moved may be judged from the fact that a batted ball, hit towards a second baseman playing 135 feet from the plate reaches his hands in from four-fifths of a second to three seconds, depending upon the force with which it is hit and the way it bounds. The ball hit to Egan was hard hit, bounded four times on solid turf, and probably struck his hands one and one-fifth seconds after it left Van Haltren's bat. The entire play was made in less than three seconds, and this is the process through which Egan's brain went in that time. His first thought was direction; second, speed; third, how the ball was bounding and whether to "back up" or "come in on it." He knew Van Haltren could reach first base in three and two-fifth seconds, and that to throw there he would have to recover the ball, make a half turn and then throw.

The moment the ball bounded away from his hands he knew Van Haltren could beat it to first base. Then, while springing after the ball he thought: "Clark, who is going to third, will turn ten feet around the base, hesitate and look to see whether the ball has rolled on to the outfield and, if I can get the ball to Dahlen while Clark is hesitating, we will catch him." So he made the play, and if Dahlen's brain had worked at the same rate of speed Clark would have been out—and Chicago would have won.

Some of the quickest thinking on a baseball field was done by Tommy McCarthy, the Boston outfielder of years ago. He made a play that called for such rapid thinking that he would have tangled up Professor Munsterberg's instruments. Tom Browne, one of the speediest runners that ever played baseball, was on second base and New York needed one run to tie the score. Jack Doyle, then a great batter, was at bat, and it seemed certain that a base hit by Doyle would tie the score and perhaps win the game, as there was only one out and Browne was so speedy he could score from second base on almost any kind of a safe hit. McCarthy crept closer to the infield in left, realizing that although he could throw with wonderful rapidity and accuracy, the chances were all against throwing Browne out at the plate unless he was close and the ball came to him quickly. Doyle drove a hard line hit straight to left field, Browne went scudding toward third base, Doyle raced for first and McCarthy plunged forward at top speed. The fielder reached the ball on its first bound, grabbed it and without stopping or looking threw with terrific force and perfect aim across the diamond into the first baseman's hands. Browne had stopped at third base, Doyle, who had turned first with the intention of sprinting to second, was caught standing still ten feet from first. The next batter went out on a fly ball and Boston won the game.

After the game McCarthy was asked concerning the play. "Well," he explained, "Browne is a quick thinker. He saw how hard that ball was hit and knew he would be thrown out at the plate unless I fumbled. Doyle doesn't think fast and, knowing that he would turn first and stop to see if I was throwing home, I threw across to first and caught him."

He figured that out while the ball was screaming through the air toward him, probably reaching his conclusions and making the decisions in four-fifths of a second.

But the victories that are won and lost by fast individual thinking are few compared with those won and lost by the managers who direct the plays. Managers spend hours figuring plays, situations, and calculating days and even weeks ahead on their pitchers, using those they deem effective in one series, saving up others for coming battles, and planning new tricks and new plays. Before each game the manager and his players, especially his pitchers, go over the characteristics of the players of the opposing teams. Of course, with veteran teams and with pitchers who have been through many hard campaigns, this is unnecessary.

The study of pitchers—his own as well as those of the other fellow—is the chief duty of a manager. He must know their condition, their superstitions, their courage, nerve in the face of trying circumstances, what batters they "have on their string" and what one "has something on them." He must change batting orders to meet emergencies, drag a left-handed hitter out to let a right-hander bat against one pitcher, and a right hander out to put a left hander in against another.

During the progress of a game the manager, both on the field and the bench, directs all plays, moves his men around, instructs each batter what he is to attempt, signals to coaches on what ball or strike a base runner is to attempt a steal or "hit and run," and frequently he issues three or four orders from the bench to one batter, trying to "outguess the other fellow."

Each man on a team has his private signals with the batters who precede or follow him, and the batter, receiving orders from the manager, signals the base runner exactly what to do. In 1908, while the Chicago team was badly crippled and changing batting order almost every day, Sheckard reached first one afternoon and Chance was following him. As Chance came to bat he was swinging two bats, and he tossed one back of him with his left hand. On the first ball pitched Sheckard attempted a steal and was thrown out. "What did you go down for?" demanded Chance later. "I thought I got the signal," said Sheckard. "I didn't give any signal." "Well, you tossed that bat away with your left hand, and you usually throw it with your right, so I thought you'd made a new signal while I was out of the game."

Sheckard's blunder shows how closely every movement of a

batter is watched, not only by his fellow players but by his opponents. In one game in 1909 Evers and Kling analyzed and discovered every hit and run signal used by the Cincinnati club merely by
their powers of observation. Ganzel, then manager of the club, signaled entirely by words, and by close attention and listening for
every unnatural phrase or expression the Cubs secured the entire
code used by their opponents, and knew as well as the Cincinnati
players what Ganzel was ordering.

But the science of signaling is but part of the generalship of the
game, for a dozen times in each struggle, if it is close, the manager
must decide points, and his decision each time may result in victory
or defeat. Taking men out of the game, knowing when to do it and
when not, is the hardest task. Fielder Jones, manager of the Chicago
White Stockings, and one of the best field generals in the world in
his last season in baseball used more pitchers and changed players
more frequently than any other manager. In one game he changed
pitchers five times and won. With the team badly crippled, and only
one pitcher to rely upon, Jones, by using that pitcher (Walsh) in
every emergency, came within one game of winning the pennant.
Three times in the late season he summoned Walsh to pitch just one
ball, and two of the games he saved. McCloskey, then managing St.
Louis, in a game against New York took out a pitcher with two
strikes on a batter, sent Raymond to pitch one ball, a spit ball, struck
the batter out, and then sent Karger in to finish the game—and won
it.

Generalship by the manager is not all. A good team needs the
fewest orders and what perhaps was the most brilliant half inning
ever played in a ball game, from the standpoint of headwork, and
perfect execution was one in which the managers had small part.
That was the last half of the fourth inning of the game between
Detroit and Chicago on October 13, 1908. Chicago had made two

runs in the third inning and with Brown pitching, appeared to be winning easily until O'Leary and Crawford opened the fourth inning with line singles to left, putting runners on first and second, no one out, and Cobb, the best batter in the American league, at bat.

O'Leary is fast, Cobb is extremely fast and Cobb is a natural bunter. Everyone knew Cobb intended to bunt, and that failure to retire him or one of the other runners probably meant victory for Detroit. Jennings sent Cobb to bat with instructions to bunt toward third base. They knew Brown intended to make the play to third base to force O'Leary, and O'Leary was signaled to take as much lead as possible and start running when the ball was pitched. Brown, past master in field generalship as well as execution walked over to Steinfeldt at third base and said: "Anchor yourself to that bag. The ball is coming here." Kling signaled for a fast ball close in at the waist. It was his plan to have Cobb miss the ball on his first attempt to bunt and then by a quick throw to Tinker on second, to catch O'Leary off the base. Brown shook his head and signaled Kling his intention to pitch a curve ball low and on the outside corner of the plate. Cobb was hoping that Brown would pitch precisely that kind of a ball, and Brown knew that Cobb was hoping for it, and it was Brown's plan to force Cobb to do exactly what he was most anxious to do—to make a perfect bunt and toward third base. Brown pitched perfectly, and Cobb bunted perfectly, thirty feet toward third base and about five feet inside the foul line. As Brown pitched he went forward at top speed, "following the ball through," and he was in front of the ball when it bounded along. Still running he scooped the sphere, and whirling made a terrific throw straight to Steinfeldt and O'Leary was forced out by fifteen feet on a seemingly impossible play, executed chiefly because Brown knew exactly what Cobb would do.

Chance's magnificent machine was not through. Knowing that

the failure of that play would "rattle" the Tigers they instantly seized the psychological situation. Kling gave a quick signal for a fast inshoot across Rossman's shoulders, and Brown, without waiting for Detroit to rally and plan a play, drove the ball fast and high. Rossman struck at the ball and missed it. Like a flash Kling hurled the sphere toward second base, Tinker met it at top speed, touched Crawford three feet from the base and standing still, and Detroit was beaten and in panic. An instant later as Rossman struck out, Kling threw to second, and Evers, leaping, stuck up one hand, dragged down the ball, and while descending touched Cobb as he slid. The big crowd, frenzied over the brilliant series of plays, and only half understanding them, cheered for five minutes.

A few years ago a play suggested by a reporter came near beating the Chicago White Stockings out of the American League pennant. "Dutch" Schaefer with several other players and the reporter, were forgathered one evening in Chicago "talking shop" as usual, and the scribe was lamenting the lack of inventiveness and ingenuity in the later generations of ball players. "Why," he said to clinch the argument, "to-day three of you fellows let Altrock sneak strikes over on you. After he had done it once why didn't a batter walk up to the plate, pretend not to be watching, and when he tried that quick straight ball slam it out of the lot?"

At that time Chicago was fighting desperately for the pennant and every game counted. It looked as if one defeat would mean the loss of the championship. The next afternoon, in the ninth inning, with the score 1 to 0 in favor of Chicago, Schaefer, who had been crippled, was sent to bat. As he came slouching up to the plate, carrying his bat in his left hand and pretending not to be watching the pitcher at all, the reporter hastily regretted the argument of the previous evening. Schaefer actually turned his head away, and "Doc" White, thinking he saw an opening, drove a fast straight ball over the plate. Schaefer waked up, mauled that ball clear into the left field bleachers, drove home a runner ahead of him and beat Chicago 2 to 1. The newspaper man didn't dare tell Comiskey about that argument until the pennant was won.

Each winter the "magnates" meet and solemnly make rules for baseball, amend old ones, and all summer every ball player in the business spends hours of time and thought to see how he can beat the rules, to discover some way to gain an extra base, or some slight advantage over their opponents. Showing how deeply some of them study the rules, and how to get around them, is a play devised by Evers.

There is a rule that a base runner may advance on the bases after a fly catch provided he touches the base after the ball strikes the fielder's hands. Another rule provides that an "infield fly" is out, whether or not the ball is caught, if first and second bases are occupied and fewer than two men out. This rule was made necessary by fielders "trapping" fly balls and then doubling base runners because they were compelled to hold their bases until they saw whether or not the fielder caught the ball. Whether or not a batted ball is an infield fly is left to the judgment of the umpire and the rules order that the umpire must call "Infield Fly" while the ball is in the air in order to protect the base runners.

Evers reasoned that, as a base runner may run on a fair catch, he may also run as soon as the umpire calls "Infield Fly," because, technically, the ball is caught the instant the umpire calls. So he waited his opportunity which came with him on second, another runner on first and Chicago leading by such a large margin that losing the decision would not hurt. O'Day was umpiring and when the batter drove a high fly into the air Evers waited at second, with one foot on the base. The ball was sixty feet in the air when O'Day called "Infield fly, batter out." At that instant Evers dashed for third base and reached it in safety before the ball dropped into the fielder's hands and could be relayed. O'Day, unlike civil judges, refuses to be hampered by legal technicalities, and called Evers out, although technically he was entitled to the base.

Fielder Jones once deliberately tested a rule in Detroit and stirred up one of the biggest discussions baseball has had in many years. With a runner on third Jones ordered him to steal home as the pitcher was in the act of delivering the ball. The pitcher hesitated, changed his pitching motion, and threw the ball to the catcher who ran in front of the batter, caught the ball and touched the runner. The umpire called the runner out. Then Jones raised this point: Was not the runner safe because the catcher interfered with the batter by running in front of him, thereby preventing him from hitting the ball? The umpire ruled that he was not out, as the ball was thrown to the plate and not pitched, therefore the batter had no right to hit it. Jones yielded the point and then argued: Did not the pitcher make a balk, if as the umpire had ruled, he changed his motion and threw to the plate instead of pitching. The umpire was cornered and refused to discuss the case further, beyond ruling the runner out.

The case stirred up a long discussion. The presidents of the two major leagues ruled in different ways, and the umpires received conflicting orders. Four-fifths of the umpires admit, after studying the play, that Jones was right and that the runner was safe, either on the grounds of interference or because the pitcher balked. But they decided to call all runners out in such cases, because, they argue, if they did not, every runner who reached third base could steal home.

If you watch a baseball game this season watch and listen. Behind the "E-Yah" of Jennings and the way he kicks up one foot, or plucks a blade of grass, you may catch his signal to the batter or runner. Back of the war cries of Chance: "At-a-boy," and "Now, you're pitching," may be hidden a whole command to his team. When "Matty" shakes his head one way he means "No," and when he shakes it just a little differently he means "Yes," and is making the batter believe his "Yes" is "No."

So, if you sit real still, and watch the game closely every second, and see every move, and study its meaning, you will enjoy the game lots more. But you won't watch. The very first time Speaker bangs a two bagger down that right field line you'll stand up on your seat and yell the top of your head off.

CHAPTER XVII

On the Bench*

Runners were on first and third bases. The game was close, and one score for either team meant probable victory. At the plate a batter, tense and alert churned the inoffensive air with short nervous motions of his bat. Out on the whitewashed lines by first and third bases two coachers ranted and raved, pawed the dirt, ran up and down howling encouragement to the batter and words of caution to the runners. Stretched sprawlingly along the bench a row of white-garbed athletes watched the field before them, holding their poses as if frozen into position. Above and on both sides of them the noise waves of the great crowd broke deafeningly as the rooter's chorus sang the song of hope of another pennant which might be decided in the next minute.

Suddenly, at the end of the tense line of athletes on the bench there was a movement. A player with earnest, but rather weary face, immobile even in the moment when the whole result of his year's work might be ruined, raised his right hand to his cap, lifted it an inch from his head, replaced it and without a muscle of his face twitching sat watching.

*Reprinted from *The American Magazine* and copyrighted by it. Additions and corrections by Evers.

Touching Second

Like a flash the coacher at third base sprang down the line. "Look out, Steiny," he screamed. "Look out, Frank," came the echo from the first base coacher's box.

The pitcher wound himself into fantastic contortions. From somewhere out of the tangle of revolving limbs a ball shot like a flash to the plate, into the catcher's mitt. As the pitcher started to wind up, the runner at first base leaped twenty feet towards second, stopped, hesitated, and took a step back towards first base. The catcher, who had caught the ball in perfect position, leaped forward, right arm drawn back, watchful, alert, in perfect position to throw to second base. The crowd groaned. Another strike on the batter; the effort to steal balked. Slowly the catcher relaxed from his tense poise. His arm dropped and he started to throw the ball easily back to the pitcher. In that instant the runner at first base was galvanized into action. Two tremendous leaps toward second, and he was flying at full speed down the line. The catcher hesitating a trice, tightened again into throwing position, and threw like a rifle shot to second just as he caught a glimpse of a figure tearing homeward from third. An instant later, in a whirling cloud of dust, a runner pivoted around the plate, his foot dragging across the rubber just as the ball, hastily hurled back to the catcher, came down upon his leg. The umpire's hands went down. The run had scored. The game was won. The crowd in a tumult of enthusiasm roared and screamed and shrilled its joy. The man at the end of the bench let a shadow of a smile flit over his face, and watched more intently than ever. The crowd had forgotten him, and was cheering the others.

Let us see what really happened, for the play described is the one by which Frank Chance saved the championship of 1908 by beating New York one game on the West Side grounds. The crowd saw everything—that is, everything it could see. What it did not see was this:—Tinker was batting, Steinfeldt was on first base, Schulte on third. The orders were for a hit and run play when Tinker went to bat. After one strike had been called Chance raised his hand, lifted his cap from his head and quickly replaced it; the signal for his men to attempt a delayed double steal. Marshall, coaching at third cried: "Look out, Steiny," and Evers, coaching at first, "Look out, Frank." No one noticed in the jumble of their yells, that they used the names of the base runners for the first time. The use of the name of a runner was the signal for the delayed double steal. All that happened afterwards was only mechanical, and although Schulte scored, and Steinfeldt reached second and Tinker helped them by his motions as he struck at the ball, intentionally missing it, they were but puppets carrying out the orders of the general. Chance had won the game from the bench when he lifted his cap from his head.

When Chicago and Detroit met for the championship of the world that same fall, Chance planned and won one of the most beautiful strategic struggles ever fought and the campaign that he planned and that his men carried out was worthy a baseball Napoleon. The game was the second one of the series and was played in Chicago before a huge Sunday crowd. Both teams realized that the game meant almost everything; to Detroit an even chance for the title, to the Cubs almost certainty of retaining their honors. Before the game meetings of both teams were held. Chance planned his campaign depending entirely upon which pitcher Detroit used, and his orders, issued the moment "Wild Bill" Donovan was selected, were conveyed to his men in one word: "Wait." They waited—waited—waited, while the huge crowd went wild as inning after inning reeled away and neither side was able to score a run. Donovan in that game had perhaps as much speed as any human being ever possessed. His fast ball jumped and darted and his curve, pitched with tremendous power and speed, broke almost at right angles.

Inning after inning as Chance sent his men to face that human gatling gun which was firing the National cannon ball at and around them, he monotonously commanded: "Wait," and they went up— and waited. One strike, one ball, two strikes, a foul, two balls, foul, foul, sometimes three strikes, sometimes a weak fly that netted nothing. To the crowd it seemed as if Donovan never could be beaten, as the Champions appeared helpless before his tremendous speed. Still Chance commanded: "Wait—wait him out." Every batter went to the plate intent upon making Donovan pitch as many balls as possible. They fouled, they waited, sometimes even let him strike them out, sometimes they hit, but never until they were compelled to do so. When the eighth inning came neither had scored. Hofman led off that inning and still his orders were to wait, and he waited until he could wait no longer, then rolled a safe scratch hit down towards third. In that moment Chance, commanding general, ordered the charge. Tinker was the next batter and the order for the assault was the single word: "Switch." That was all, but Tinker, rushing eagerly forward to the batter's position, knew that the leash that had held the champions had been cut and that he could hit when he pleased, even the first ball. Crash, Tinker smoke the sphere a terrific blow and like a swallow the ball darted out to right field, high, higher, until, soaring far over the heads of the crowd it struck the sign above the right field seats and the crowd went wild. Then, like soldiers attacking a breached wall, the champions rushed to the assault and, before the inning was over, they had made six runs and their waiting game had won.

Chance had calculated from the first that Donovan was pitching with too great speed, and that no human being could hold such a pace through nine innings, and during all the time that the crowd thought Detroit would win, the leader of the champions was sitting watching every move, waiting for the first sign that Donovan was tiring or beginning to lose his speed. At the start of the seventh inning he thought he detected signs of weariness, but the Smiling Tiger still was strong. After Hofman scratched that hit at the start of the eighth, Chance saw Donovan lower his pitching arm as if weary, and he issued his order—and after Tinker drove that home run he ordered, "Take a crack at the first one." Like a general, he had found the breach and ordered the charge, and his men leaped to the plate and began the bombardment that brought victory.

It is seldom that spectators at any game get a glimpse of the brain work behind the movements of the players and even to hardened "fans" the game looks haphazard. They criticize because they do not understand. They see only the individual, what he does, where the ball is hit, or caught, or thrown, and the intent and purpose of it all is lost, without thinking how much thought may have been wasted on the play that the individual attempted to carry out, or how well planned the game may have been. They imagine, most of them, that the players are individuals who walk to the plate, hit or miss the ball, make a safe hit or go out; they do not know that behind the way the man hits, behind the movements of the base runner, behind the position the men take, are hidden a code of signals, and a series of orders to be obeyed without question, for the general good. They scarcely imagine that games are planned before they are started, or that as soon as a pitcher is named the manager and his advisers map out a scheme of action and plan an attack upon the weakest point of the opposing team.

They do not realize that as soon as Marquard, of New York, or Pfiester of Chicago, is named to pitch, the opposing manager orders a bunting game, or that as soon as a catcher known to have a weak arm, or to throw badly, or a pitcher who does not watch base runners carefully is elected to perform battery duty for the day the opposing manager signals "steal," "steal," "steal," to every fast man who reaches a base.

Touching Second

Listen to a coacher, "Doc" Marshall, of Brooklyn, for instance, on the line at first base, running up and down, pawing the dirt, acting like a madman, and perhaps one not deeply versed in the game imagines he is trying to "rattle" the opposing pitcher, or spur his own men to greater efforts. A hundred of the words or phrases he uses may mean nothing, but somewhere among them the base runner hears, "Careful, Harry," which tells him Marshall has seen a signal for a fast ball, flashed the batter a signal to hit and is warning the runner to start as soon as the ball is pitched. Or he may catch, "Now we're at 'em," and leap forward to save himself from being forced when the batter bunts a sacrifice.

Sometimes, however, the best laid and most carefully planned campaigns go sadly amiss and one of the instances of this was the miscarriage of a plan Chance once laid to beat St. Louis. Sallee, "The String Bean," a tall rangy pitcher who is about nineteen hands high and left-handed, was pitching a strange game. Regardless of who was batting he pitched the same way to each man, a curve over the plate, another curve either on the inside or outside corner, two fast side arm balls high and outside, and then a curve low and over the plate. His pitching, although monotonous, was effective, and for an odd reason.

Chance had a theory that Sallee lacked control, in spite of the fact that he was showing almost perfect control, so he counseled a waiting game and told his men to "take two," which means they were not to strike at either of the first two balls pitched. As a consequence Sallee had the batter "in the hole," all the time—that is, had the advantage, and when they finally were compelled to hit, they were forced to hit his curve so they did not do much hitting.

By the middle of the game Chance realized Sallee was not going to be wild,—and right there the game ceased to be baseball and became a guessing match. Chance, seeing Bresnahan's plan of

◆ 230 ◆

pitching, expected him to change it, so he stuck to his original plan. Bresnahan knowing Chance expected him to change, decided not to change, and waited for Chance to switch his plan of campaign. The game was almost over before the Champions, made desperate, began hitting the first ball, and then Bresnahan changed on every batter, outguessing them all the time.

It was just like men matching heads and tails, each manager sticking to his own plan, Bresnahan turning heads every time and Chance tails, each expecting the other to change.

The man who, perhaps, is past master of directing ball clubs from the bench is John McCloskey, who has managed many clubs. As many of his campaigns have been poorly executed by inferior players, he often has failed, but if ever he gets a team together that can and will carry out his orders, that team probably never will lose a game.

One of McCloskey's most brilliant plans was conceived when he was managing the St. Louis Cardinals. He had an idea his team could beat Reulbach, of Chicago, by bunting and he sent the first seventeen men to bat with orders to bunt or push the ball down the infield, no batter being allowed to hit the ball hard until after two strikes had been called. The first six innings passed without a run being scored by St. Louis. Then two bunts went safe in succession, another advanced the runners and the next man pushed the ball towards first base. It was thrown wild to the plate, two runners scored, and St. Louis continued bunting until five runs counted and the game was won. All during the early stages of the contest the players were frantic, begging to be permitted to hit hard but McCloskey stuck to his plan of campaign and won.

On the attack, when his own team is at bat, the manager has the opportunity to speak to each man as he leaves the bench, to tell him what he is expected to do, but if he changes that plan after the man is in batting position he signals either the batter direct, or the coacher his change of plan, so that every man on the team may know what is to be attempted. With experienced men few signals are necessary, except those of the manager, who must decide which of two possible plays the batter shall try.

After a team has played under one manager several years, the players know, almost without a glance toward the bench, what the orders will be under given circumstances. Often, too, when a manager and batter suspect that the opposing team has learned their signals, the batter will look towards the bench, even when he knows perfectly what is expected of him, and receive a false order intended to "cross" or deceive the trickster who is stealing signals. It is when the batter "crosses" the opposing team, leading them to think he is going to do one thing when he does another, that disastrous consequences are likely to result to the defenders.

In a game between Pittsburg and Philadelphia years ago, when Tommy Leach was a youngster, he thought he detected a signal for Larry Lajoie to bunt and he came creeping forward expecting to get a good start on the bunt if it came towards third. Lajoie slashed a line drive down the third base line, the ball struck Leach on the shins, and his head was the first thing that hit the ground.

The lengths to which clubs will go to learn the signals, especially the signals of managers from the bench, is astonishing to those not familiar with the game. To catch a signal legitimately, by observation, quickness of eye or quickness of thinking is part of the sport, Marshall of Brooklyn, Kane of Chicago, Dooin of Philadelphia, Bridwell of New York, Hartsel of the Athletics, of the present generation of players, are past masters of the art of seeing what the opposing batsmen are trying to do before the effort is made. In one game at Cincinnati in 1909 Manager Griffith said he was compelled to change his signals six times during the contest because Pat Moran was getting them.

XVII. On the Bench

Efforts have been made in the past to steal the signals by the most brazen trickery and unsportsmanlike methods. Perhaps the worst case of this kind ever revealed was that of the old Philadelphia team in the National League. Here was the greatest aggregation of batters ever assembled on one team, but, not satisfied with their natural batting ability, they wanted to know in advance what kind of a ball the pitcher was going to serve in order to increase their hitting. Morgan Murphy, one of the cleverest men at interpreting signals who ever played in a ball game, formulated the plan. Stationing himself with a confederate in the club house in center field, he armed himself with a pair of powerful field glasses with which he watched the signals of the catchers as well as the signals of the managers from the bench. It was afterwards learned that he frequently watched the pitcher, catcher and manager making up their signals before a game and frequently knew before play started every signal that was to be used.

At first the signals were given by the confederate, who stood in a club house window, and passed the signals by the positions of his arms against the sides of the window. One arm was for fast balls, the other for curves, and the code included many positions of the man. The opponents, knowing their signals were being "tipped off," grew suspicious and Murphy, learning of their suspicions and fearing detection, changed his plan and gave the signals by raising or lowering an awning on the club house. If the awning was raised a few inches and held there, a fast ball was to be pitched and if it was raised and dropped quickly a curve had been signaled for. Not content with the success at home the club took Murphy on the road, and he worked from windows overlooking the park, often hiring rooms in order to carry on the unsportsmanlike practice.

It is remarkable how quickly a catcher suspects the opposing team is getting his signals, or those that are being given from the bench. He judges chiefly from the unnatural actions of the batters. After even two men have batted the catcher begins to look in all directions to see who is "tipping off" the signs, and he immediately signals the bench what is going on. Then all eyes on the bench scan the field, fences and adjacent buildings to discover what scheme is being worked.

Murphy's awning worked well, until it was discovered by sharp eyes on the bench and then Murphy and his associates invented something entirely new in baseball. They put electric wires underground, connecting the club house with the coacher's box at third base and buried in the ground a small wooden box containing a "buzzer." A certain noisy, obstreperous player was stationed at third base with one foot directly over the box containing the "buzzer" and as the signal sounded he could feel the tapping under his foot, whereupon he called a code word warning the batter what the pitcher was going to pitch or what the opposing manager had ordered from the bench.

Not a regular player on the Philadelphia team batted under 300 per cent. while the "buzzer" was in operation, and several of their pitchers and catchers were among the leading batters of the National League. Opposing teams knew that, in some way, the Philadelphians were getting the signals, but how they could not discover until one day the Cincinnati club was playing on the Philadelphia grounds. Every man on the Cincinnati team was watching to see where the signals were coming from and they saw that one player stationed near third base no matter how he moved, always kept one foot in the same position.

In the middle of the game, one of the Cincinnati team wandering apparently aimlessly toward third base, made a sudden rush, pushed the guilty Philadelphian out of the coachers' box and dug up the device which was winning games for Philadelphia. The discovery created a big sensation in baseball and aroused a vigorous protest against such unsportsmanlike methods. But instead of stopping, the Philadelphia club moved the buzzer to their bench, and continued using it until stopped by league action.

Not satisfied with having that much advantage on the home grounds, the man who planned the thing followed his team around the country, renting windows overlooking the grounds in each city and wigwagging signals to the batters. He was caught at Brooklyn by some of the Brooklyn players, and trounced, and after that the method of spying gradually was abandoned.

Pittsburg, however, tried the same thing a year later, using an ingenious device; a semiphore arrangement fastened to the center field fence which was raised at right angles for a fast ball and straight up for a curve. The arrangement was not in use for a week before the keen eyes of the opponents discovered it and began changing signals so rapidly the spies could not follow them. After seventeen batters had been hit by pitched balls in four days and some of them hurt because they expected one curve when another was being pitched the scheme was abandoned.

The defensive game of all teams is ordered by the manager either from the bench or from his field position and the manager who also is a player has an immense advantage over the bench manager in that he can reach his men more readily and moreover without a signal, sign, or spoken word his players can tell from the position he assumes where he wants them to play and how he expects the play to be made.

Observe the New York ball team. McGraw from the bench flashes a signal to Tenney. Devlin creeps forward fifteen feet inside of third base, Tenney moves forward almost twenty-five feet, the entire outfield advances while Doyle and Bridwell remain as they were. There is a man on first base, another on third, one batter out and New York has one run more than the opposing team. Any one who knows the game knows the batter is not a fast man and understands the entire plan of action. If the ball is hit to Tenney, to Devlin or to the pitcher, it will be thrown to the plate to prevent the runner from scoring from third base. If it is hit either to Doyle or to Bridwell, the other will cover second base, take the throw and attempt by a quick throw to complete the double play and retire the opposing team.

The batter makes a base hit, the runner scores from third, the man who was on first reaches third, and gain runners are on first and third bases, with one out, and the opposing team needs a run to win. But the infield instead of playing the same way gets a signal from McGraw and while Tenney and Devlin remain as before, Doyle and Bridwell move forward onto the grass, twenty-five feet nearer the plate than they were before. The fan may not understand, but a fast man is coming to bat; there is but a slight chance of a double play being executed successfully and the Giants driven to the defensive, are signaled by their manager to close up the inner line of defense in the desperate hope that the ball will be hit straight at one of them who may cut off the runner at the plate and save the day. McGraw has issued the order, and whether it wins or loses the game he accepts the blame.

There was a game played in Cincinnati in 1909 which Chicago came near losing after having saved it three times by magnificent generalship. McLean, the heavy hitting Cincinnati catcher, is one of the most dangerous of batters when his team needs runs, and four times during the game he came to bat when a safe hit, it seemed, would win the game for Cincinnati, and each time Chance, on the bench, raised his hand with four fingers up and the thumb turned in, which was his signal to give McLean a base on balls and not allow him to hit and to rely upon retiring the next batter, who was not so dangerous as a batter. Three times Reulbach purposely pitched four balls wide, allowing McLean to take first base and each time the succeeding batter failed to hit, so Cincinnati could not score. The other time Chance shoved up four fingers just as one of the umpires passed between him and the field, and Reulbach missed the signal and thinking Chance had not signaled at all he broke a curve over the plate for a strike. Again Chance flashed four fingers and again the umpire obscured the view, and Reulbach drove over another strike.

Moran, who was catching, was angry. He thought the proper thing to do was to give McLean a base, and he turned to Chance for orders to pass the batter even then, but having escaped twice Chance had a "hunch" that he had been wrong, and signaled to make the batter hit. Reulbach pitched a high fast ball and McLean hit it safe to center, scoring a run and tying the score, and the Cubs were compelled to play eleven innings before they finally won the game.

Many spectators who see players go through season after season and play perhaps 175 games a year imagine that they would get hardened and become indifferent as to whether they win or lose. The opposite is the case. The young players endure defeat better than the old ones and it seems the longer the player is in the game the more he hates to lose.

The bench, during a defeat, is like an army in a rout, everyone raving, swearing, blaming each other, and hurling abuse and invective back and forth. But while the result hangs in the balance the men seem impassive, almost indifferent. Conversations are carried on in low tones, orders are issued quickly and incisively, and everything is deliberate and calm. The storm that follows either victory or defeat comes as quickly as the hit or the error that starts it. The moment that the hit that brings victory, or the error that means defeat comes, all the pent up and repressed excitement of the day breaks loose and then the wildest fan in the bleachers is sane compared with the players—and usually the manager is worst of all.

But the bench is not always calm or angry, for at times it is like a crowd of school-boys, up to all sorts of pranks, from nagging the umpire to playing jokes on each other. One of the funniest situations arose in Cincinnati a few years ago when the Reds were being beaten. One of the players was an inveterate joker, and even in defeat he could not withstand the temptation to turn the laugh upon some one. There was a water pipe from the stand that divided directly over the players' bench, one end being at the side of the bench, the other directly over the water tank where the players drank. The joker had discovered that the pipe could be used as a telephone and while his team was going to pieces he sat where he could lean over and speak into the open end of the pipe. Lobert had made a couple of bad misplays and as he went to the water tank to get a drink after the disastrous inning the joker leaned over and spoke into the pipe, saying: "You big, bowlegged, Dutch slob, who ever told you you could play ball?" The words seemed to come directly from over Lobert's head and he dropped the drinking-cup and leaped back, glaring up into the stand to see who was "roasting" him. The party in the box overhead looked supremely innocent and unconscious, but Lobert remained in front of the bench all during the inning, to see if he could discover the offender.

The joker remained quiet until the next player went to the tank, and then he hurled more insults through the tube. He kept it up during the entire game, abusing, criticizing and insulting every player who went to get a drink, and by the middle of the contest he had the players fighting mad, and sending spies into the stand to try to find the man who was abusing them.

So the most interesting part of the game; the brain work, the generalship of baseball is hidden under those coops behind first and third base where the masters of baseball use fingers, eyes, head, feet, hands, cap, strange phrases and senseless words, all of which are in the code, to direct their wonderful puppets. The public never gets a chance to find out what is behind all the running and throwing and batting unless some one tells and then it is impossible to tell even the half.

One knows that when he sees Chance raise his cap, a double steal is to be attempted, that if he raises four fingers, the batter is to be given a base on balls. One knows when McGraw changes places with the man next to him on the bench he is ordering his players to hit and run. One knows that when a Chicago coacher uses the given name of the base runner the given name is part of that code. One knows that when "Doc" Marshall yells, "That's getting them," that "getting" is the catch word, and that when Hughie Jennings pulls grass with his right hand, he means one thing, with his left another, and one can hear behind Griffith's "Watch his foot," an order to steal. But no one knows it all.

CHAPTER XVIII

Deciding Moments
of Great Games*

Nearly every baseball game is won and lost on one play; a play that comes at the psychological instant. Among the players (who do not study psychology) the crucial moment is known as "the break," a phenomenon which no one has analyzed and which the players themselves do not understand.

Twenty men on the bench are watching closely and intently every move of the pitcher. The tide of battle rises, ebbs—and then suddenly, at the start of some inning, something happens. What it is no one outside the psychic sphere of influence ever will understand, but the silent, tight-lipped, alert fellows on the bench see something, or feel something and the mysterious "break" has come.

"One ball!" The players on the bench suddenly stiffen and prepare for action. "Two balls!" Two players jump for bats and begin swinging them; the coachers who have yelled only because it was their duty, suddenly begin raging, screaming and pawing the dirt.

*Reprinted from *The American Magazine* and copyrighted by it. Additions and corrections by Evers.

The manager who has appeared half asleep, makes a trumpet of his hands and leads his men, bawling orders to his players and wild taunts to the opponents.

The spectators do not understand anything has happened. Other batters have had two balls called many times—and the situation looks the same to the spectator who is beyond the "break" influence. In two more minutes the bench is a madhouse with twenty men shouting, screaming, ordering and moving. "Three balls." A madman rushes out to the "deck." "Four balls!" And the spectators join the players in the demonstration, not understanding why. The madness is spreading. Crack! A base hit, a bunt, a wild throw; another base hit; screams! Shouts! Imprecations!—a roar of frantic applause! a final long fly. The manager reaches for his glove, spits into it, and says quietly: "Four runs. We've got 'em." The break is over and the players' bench is again the quietest part of the grounds. The surge of enthusiasm, confidence and noise subsides and the game is won.

Baseball is almost as much psychological as athletic. Why one team can beat a stronger one regularly, and lose to a weaker with the same regularity; why one batter can hit one pitcher and is helpless before another; why one pitcher is effective against a strong team and at the mercy of another that cannot bat half as hard, are psychological problems.

In 1908 Joe Tinker, who is only an ordinary batter, became imbued with the idea that he could hit Mathewson's pitching at will. The confidence born of this idea enabled him to beat Mathewson out of several games, and after that Mathewson seemed to have the same belief, for Tinker during the season won five games from New York by his individual hitting, and in four of them Mathewson was the victim. One of the hits that Tinker made off Mathewson will be part of Chicago's baseball history for generations. The teams, with Mathewson and Brown pitching, had battled for four innings, neither being able to score, and in the fifth Tinker came to bat, first in the inning. Tinker drove the ball on the line into the far left field corner—and raced around the bases. At third base Zimmerman who was coaching, leaped out, tackled Tinker and threw him, trying to drag him back to third base, but Tinker broke away and scored with the only run of the game, beating Mathewson 1 to 0. Twice later in the year, Tinker beat Mathewson by long drives.

One of the hardest games Chicago lost in that season was to Brooklyn late in the year, at a time when the Cubs were fighting desperately to overtake New York and Pittsburg, and when every defeat seemed to wreck their last hope. The Champions had the game well in hand, but Tim Jordan was hitting terrifically and Lundgren seemed unable to stop him. Twice Jordan had driven the ball over the right field fence of the Washington Park grounds and yet when "the break" came in the eighth inning, Chicago was two runs ahead. With one man out, two on bases and Jordan at bat, Chance, seeing Jordan was so anxious to make another long hit that he was kicking one foot high in the air every time a ball was pitched, went to Lundgren and said: "Put it over straight. Make him hit it, if he hits it out of the lot." Four times Lundgren tried to make his straight ball go over the plate, and four times it swerved outside and Jordan drew a base on balls. Brooklyn suddenly changed plans, ordered Lumley to bat for Lewis. He drove a three-base hit against the right field fence, and a long fly that followed allowed him to score, and gave Brooklyn the victory.

Another game, lost in the critical instant to Cincinnati on the same trip seemed to end Chicago's final chance for the pennant and was the result of just such a rally. The ninth inning saw the Cubs seemingly victorious, the pennant within their grasp, but the psychic wave inspired the Reds and with two men on bases, Lobert at bat and two strikes and two balls called, Chance ordered his pitcher,

Overall, to pitch a straight low ball. The result of the entire season seemed to hinge upon that ball. Overall tried, but the fast ball went high, instead of low and Lobert sent it screaming over second, driving home two more runs and winning the game.

That hit was one of the best testimonials to the honesty of baseball ever given, for Lobert was wild for Chicago to win the pennant, and a great friend of Overall, whose heart almost was broken by the hit his friend made.

What probably was the most sensational finish ever recorded in any league was that in the Western League on the last day of the season of 1909. On that day the psychic wave struck Omaha. The situation was this: Des Moines and Sioux City practically were tied for the pennant, and each team was playing two games, the Sioux City team playing at Omaha. Sioux City had to lose two games and Des Moines had to win one to give Des Moines the championship. Sioux City lost the first game, but had the second won by three runs in the ninth inning. Manager "Ducky" Holmes, of the Sioux, did not feel the "break" coming. He leaped into his automobile after the first Omaha batter in the ninth inning went out, called the attention of the crowd to his champions, and raced away toward home to start celebrating the victory. Just then the "break" came. Omaha needed three runs to tie, four to win. Hits and errors quickly filled the bases and with two men out, three men were on the bases, and a home run drive scored four runs, won for Omaha, beat Sioux City, and gave the pennant to Des Moines.

Manager Rourke hastened to the press stand and sent a hurried telegram to the police in a town between Omaha and Holmes' home, which read thus:—

"Arrest Holmes, put him in handcuffs and a straight jacket, gag him and then break the news. Omaha won out in the ninth."

One of the plays which turned the National League tide in 1908 was one made in July and was one of the most peculiar and decisive double plays on record. Chicago was leading by a score of 2 to 1 when New York came in for the seventh inning and with Brown pitching it looked as if the game was won. Bresnahan, the first batter up, singled, and Donlin smashed a two base hit to right, sending Bresnahan to third. The "break" was on and the Cubs in panic. Seymour poked a short "Texas League" fly to right field, and Evers played a trick that stopped the break. Pretending not to see the ball, he stood still to the last possible second. Donlin, seeing the ball falling safe and far out of Schulte's reach, made a frantic dash for third, intent upon scoring behind Bresnahan and giving New York the lead instead of only tying the score. Evers, seeing his trick had worked, reached the ball by a desperate sprint, caught it and instead of tossing the ball to Tinker, whirled and without looking threw to the plate, knowing Donlin could be doubled, and intending to prevent Bresnahan from trying to score on the double play, which he might have done. Bresnahan was driven back to third, and Kling racing in, met the throw, hurled the ball back to Tinker on second base completing the double play and stopping the break.

A play which came at the deciding moment and wrecked Chicago's hope of the National League pennant of 1903, was peculiar. The Cubs, then young, were making a spurt, winning games steadily and pressing the leaders, when the play came up that broke the winning streak and robbed Jack Taylor of a record game. It was at Boston and in the ninth inning, with a runner on second base and two men out, the score 1 to 0 in favor of Chicago. Boston had made only one hit off Taylor up to that time. The batsman hit an easy fly to left field and Slagle ran over and caught the ball fairly in his hands, but at the instant it struck his hands he collided with a fence and was rendered unconscious. Before another player could reach the unconscious man and pick up the ball, two runners scored and Boston won the game.

XVIII. Deciding Moments of Great Games

The majority of games are won and lost by pitchers blundering in the crucial moment, but sometimes it is the catcher who makes the mistake. One of the funniest blunders of years was made by "Hackenschmidt" Gibson, Pittsburg's great catcher, who persisted in his error. "Lefty" Leifield is one of the best and brainiest of pitchers, but essentially a fast ball pitcher and a "waster." A waster is a pitcher who never puts the ball over the plate unless compelled so to do, but keeps it high, low, inside, outside, his plan being to make batters hit bad balls. Leifield seldom uses curves unless compelled to, and his high fast ball which breaks with an odd little jump, is one of the hardest for a batter to hit. One day Leifield had held Chicago helpless and beaten them decisively, and the following day, after the Champions in a "break" moment had started a slashing attack upon Willis, "Young Cy" Young was sent in to check them on the theory that a change from a right to a left-handed pitcher might stop "the break," although every player knows that when a team starts hitting nothing will stop them except sheer accident or a sudden change of "luck." Gibson had observed Leifield's effective use of his fast ball against Chicago and signaled Young to pitch fast ones. The champions made seven straight hits before Young was retired, and all because Gibson did not differentiate between two kinds of fast ball, Leifield's going high and out, while Young's, pitched shoulder high, angles down and low.

Pitching and studying batters is an art in itself, and the pitcher who knows the men who oppose him, and who can put the ball where he wants it to go is a great pitcher, and one who sometimes can stop "the break." In the art of pitching, the batter, so far as brain-work goes, is a failure, except in instances in which batters are men of desperate courage and fearless. The batter in matching wits with the pitcher, has no chance, because he is taking all the risk of injury, and trying to "outguess the pitcher" is dangerous, as the one who blunders may receive a blow on the head that will end his career. The pitcher, on the other hand, can study the batter, analyze his position and condition of nervousness, and, if he has sufficient control of the ball, he can prevent him from hitting.

Observe closely a pitcher when "the break" comes. Up to that time he has been pitching coolly, taking his time, studying each man—but, after "the break" he hurries, returns the ball as fast as he gets it, loses head, loses control, and loses the game. Mathewson, one of the greatest of them all, has only that one fault, and the instant the tide turns against New York, every effort of the other players is to slow down Mathewson and make him hold the ball, instead of pitching as soon as it returns to his hands.

One of the prettiest bits of brain work was done by Leifield, by which he won a hard fought game from Boston and staved off defeat by sheer cleverness. Pittsburg had been leading, but "the break" came against them and Boston started slugging and piling up runs rapidly, until one more hit meant victory, when Bill Dahlen came to bat. Dahlen is a dangerous hitter "inside"—which means when the ball is pitched between him and the plate, and Leifield knew this, so he attempted to make his fast ball go high and outside. Instead the ball escaped him and went waist high across the plate, on the inside corner, just where Dahlen likes to hit. Dahlen, expecting a high fast one, was surprised, and swung at the ball, missing it. Instantly the entire Pittsburg team was screaming at Leifield, abusing him for making the blunder and ordering him not to pitch inside again.

Leifield instantly decided that, as Dahlen had heard him ordered to keep the ball away he would expect a fast ball outside, so instead of pitching there, he deliberately repeated his blunder and Dahlen struck again. Clarke, angry and fearing Leifield had lost control and would lose the game, rushed in and ordered him to keep the ball outside. Leifield nodded assent, but pitched the ball where

Dahlen likes it best for the third time and Dahlen struck out because he had been out-guessed and outgeneraled.

Another game which Leifield won late in 1908 after one of the hardest struggles of the year, was won by his brainy pitching to John Kling, Chicago's heavy-hitting catcher, who came to bat in the eighth inning with men on second and third bases, and one out. Leifield pitched three balls so far from the plate Kling could not reach them, and Kling naturally supposed that Leifield was going to give him a base on balls, fill the bases and increase the chances for a double play, so he was stretching as far as possible, hoping Leifield would pitch close enough to the plate for him to hit to right field. Instead Leifield shot a fast ball straight over the plate, and followed this up by curving two over, striking Kling out, and the result was that Brown lost his first game in three years to Pittsburg.

There are three decisive moments that stand alone in baseball history. Possibly the greatest of these was the famous tenth inning at Columbus, Ohio, when, with one hit, "Big Dave" Orr decided the American Association race, and kept St. Louis from breaking all records as a pennant-winning team. Brooklyn and St. Louis practically were tied for the championship on the last day of the season. If both teams lost, or both won, St. Louis would win its fifth pennant. If St. Louis won and Brooklyn lost, the Browns would have the honors—but if Brooklyn won and St. Louis lost, Brooklyn would win. Brooklyn, playing in the East, already had won, and St. Louis and Columbus were tied in the ninth inning. St. Louis scored one run in the tenth—and with a runner on second base, two men out—and three balls and two strikes called—Orr stood at the plate with one ball left to decide the season. He drove it over the center field fence—sent home a runner ahead of him, and won the pennant for Brooklyn, his hit, according to many, being the longest ever made.

The famous spit ball pitched by Jack Chesbro, which slipped

and beat New York out of a pennant, the pitch of Theo Breitenstein, the veteran, which gave Nashville victory in the ninth inning of the last game of the season, and with it the pennant, are historic events of recent years.

The greatest individual feat ever performed in a decisive moment—probably in any moment—was a catch by which Bill Lange, now retired, saved a game for Chicago and $200 for himself at Washington years ago. There is a story leading up to that play. Lange had missed a train in Boston two days previous, and failed to arrive in New York in time to play there and Anson had fined him $100. Thereupon Lange missed a train to Washington, arrived on the grounds after the teams had practiced, and just in time to start the game, and for that Anson fined him another $100.

The game that afternoon went eleven innings, Chicago scoring one run in the eleventh. There were two men out, a runner on bases, when Selbach, one of the hardest hitters of his time, smote the ball a fearful blow and sent it flying over Lange's head toward the center field fence. The hit seemed a sure home run but Lange, a man weighing 225 pounds, turned and without looking, sprinted desperately straight out towards the fence, racing with the flying ball. At the last instant as the ball was going over his head, Lange leaped, stuck up both hands, turned a somersault and crashed against the fence. The boards splintered, one panel crashed outward, and out of the wreckage crawled Lange holding the ball in his hand. Lange came limping in with the crowd standing on seats, shouting madly, and said to Anson: "Fines go, Cap?" "Nope," said Anson, and the catch had saved the big fielder $200.

Scores of miraculous individual feats have been made in deciding moments. On one occasion Jimmy Ryan leaped entirely over the bleacher barrier in the right field at Washington and caught a fly ball while falling into the crowd. One of the greatest exhibitions of nerve and courage of that sort was given by Hughie Jennings, now manager of Detroit, in a game at Chicago, when he was playing short stop for the famous old Baltimore team. The crowd had encircled the playing field, and was surging closer and closer to the base lines as the battle progressed and, when the ninth inning came with the score tied, one out and Bill Everett on third base, it looked as if Chicago had won and that Baltimore, by losing would be compelled to surrender the pennant. The batter hit a foul ball, high, and into the crowd back of third base, a crowd ten deep, part seated, part kneeling with rows of standing spectators behind. Jennings, tearing across from short, did not hesitate. Hurling himself through the air he caught the ball over the heads of the spectators and plunged down upon them. Everett meantime had touched third base, turned and was sprinting for home. Jennings, climbing upon the heads and bodies of prostrate spectators, threw to the plate, cut off Everett, and in the next inning Baltimore won the game.

That Baltimore crowd, a team of only fair players winning by dash, nerve and courage, gave many exhibitions of individual daring, but one of the greatest was the feat of "Wee Willie" Keeler on the home grounds. Right field on the Baltimore grounds of those days was the terror of visiting players. It was down hill, rough and weedy, and back of it was a high fence, peculiarly constructed for advertising purposes. Inside the fence sloped at an angle of about 65 degrees, being straight on the outer side. Boston was playing there late in the season in which the two teams had their frantic struggle for the pennant, and late in the game, with runners on bases, Stahl drove a long fly to right that seemed likely to win the game for Boston. Keeler, one of the fleetest men in the business, seeing the ball was going over his head, leaped upon the slope of the fence and started to run along it, going higher and higher, and just as the ball was going over the fence he caught it. His momentum carried him higher along the incline and before the big crowd realized he had caught the ball, he was running along the top of the fence, and then holding the ball aloft, he plunged over and fell outside the grounds. Probably never a ball player received such an outburst of applause as he did when he climbed over the fence and tossed the ball to the infield.

Another magnificent individual feat was that of "Dutch" Schefer, then Detroit's second baseman, in the opening game of the World's Championship series between Detroit and Chicago in 1907, a game which, for thrills and excitement, was the greatest ever played. An immense crowd watched the battle and both teams were near exhaustion in the twelfth inning from the succession of tense situations and desperate plays. The crowd seethed and bubbled with excitement and spouted volcanoes of noise at every move of the players. The score was tied. Chicago had a man on first base and two out when Chance hit one of the fiercest drives of the year, a line smash between first and second which, if it cleared the infield, was certain to go to the corner of the grounds and bring home the run for which the clubs had fought for over two hours. Schaefer, playing down near second base, raced back ten steps, leaped, twisted, stuck up his gloved hand, with his back to the stand, and while twisting, dragged down the ball, and the crowd was so stunned by the wonderful catch that it forgot to applaud until the umpire had stopped play and called the game a draw.

That same game, however, was thrown away by Chicago in the critical instant by Steinfeldt, who, in the stress of excitement, lost his head and the game at the moment of victory. That was in the tenth inning when a wild throw let Slagle sprint for the plate, as Steinfeldt was batting. The ball was recovered and thrown back to the plate, too late. It came high and five feet to the left of the plate as Slagle raced across, and, in that instant, when the crowd thought the game over, Steinfeldt hunched his shoulder, made the ball hit him, preventing the fielder from getting it. Slagle promptly was called out because of Steinfeldt's interference and the struggle continued until Schaefer saved it by his wonderful catch.

Sometimes the turning play of a game, the one that decides it is freakish, and one of the oddest freaks of recent years happened in one of the bitter contests between the Chicago and New York teams, an accident that gave New York a victory, and almost gave them the championship. Chicago had runners on first and third bases, one man out and "Del" Howard at the bat, when the fates interfered. Howard hit a vicious bounding drive near second base, and Doyle was in front of the ball, with Bridwell standing on second base to receive the throw and relay the ball to first base to complete the double play. The ball broke through Doyle's hands and struck his shin bone with terrific force. Instead of the error making Chicago's victory easy, it beat the Cubs, for the ball, bouncing off Doyle's shin, went straight into Bridwell's hands and resulted in an easy double play that deprived the champions of the victory.

In that same series there was one of the grandest exhibitions of generalship and pitching ever recorded. Crandall was pitching for New York, and the Giants gained a big lead early in the game. When the ninth inning started with New York four runs ahead, Mathewson, who had been warmed up and ready to rescue Crandall, thought the game safe and, retiring to the club house, disrobed, got under the shower bath, and prepared to don his street clothes. Just then "the break" came, the Cubs began a slashing batting assault upon Crandall and before McGraw could make a move Chicago had two runs and a man on bases. Tenney, Bridwell and Devlin were striving desperately to steady Crandall, who was getting worse and worse, and McGraw sent out a C. Q. D. for Mathewson to save the day.

Delaying, arguing, using every trick and device, McGraw played for time. Reports came from the club house that "Matty" already had his shirt on. Two substitutes were acting as his valets, and he was dressing rapidly as possible, when the cruel umpire ordered McGraw to play or forfeit the game and McGinnity was sent in to pitch. He used up as much time as possible, but finally was compelled to pitch one ball. Slagle rammed a safe hit past first base and Chicago needed only one run to tie the score. Meantime Mathewson's lost trousers had been found. Half a dozen substitutes were helping him dress and before McGinnity would pitch another ball, Mathewson, half dressed, with shoe strings unloosened and uniform awry came racing across the field. There was no time to warm up, for already McGraw had wasted eleven minutes and the umpire was getting peevish. Mathewson's arm was "cold" and to attempt to use either curves or speed with "Del" Howard at bat meant almost certain defeat. Mathewson dropped three slow, twisting fadeaways near the plate, two of them fading until they hit the ground. Howard took three desperate swings at them, struck out and the Giants were saved.

Pitchers of the Mathewson stripe hold the key to the situation in the deciding moments of games, and upon their coolness depends the success of the efforts to resist "the break" influence.

Clark Griffith, now manager of Cincinnati, than whom no brainier pitcher ever lived, was past-master of handling batters in the psychological moments. Once in Washington, with the Senators needing a run to tie—and with men on second and third, Al Selbach came to bat. Griffith's best line was taunting and nagging at batters, delaying and "stalling" to make them nervous and over anxious. He taunted Selbach thus: "You big stiff, you couldn't hit this one with a board," and then he pitched wide and high, and he kept up that kind of work until two strikes and three balls were called and Selbach was wild with anxiety to hit, and rising onto his toes with eagerness. Then Griff, smiling and exasperating, said: "Hit this, you big bloat," and he deliberately tossed the ball underhand toward the plate, so slowly that Selbach, in his eagerness to hit, over-balanced, fell to his hands and knees before the ball reached the plate and was called out on strikes.

Griffith's greatest feat, though, was in a game between Portland and Seattle in the old Northwest League, when he and the afterwards famous "Dad" Clarke were opposing each other in the final game of the season. The game went fourteen innings, with neither side able to score, and in the first of the fourteenth, before a man was out, a hit and two errors filled the bases with Portland players. Clarke was running around, taunting Griffith, who walked out of the box, went over to "Dad" and said, "I'll bet you $10 I strike out the next three men." He did, and Clarke was so angry he refused to pay the bet until years afterwards when both were in the National League.

There is one more interesting incident that stands unique, and it is one by which Jimmy Slagle staved off disaster to the Chicago team in a twenty-inning battle between Chicago and Philadelphia, which Reulbach finally won two to one. In the eighteenth inning of that struggle, with a runner on first base, Sherwood Magee drove a hard line hit to left center. Slagle had just shoved his hand into his hip pocket to get his chewing tobacco when the ball was hit, and as he started in pursuit of it, he discovered to his horror that his right hand was caught in the pocket and refused to come out. A quick jerk failed to release the hand, and Slagle, racing on, leaped, stuck up his left hand, and caught the ball, saving the Cubs. Then he pulled out his tobacco, bit off a piece, and grinned as the crowd applauded.

CHAPTER XIX

Scoring

Scoring is the process of transferring a baseball game from the field onto paper, and the scorers are the recording secretaries and historians of the game. I (Fullerton) started recording the doings of the big boys by cutting notches in a pine stick with an IXL two-bladed knife. A pine stick a foot long with twenty-seven notches on one side and sixteen on the other, which was the basis of a library of score books occupying two shelves, still remains to tell the story of the triumph of the North Enders over the South Siders the day "Sharp Head" licked "Jack Rabbit" Smith.

From the first the idea was impressed upon me that a score of a game should be a lasting record of that game, and going beyond the common rules, I evolved a system by which I can record every ball and strike pitched, every foul, every fly, every move made in a game. It is trouble, and except in important games, upon which a pennant may hinge, or in World's Championship contests, it is not necessary, save perhaps to decide arguments years later. Yet scoring in that manner is a source of much pleasure, for on long winter evenings, sitting near the cheerful sizz of a hard-working radiator, I can draw out the score books of long ago, and have another game with Anson, root for poor Mike Kelly, or get all worked up for fear

PLAYER'S NO'S.

1 – PITCHER
2 – CATCHER
3 – 1st B.
4 – 2nd B.
5 – S.S.
6 – 3rd B.
7 – R.F
8 – C F
9 – L.F.

PITCHED Balls.

ʟ curve
ʟ Curve. low.
ᴛ curve. high.
ᴇ curve, outside.
ᴄ curve inside
ʟ curve high and in.
⊥ straight ball, low.
5 slow ball high.
S Spit ball low and out.

ERRORS AND MISC.
E6 ⌇⌇ Error third
baseman on hit to his left.
E3 ⌇⌇ᶠ Fumble by 1st B.
⌇⌇4E3. Second baseman
throws to first, who muffs.
⌇⌇5⊤2-6-5-2? Grounder
to S.S. Throw home, Runner
out SS to C. to 3B to C.

MARKS FOR HITS

/ Single to right field
| Single to center.
\ Single to left.
// Two base hit to right.
|| Two base hit to center.
\\ Two base hit to left.
/// Three base hit to right
||| Three base hit to center.
\\\ Three base hit to left
//// Home run to right
|||| Home run to center
\\\\ Home run to left

BATTED BALLS.

⌇⌇⌇⌇
∿∿∿   Ground balls.

⌒   Fly ball
      Line fly
∧   high fly.

6 ⌇⌇ 5 Ground ball
between SS and 3rd B.
⌇⌇ Ground ball
5
to right of SS.

F8 ⌐ Fly ball caught
by center field to his right

⌐8 Fly ball that
hit ground and bounded
over center fielder.

⌇⌇ 8
|||| ⌇⌇ 9 Home run
between left and center
that passed over SS on
line and went in "groove."

"Willie Bill" Hutchinson will "go into the air." And in the days when I begin to drool and contend that the players of the present are mere school-boys compared to those of MY day, I can get out the old score books and prove it.

The records of thousands of long-forgotten games are scrawled in signs that mean nothing to anyone else, but bring a flood of recollections, and memories of old friends. (Odd, isn't it, how they all are friends when they are scattered and gone?) Anyhow, it is worth while to save them, to record the games, ball by ball, for, even if the sight of the old score books does not bring back memories of brilliant plays, of fierce strife, of sad failure; even if they do not recall glad days, and gladder nights with men who were worth calling friends, weary rides, and joyous outings; why then maybe some day some fresh guy will want to bet on something, and you can just dig up that score and grab his kale seed.

The system of scoring used varies with every-man, yet all have the numbers of the players as the basis. Everyone knows that "4–3" means that the second baseman fielded a ground ball and threw to the first baseman, and if the number in the little central square is 2, everyone knows it made the second out in the inning. Everyone, almost, makes a straight mark for a hit, two straight marks for a two base hit, and slants them in the direction the hit was made.

My system is simple. I strive to make the marks express in themselves what happened. I draw a wavy line for a grounder, and try to approximate by the waves the number of bounds. A long arch means a long fly, a high curve a high fly, a sharp line, curving downward at the end, a line fly. If the ball goes between the short stop and third baseman I merely mark the way it bounded, and put 6 on one side and 5 on the other.

It is the same with pitched balls. The curve symbol curves in the direction the ball curved. If the curve went low, a little scratch at the bottom of the symbol shows that it did. If it goes outside the plate, a little line runs on that side of the curve mark at the height the ball went. A slow ball is a lazy "S," a fast ball a straight line. The little marks indicating strikes are put in the upper left-hand part of the scoring square, the little marks meaning balls in the lower right-hand space. If the first ball was a strike, a minute figure 1 reveals that fact. If the next was a ball there is a minute 2 after the symbol indicating what kind of a ball was pitched and where it went. The sign for the spit ball slobbers down in a triple curve.

The accompanying key, together with the explanation, ought to enable anyone to read the score without much trouble. It simply is picture writing, and anyone can make their own pictures of what a hit looks like. To those who know the game a full score including every ball and strike and foul sometimes is almost as exciting as watching the game. The foul strike rule disrupted my scoring system for a little time, but by adding a little round "o" at the top of a strike it became simple. There are times, too, when a person wants to know whether the batter struck at the ball, or the strike was called, and a little k (which means strike in baseball, for some strange reason), placed after the strike at which the batter swung, clarifies it.

One really gets interested in adding to the system whenever any play that comes up seems to need recording. For instance, if there is a mark waving down to 5, and after that the fatal letter E, which means error, one wants to know whether he fumbled or threw wild. A line making an inclined plane immediately following will show that the short stop scooped the ball, but made a high throw over the first baseman's head. "BB" of course, can mean nothing but bases on balls, especially with those four odd little marks down in the lower right hand space. The number of times at bat I mark alongside the number of the innings at the top of the score blank carrying forward the total each inning, to make certain the finals are correct. If pitchers

CHICAGO CUBS vs. PITTSBURGH (cancelled) AT CHICAGO DATE September 5 1909.

CUBS	Pos	1	2	3	4	5	6	7	8	9	10	11	AB	R	1.B	S.B	P.O	A	E
Evers	4												5	0	0	0	0	0	1
Sheckard	9												3	0	1	0	3	0	0
Schulte	7												2	0	1	0	4	0	0
Chance	3												4	1	1	0	9	0	0
Steinfeldt	6												4	0	1	0	0	2	0
Hofman	8												2	0	0	0	3	0	0
Tinker	5												4	0	1	0	0	6	2
Needham	2												3	0	0	0	8	1	0
Brown	1												3	0	0	0	0	4	0
Howard	X												1	0	0	0	0	0	0
Zimmerman	XX												1	0	0	0	0	0	0
Total		0	0	0	0	0	0	0	0	0	0	0	32	1	5	0	27	13	3

Entered according to Act of Congress, in the year 1877, by A. G. Spalding & Bros., in the office of the Librarian of Congress, at Washington, D. C.

x Batted for Pfiester in 11th inning, x x Batted for Brown in seventh inning

BASES ON BALLS. 7 .... TWO-BASE HITS. 3 .... THREE-BASE HITS. 0 .... HOME RUNS. 0 ....

DOUBLE PLAYS. 5 – 1,6,5 & 3 .... HIT BY PITCHED BALL. 0 .... STRUCK OUT 4 7.3², 2 .1 .... PASSED BALLS. 0 ....

WILD PITCHES. 1 .... UMPIRE Klem and Johnstone .... SCORER. (E) .... TIME OF GAME. 2.01.

CHICAGO CUBS vs. PITTSBURGH _____ AT Chicago _____ DATE, September 5, 1909

	Pos	1	2	3	4	5	6	7	8	9	10	11	AB	R	1	RI.	BS	BH	PO	A	E
Byrne	6												4	1	1	0	1	1	1	0	0
Beach	8												5	1	1	0	0	1	0	0	0
Clarke	9												5	0	1	0	0	4	1	0	0
Wagner	5												5	1	2	0	0	4	2	0	0
Miller	4												5	1	1	0	0	1	5	0	0
Abstein	3												5	0	1	0	0	11	0	0	0
Wilson	7												4	1	2	0	1	2	0	0	0
Gibson	2												5	0	1	0	0	9	3	0	0
Hyatt	X												1	0	0	0	0	0	0	0	0
Camnitz	1												1	0	0	0	0	0	0	2	0
Leever	1												2	0	0	0	0	0	0	2	0
Total		0	0	0	0	0	0	0	1	0	0	4	42	5	10	0	2	33	15	0

X Batted for Camnitz in eighth inning

BASES ON BALLS.1............TWO-BASE HITS.5..9..6...........THREE-BASE HITS. 0...........HOME RUNS. 0

DOUBLE PLAYS..0............HIT BY PITCHED BALL... 0.......STRUCK OUT.4.3.1.1......PASSED BALLS. 0..........

WILD PITCHES.0............UMPIRES. Klem and Johnstone........SCORER...........TIME OF GAME. 2 hr 7 min

♦ 259 ♦

change, I carry the total at bats on one side and the total at bats against the second pitcher on the other. Also it is imperative that a scorer credits fielders with their put-outs, assists and errors at the end of each half inning and immediately checks off that inning, so that, in case of error, it may be discovered in an instant.

The sample score chosen to illuminate the scoring system is not the most perfect score possible because that certainly was an exciting game and exciting games sometimes disturb even scorers. It was the game that really decided that the Pittsburg team was to be the Champions of the National League in 1909 season. If Chicago had won that game, which it many times came near doing, as the score will show, the moral effect of the victory upon both teams probably would have reversed the final result. The set-back, coming just at the moment when the Champions seemed finally about to pass their rivals, was a death blow to Chicago's hopes, and revived the apparently waning courage of the Pirates. If not the deciding game of the season, it was one of them, and as an individual game it was one of the most thrilling and sensational ever played.

Look on the Chicago side in the seventh inning. See those marks? Read them. They mean that Schulte opened against Camnitz with a slashing line drive and that Chance followed with a long fly into the crowd that hemmed in the field—a two-base hit under the rules putting men on second and third and no one out. Notice that scrawly, indistinct "5–2" in the upper left hand corner of Schulte's square? Know what that means? It means WAGNER, consarn him! That was when, driving forward he scooped off the ground a slow, high bounder hit by Tinker and with a wonderful throw to Gibson, cut Schulte off at the plate. You can see by the high curley-cue over that F C which means fielder's choice in Tinker's square, how that ball bounded, and it was one of the greatest plays of the day. Hofman's square says "F 8" and you can tell by the length of the curve over it how far Hofman hit that ball. Leach got it five feet from the crowd, or the game would have been over right there, but Leach did not have a chance of throwing Chance out at the plate, being too far out. Here! Don't forget to mark "Sac" over that "F 8." Don't forget that the rules give a batter a sacrifice on flies when runners score.

Now look over in that Pittsburg's eighth inning, in Wilson's square, and if you love the Cubs, weep. Brown had the game won 1 to 0 in spite of all that great playing of Wagner, and here was Wilson at bat. Humph, Wilson can't take it in his own hands and hit 200. But—look at that mark. Straight as a die, a line single to the right of center. Wouldn't that jar you? And he had two strikes on him, too, and was fishing after the curve! Never mind, Brownie will get them yet. Wow! Wow! Punk! Punkerino!! Rotten plus four!!! DID you see what happened? Aw, nothin'! nothin'!! Only this ham, Needham—What do they let that fellow catch for, anyhow? Oh, Archer and Moran both hurt, eh? WHY don't Kling come back? What DID happen, eh? Why, Brownie pitched high. Needham knocked the ball down all right. It fell right at his feet in front of him and Wilson never moved. Then what does he do but think the ball has gone to the stand and turn and chase after it and let Wilson go to second! Wouldn't that—Oh, what's the use? There he goes to third while Schulte is clawing Gibson's line drive out of the crowd. Great catch, that, Frankie, old boy! You're the child wonder who can do the stunts, eh?

They'll never score now. Say, who's this coming to bat? Hyatt? Never heard of him. Wow! Brownie's got him. Two strikes!

Rotten! Rotten! SAFE? Why he was out as far as from here to the Lake Front. What DO you think of that umpire? Letting them score on that after Tinker made that stop and throw to the plate! Say, if they haven't got the worst bunch of holdup men, yeggs and sandbaggers for umpires I ever saw! Well, anyhow, they only tied it. We'll lick 'em now.

Do you see those marks in Chicago's tenth inning? Look at them closely for never again will you see them. In that inning Fred Clarke made three of the greatest catches ever a man made, and he alone stood between Chicago and its fourth Championship. Steinfeldt hit a low, vicious, line drive down the left field line. Like a madman Clarke came racing down along the wall of humanity banked around the field, almost brushing against the spectators, touching their feet as he sped to save Pittsburg. At the last moment, as the ball was going into the crowd a few feet inside the foul line, Clarke lurched, threw himself through the air, dived at the ball and, turning, rolling and whirling, he crashed into the crowd, and came up with the sphere clinched in his fingers.

The crowd, as he limped back to his place, paid the Pittsburg leader one of the greatest tributes ever given a foeman, cheering for minutes. While the cheers still were echoing Clarke again smashed into the crowd and hauled down Hofman's hard drive and then, sprinting far out to left center, against the crowd, he caught Tinker's smash which deserved to be a home run, and the inning was over.

Those rows of straight marks in Pittsburg's eleventh inning tell the rest of the story of how Brown, worn down by the fierceness of the struggle, pitching desperately, wavered, and how, helped by fumbles and failures of the broken infield, Pittsburg pounded the way to victory.

Now, honestly, isn't that almost as much fun as paying fifty cents to sit in the sun with pop peddlers crawling over your back and policemen jabbing you in the ribs with clubs? Wouldn't you rather sit at home by the fire, and see it all over again in scrawly little marks? If you would, then take a book next summer and store up

XIX. Scoring

some games against the hard winter. It's easy, if that fat man in front will only sit down and let you see what is being pitched.

And then, next winter, when the missus says she thinks you might at least stay home ONE night in winter, when you go gadding around ball games all summer, you can dig up the score, and get a big, easy chair, and toast your shins, and just root, and root and root.

FINIS

Index

Index

Index

Index

Index

Index